THE COMMUNITY COLLEGE LIBRARY

FRITZ VEIT

Contributions in Librarianship
and Information Science, Number 14

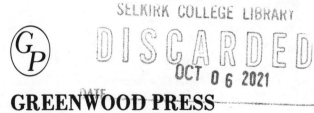

GREENWOOD PRESS

Westport, Connecticut ● London, England

Library of Congress Cataloging in Publication Data

Veit, Fritz, 1907-
    The community college library.

    (Contributions in librarianship and information
science ; no. 14)
    Includes bibliographical references and index.
    1. Junior college libraries. 2. Municipal
university and college libraries. I. Title.
II. Series.
Z675.J8V43   027.7   72-843
ISBN 0-8371-6412-5

Library of Congress Catalog Card Number: 72-843
ISBN: 0-8371-6412-5

First published in 1975

Greenwood Press, a division of Williamhouse Regency Inc.
51 Riverside Avenue, Westport, Connecticut 06880

Manufactured in the United States of America

THE
COMMUNITY
COLLEGE
LIBRARY

CONTRIBUTIONS IN
LIBRARIANSHIP AND INFORMATION SCIENCE

Series Editor: Paul Wasserman

Urban Analysis for Branch Library System Planning
Robert E. Coughlin, Françoise Taïeb, and Benjamin H. Stevens

Frontiers in Librarianship: Proceedings of the Change Institute, 1969
School of Library and Information Services, University of Maryland

Subject Retrieval in the Seventies: New Directions. An International
Symposium
Hans (Hanan) Wellisch and Thomas D. Wilson, Editors

Quantitative Methods in Librarianship: Standards, Research, Management
Irene Braden Hoadley and Alice S. Clark, Editors

Public Relations for Libraries: Essays in Communications Techniques
Allan Angoff, Editor

Human Memory and Knowledge: A Systems Approach
Glynn Harmon

Libraries in the Political Scene: Georg Leyh and German Librarianship,
1933-1953
Marta L. Dosa

Information Retrieval and Documentation in Chemistry
Charles H. Davis and James E. Rush

Illustrative Computer Programming for Libraries: Selected Examples for
Information Specialists
Charles H. Davis

To the Memory of My Parents
and My Sister

CONTENTS

FIGURES

FLOOR PLANS

TABLES

PREFACE

This study deals with the learning resources programs of the public two-year colleges. In former years these institutions were commonly called junior colleges, and the college departments or divisions that assembled, organized, and interpreted the learning resources (mainly books) were commonly called libraries. In keeping with traditional terminology I could have chosen "The Junior College Library" as the title for the study; however, I decided to modify the title to make it correspond more closely to prevailing current terminology.

Today, many of the publicly supported post-secondary two-year institutions have more varied and diversified functions, stressing service to the community in which they are located; they are commonly known as community colleges. "Community college" has therefore been substituted for "junior college" in our title. However, "library" has been retained even though it could have been replaced with perhaps equal justification by "learning resource center." The original form was retained because in practice a good many of the libraries—even though they have extended their concern to nonbook materials—are still so designated. And the library profession still prefers the short word "library" to the longer designation "learning resource center." The succinct title we have selected for our study thus reads: "The Community College Library." It should be understood that in the title "community college" should be construed broadly to embrace all public post-secondary two-year institutions whatever their official name; "library" is also meant in the broad sense which includes responsibility for books and other learning resources. Our preference for "library" as part of the title will not affect the use of the term "learning resource center" in the text whenever this seems indicated.

In the preparation of the study I have drawn on many sources as well as on my professional experience: literature, including handbooks, reports, lists, and other publications of individual institutions; replies to questionnaires; correspondence to clarify special situations; meetings with colleagues at conferences; on-site visits; directing seminars dealing with the community college library; and administering a joint library which served a five-year college (now university) and a community college.

In quite a few respects the community college library has characteristics similar to those of a senior college or a university library. However, there are certain significant differences between libraries serving community colleges and those serving other levels of higher education, engendered largely by differences in institutional objectives.

Since a library is inextricably intertwined with the institution of which it is a part, the community college itself will be briefly described in the first chapter. Subsequent chapters deal with personnel, administrative organization, technical services, learning materials, user services, cooperation, standards, buildings, and movements and developments that have had a strong impact on community college librarianship.

The book is addressed to several groups: to the student of the community college and its learning resources program; to community college learning resource center staffs who may wish to compare their goals and practices with those of other institutions; and to others who may wish to deepen their understanding of the field.

I am grateful to colleagues from various parts of the country who have generously shared information I requested. Their helpfulness is recognized as the information they supplied is utilized in the text. Extensive use has been made of the *Library Statistics of Colleges and Universities, Fall 1971,* a United States Office of Education publication. As the source notations will show, a number of the tables and charts included in the text are derived from the U.S. Office of Education data.

I am especially indebted to my wife Lucille for careful reading of the manuscript and valuable editorial suggestions.

Chicago, Illinois
May 1974

THE
COMMUNITY
COLLEGE
LIBRARY

1

THE COMMUNITY COLLEGE

In an ideal situation the objectives of a library are determined largely by the objectives of the institution it serves. It is therefore highly desirable that we gain an understanding of the nature of the public post-secondary two-year institution, as a preliminary to an evaluation of its library.

THE DEVELOPMENT OF THE TWO-YEAR COLLEGE

As we follow the development of the two-year post-secondary institution we shall see that it has undergone changes in scope and objectives and that these changes are also reflected in terminology. The scope of the institution has been enlarged and so has the scope of the library. The junior college has been transformed into a much more broadly based institution and is now widely known by such names as community college, community junior college, or just college. And the library's base likewise has been extended; the libraries of most two-year institutions have become comprehensive resource centers. Initially we shall use the term "junior college" and "library"; later we shall often shift to the use of the terms "community college" and "learning resource center." We must be aware of the fact that many junior colleges have retained their original designations, as did many of their libraries, even though in fact both the colleges and the libraries have become more comprehensive in character.

The junior college is the youngest segment of American higher education. While there were a few private post-secondary institutions as early as the eighteenth century, public post-secondary education had its beginning in the last decades of the nineteenth century.[1] Its chief proponents were William R. Harper (the first president of the University of Chicago) and other educational leaders who had studied abroad, especially

3

in Germany. These educators found that in Germany specialization began at a period roughly corresponding to our third year of college, while the first two years were still limited almost entirely to general education. Harper therefore advocated that the four-year sequence of the college be split into two distinct parts: a junior college comprising the first two years, and a senior college comprising the second two-year period. Harper carried this plan through at the University of Chicago in the late 1800s. It is noteworthy that the first American public junior college was established in 1901 in Joliet, Illinois, not far from Chicago.

The early junior college represented a sort of replica of the first two years of a four-year college; the courses offered were parallel to those offered in the first two years of a four-year college. The junior college gained ground only very slowly. As an institution it was generally not furthered by state or local authorities.

Most junior college programs came into being as outgrowths of secondary school programs. In quite a number of instances a secondary school principal felt that some of his faculty members had the preparation and the desire to teach college-level courses, and he authorized the offering of such courses on the high school premises. Frequently, junior colleges developed from such modest beginnings, with the high school principal in charge of the junior college programs. Because of the very close ties of many junior college programs with secondary education, it is not surprising to find the early public junior college under the jurisdiction of the local school boards. It is also not surprising that because of its close ties with the common school system, many viewed junior college education as a phase of secondary rather than of higher education.

Junior colleges, which for many years had struggled for recognition, or even their very existence, became institutions turned to by more and more individuals in search of college education. They were attractive because admission was either free or at low cost and the junior college was usually nearer the students' homes than the state college or university.

Responding to demand, their number increased steadily. The development was not uniform throughout the nation. However, some of the largest and most populous states began encouraging the establishment of this new type of institution. The states in which large numbers of students attended junior colleges were California, Illinois, Florida, Georgia, Texas, and New York. These states still lead in the number of junior college students.

With the passage of time the junior college became generally accepted and gained increasing support from local and state authorities as well as from teachers and writers in the field of education. Significant factors in the growth and expansion of the junior college were the increase in age of the college-age population, the pressure from returning veterans who wanted to attend college, and the need for further college-level study by persons who wanted to succeed professionally in a society that had grown more complex and technically advanced. Pressure toward broadening junior college education also came from groups who previously had not been given the opportunity to pursue college education: the minority Americans, the urban disadvantaged, and the poor. Generally, it was felt that two years of post-high school education should be available to anyone who desired to obtain it.[2]

To fulfill the demands made upon the junior college, it had to extend its scope. It necessarily became an agency that provides college-parallel education. It had to serve the wide range of educational, college-level needs of all of its constituents. In other words, it had to develop into a community college.

The phenomenal growth of the junior college during the past decade is evident from the enrollment increases. The trend is illustrated by Figure 1. Since 1964 enrollment grew by more than 100,000 each year. In 1965 the enrollment was about 565,000; by 1970 it was about 2 million. Now about one-third of all students enter higher education through a junior or community college. In certain states the figure is much higher than the national average. In California, for instance, it is 80 percent. Nationally, junior college enrollment represents about 28 percent of the total undergraduate enrollment.

The idea that a college should offer more than the usual academic subjects is not new. The junior college has inherited some of the character traits and some of the functions of the early land-grant colleges. The land-grant movement, spurred by the Morrill Act (1862), stressed new kinds of subjects: technology, agriculture, and applied sciences. Many of the land-grant colleges became universities and consequently they treated these service tasks as secondary obligations or even dropped them. The junior college, as it has become comprehensive, has accepted and reshaped the service philosophy of the land-grant colleges.[3] The impact of the Smith-Hughes vocational education legislation is especially noteworthy since it brought vocational education into the orbit of the junior college.

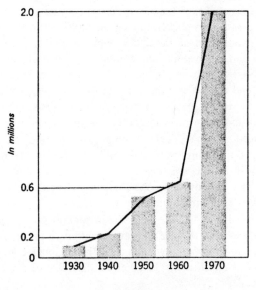

Figure 1
Enrollment in Two-Year Colleges, United States, 1930-1970

SOURCE: Leland L. Medsker and Dale Tillery, *Breaking the Access Barriers* (New York: McGraw Hill, 1971), p. 17. Reproduced with the permission of the Carnegie Commission on Higher Education, ©1971 by The Carnegie Foundation for the Advancement of Teaching.

The development of the comprehensive junior college was preceded by the development of the comprehensive high school. As Clifford G. Erickson notes, there were academic high schools, technical high schools, trade schools, continuation schools, and separate adult education divisions.[4] This diversity of types was replaced by one comprehensive high school. Similarly, on the junior college level technical institutes added academic offerings, and academic junior colleges increased their curricula by adding technical subjects. This development has been in accord with the educational philosophy that students pursuing various vocations should have equal status and that they are most likely to have it if technical and academic curricula are within one institution. But, more importantly, in a comprehensive institution a student may change from one curriculum to another without having to interrupt his schooling.

THE COMMUNITY COLLEGE TODAY

The two-year college of today is expected to provide a very broad range of learning experiences, including many which other institutions will not or cannot offer. The literature commonly notes the following as the six main functions of the community college: preparation for advanced study, career education, guidance, developmental education, general education, and community service.[5] The early junior colleges were established to provide preparation for advanced study, i.e., to offer courses which were parallel to courses offered within the first two years of a four-year college. The junior college courses were patterned very closely after these courses; an effort was made to have them identical in name and content in order that they be transferable. Since a four-year college was viewed by many students and instructors as an institution of higher rank and prestige, the aim of many students was to pursue college-parallel study in order that they might be able to transfer to a senior college or university.

However, there has been a slow but steady recognition of the great value of the other frequently unique offerings of the two-year college. Career education, especially, has gained more and more ground. The number of career fields for which college instruction is now available is very large. The course announcements and catalogs of the colleges reflect this. For instance, the 1972-1973 catalog of Triton College, "a Public Community College and Technical Institute for all the People," located in River Grove, Illinois, lists well over fifty career curricula in such diverse fields as air conditioning and refrigeration, architectural technology, beauty culture, dental assisting, marketing mid-management, medical laboratory technology, nuclear medicine technology, operating room technology, restaurant training, secretarial training, and welding technology.[6] A similar wide variety of career courses is offered in the Central Piedmont Community College catalog for 1972-1974.[7]

From an examination of these and numerous other catalogs it is evident that career education has various levels and periods of duration. The Central Piedmont catalog, for instance, lists occupational extension courses for those who need only short-term training, retraining, or upgrading in a vocational or professional area.[8]

In technology and career education the interdependence of the college and the business, professional, and industrial community is obvious.

Most colleges have advisory committees for technical and career programs, the committee members being drawn from their respective fields. Most of the colleges which offer library technical assistant programs, for instance, have advisory committees composed of practicing librarians. Some college catalogs list the various advisory committees and their members with their professional affiliation.[9] It may be highly advantageous for a college to involve business, industrial, and professional leaders as advisors since they often become strong supporters of the colleges in addition to providing counsel in professional matters.

Many states require that community colleges further career education by devoting a stated minimum percentage of their curricula to this purpose. In Illinois, for instance, full state support depends on an institution's assigning at least 15 percent of its programs to vocational education of which no more than 50 percent may be business courses.[10]

Guidance is a most important service of a community college, since the college attracts many persons who have not been previously exposed to college life. Such persons must often be helped in discovering their abilities and skills as well as their deficiencies. The community college acts as a sort of distributing agency recommending vocational education curricula to some and academic education to others, and courses for cultural enjoyment to still others.

Inasmuch as the community college has an open-door policy, it welcomes all who wish to obtain post-high school education. The student body therefore usually is not a homogeneous group; the individuals within one college usually differ from each other in social and economic background as well as in academic preparation and in levels of achievement. Many need assistance to reach a level at which they can pursue regular college study.

Another task of the community college is to provide general education. This function has been defined in many ways but may be succinctly described as a body of common course experiences, or a set of courses designed to help an individual orient himself in society.[11]

True to its expanded and extended function, the community college provides community services. It is the center for community life. Lectures, concerts, and art exhibits are open to the community at large. Each college gears its offerings to the cultural and educational preferences of the community.

THE FACULTY

The community college needs a staff for its task.[12] It needs a staff that agrees with and advances the goals of the junior college. An analysis of the background and employment preference of the junior college faculty reveals that the majority of the faculty are in the 31-to-50-year age bracket, that 23 percent are over 50 years old, and 18 percent are under 30. From this age breakdown it is evident that most of the faculty themselves have not attended a junior college because relatively few were in existence when the majority of those who now are junior college faculty members attended college.

The degree held by most is the master's; 8.6 percent hold the doctorate, 10 percent hold the bachelor's degree, and 3.5 percent have still less formal education. Many—in Illinois, e.g., more than half of the faculty—have hours beyond the master's. Of great importance is the instructor's professional affiliation before he joined the junior college faculty. His style of teaching is bound to be influenced by the style of teaching he has followed before he became a junior college instructor. Over one-third were teachers in public elementary and high schools, 11 percent came from four-year institutions, and 22 percent from graduate school. For many teachers the junior college was a second choice. If given the opportunity, about 45 percent of the junior college teachers would have preferred to be connected with a senior college or a university. Only about half of the faculty considered occupational curricula essential. About the same proportion of the faculty deemed remedial courses essential. Sixteen percent were not even neutral regarding remedial courses, but considered them inappropriate.

As Medsker and Tillery emphasize repeatedly in their *Breaking the Access Barrier,* a community college can fulfill its broad range of objectives only if the faculty is in agreement with them. When academic staff is recruited it must be made aware of the goals of the junior college. A major requirement for selection should be enthusiasm for the attainment of these goals. Having been engaged, faculty members can be given orientation towards the junior college in regular courses, in workshops, or by means of in-service training.

CONTROL AND SUPPORT[13]

We have noted earlier that the junior college was local in origin. It was usually considered part of the local school system. Today in practically every state junior colleges are removed from the jurisdiction of the common schools and are considered part of higher education.

Since education is a state concern, each state may shape its educational pattern to suit its needs and its preferences. In spite of the resulting great variety, two basic patterns can be found:

1. Responsibility is shared between state and local government,
2. Responsibility rests primarily with the state.

It should be noted that both patterns may exist concurrently within a state.

In some states, branches of a state college or a state university are classified as junior colleges. These units may be largely identical with the first two years of college, providing mainly college and university parallel education. Sometimes these two-year state college or state university branches are true community colleges. In some states two-year university branches are the only community college-type institutions, in other states there are separately maintained community colleges as well as two-year university or college branches. Since a two-year branch of a university (or college) is within the overall administration of the university (or college) of which it is a part, such a branch may find it difficult to develop into a true community college, although this development has occurred in a number of instances.

It has been suggested that universities should divest themselves of community college education and leave this task to institutions specifically designed for the purpose. On the other hand it is also recognized that a branch of a university usually has the resources of the whole university, including the total library resources, freely available.

Succinct descriptions of how two-year public higher education is organized in each state of the union may be found in *American Junior Colleges,* edited by Edmund J. Gleazer.[14] Its main purpose, however, is to present various data (exhibits) for all post-secondary two-year institutions that were regionally accredited or were candidates for accreditation on January 1, 1971. There are also exhibits for a number of two-year units of four-year colleges and universities. The exhibit for each institution gives its history, control, physical setting, administrative structure, financial data, and information on academic matters such as programs and staff. The section on special facilities lists the library and other learning resources for each institution.[15]

States use two basic control plans. The majority (twenty-eight) have a combination of state and local control. A smaller number of states (twelve) administer junior colleges through a state agency. Nine place community colleges under the direction of state universities or colleges.[16]

Full state control has been favored by an increasing number of people. This means that maintenance of the community college becomes the sole responsibility of the state. In such a case community colleges would be treated like the other publicly controlled institutions of higher learning. It should be noted that we find a certain degree of state control in all patterns, even in the pattern we designate as local control. The state's interest in the junior college has steadily increased. The state has assumed an ever-larger share of the financial burden of maintaining junior colleges. Where the state shares control with local institutions, the state's share has increased on the average by 10 percent from 1960-1961 to 1967-1968—more specifically, from 26 percent to 36 percent—and conversely the local share has decreased by 10 percent from 40 percent to 30 percent during the same span of time.

A development that merits notice is the multi-institution junior college district.[17] This pattern occurs when one governing board operates two or more campuses within a district. The multi-institution unit is called a multi-branch if a multi-institution or a multi-unit district operates the units as parts of one institution. The multi-institution unit is considered a multi-college if a multi-institution or a multi-unit district operates the several units largely as separate entities.

The 1950s may be characterized as the years of the independent junior college district expansion; the late 1960s through the early 1970s is notable as a period of multi-institutional expansion. In 1964 there were only ten multi-institution districts, in 1968 there were forty, and since that time the number has again increased. When the units are branches, most significant decisions are made in the central office; when they are colleges, more freedom is left to the local administrator, and more limited control and supervision is exercised centrally. The tendency is towards decentralized administration, towards shifting of power from the central unit to the local unit. The pressure to move in this direction is usually exercised by faculty and students, who can identify much more readily with a local unit than with a remote central administration.

Also of importance to library administration is the policy regarding the course offerings of the several units (campuses or branches) within

one college. The units of a multi-unit junior college district may offer
identical comprehensive programs, or the central administration may
prescribe multi-program-type institutions with each campus offering
a different curriculum.[18] In the former instance the learning resources
needed would be identical or at least very similar in all units; in the
second instance different resources would be required for the respective
different curricula. While the comprehensive junior college is generally
favored, it is recognized that even in a big city system one unit should
not necessarily be an exact replica of the other units. A program in a
specialized field, even if offered in only one unit, may satisfy the demands
of a whole city. High cost of certain programs, especially in vocational
areas, may also militate against duplication. John F. Grede suggests,
therefore, "collective comprehensiveness"—comprehensiveness afforded
by a city system as a whole—rather than "unitary comprehensiveness,"
where it would be provided by each unit of a system.[19]

In this brief survey we could not offer an exhaustive description of
the community college. However, some of its essential characteristics
are presented, especially those characteristics which may have a bearing
on library service. In the course of later discussions more details relating
to the community college may be introduced in their proper context.
There will also be occasion to discuss new educational movements and
trends such as open education and utilization of newer media, and to refer
to their possible impact on community college library service.

THE FUTURE

And what of the future? If the "goals and expectations" sketched
in the Carnegie Commission's special report on the open-door colleges
come true, the future is full of promise.[20] Goals and expectations will
be gradually achieved. The years 1976, 1980, and 2000 are designated
as steps in the continuing upward development of the community college.
By 1976, among other achievements there will be open access to all
community colleges; comprehensive programs will prevail on all community college campuses and will yield meaningful learning options.
The colleges, keeping informed of changing manpower needs, will constantly adapt their occupational programs to meet these needs. Community colleges will be within commuting distance of any potential
student and will be truly within his reach.

By 1980, according to the Carnegie Commission report, 230 to 280 new community colleges, which will have already been in the planning stage by 1976, will be completed and the whole community college network will be able to accommodate 35 percent to 40 percent of all undergraduate students.

The Carnegie Commission report projects that by the year 2000 40 percent to 45 percent of all undergraduates will be enrolled in community colleges and the additional colleges that may be needed will have been built.

Community college administrators, sensitive to changing educational and occupational needs of our society, will adapt curricula and resources to meet the new challenges.

NOTES

1. Carnegie Commission on Higher Education, *The Open-Door Colleges: Policies for Community Colleges* (New York: McGraw-Hill, 1970), pp. 9-10 (A Special Report and Recommendations by the Carnegie Commission on Higher Education, June 1970).

2. Leland L. Medsker and Dale Tillery, *Breaking the Access Barriers: A Profile of Two-year Colleges* (New York: McGraw-Hill, 1971), pp. 15-20 (Fourth of a Series of Profiles Sponsored by the Carnegie Commission on Higher Education).

3. Carnegie Commission on Higher Education, *op. cit.,* pp. 8-9.

4. Clifford G. Erickson, "The Community College–Keystone for Change," *Junior College Journal* 40, no. 6 (March 1970):12-15; and Julio L. Bertalozzo, "Defining the Need," in *Junior College Libraries. Development, Needs and Perspectives,* ed. Everett L. Moore (Chicago: American Library Association, 1969), pp. 3-8.

5. See for instance Medsker and Tillery, *op. cit.* pp. 53-74.

6. Triton College, River Grove, Ill. *Announcement of Courses,* Vol. VIII: 1972-1973. 1972-1973 Catalog (River Grove, Ill.: Triton College, 1972), pp. 52-113.

7. Central Piedmont Community College, Charlotte, N.C. *General Catalog, Vol. VI: 1972-1974* (Charlotte, N.C.: Central Piedmont Community College, 1972).

8. *Ibid.,* p. 35.

9. Triton College, *op. cit.,* pp. 41-51.

10. 3 *Illinois Revised Statutes 1971*, title 122, art. 101-2 (g).

11. B. Lamar Johnson, *General Education in Action: A Report of the California Study of General Education in the Junior College* (Washington, D.C.: American Council on Education, 1952), esp. pp. 328-44.

12. Medsker and Tillery, *op. cit.*, pp. 87-104.

13. *Ibid.*, pp. 105-23.

14. *American Junior Colleges*, 8th ed., ed. Edmund J. Gleazer, Jr. (Washington, D.C.: American Council on Education, c. 1971).

15. See Table 18: "Patterns of Control of Public Community Colleges, 1969." Medsker and Tillery, *op. cit.*, pp. 108-9.

16. Frederick C. Kintzer et al. *The Multi-Institution Junior College District* (ERIC Clearing House for Junior College Information, American Association of Junior Colleges Monograph Series), (Washington, D.C.: American Association of Junior Colleges, 1969), pp. 2, 6.

17. *Ibid.*, p. 2.

18. *Ibid.*, pp. 8-9.

19. John F. Grede, "Collective Comprehensiveness: A Proposal for a Big City Community College," *Journal of Higher Education* 41, no. 3 (March 1970): 197-94.

20. Carnegie Commission on Higher Education, *op. cit.*, pp. 51-52.

2

PERSONNEL

At the community college learning resource centers we find three principal staff categories, just as in most other libraries. The first category comprises the professional staff, the second category comprises the nonprofessional or supportive staff, and the third category comprises student assistants. Each of these categories is usually divided into subgroups.

PROFESSIONAL STAFF

The scope of many junior college libraries has been broadened through the years, especially during the last decade or so. Many libraries that dealt largely with graphic media have become the centers and focal points for a wide range of communication media. This has had an impact on the kind of personnel needed by the centers. When the concern was graphic materials and when nongraphic materials were either outside of the library's concern or represented only a minor interest, it was natural to expect that staff members receive their professional graduate preparation in library schools. This view is still unequivocally reflected in the 1960 Standards, which require that professional members of the library hold a graduate library degree.[1]

Many members of the profession have come to recognize that for certain kinds of assignments in-depth study in another area could be more purposeful. For instance, a person who is in charge of the learning laboratory that forms part of a learning resource center might need a deep understanding of the psychology of learning and curriculum construction and might obtain this proficiency by specializing in the field of education. Or a library may computerize various aspects of its operations and may need a computer expert. This person might have had to pursue graduate academic studies outside of the graduate library school. The staff member in charge of the television studio, which in some institutions forms

15

part of the learning resources complex, would need an academic background which would probably have to be obtained in a communications
department or a physics department; as evidence of this attainment, one
would usually get a degree from one of these departments rather than
from a graduate library school. (An interdisciplinary approach is at
times possible and in that case a degree might be obtained from the graduate
library school.) The new Guidelines have taken account of this situation,
and they stipulate that the "professional staff members should have
degrees and/or experience appropriate to the position requirements"[2] –
degrees in library science or in another field, depending on the tasks to
be performed.

Director of Learning Resource Center

Two very recent investigations reveal that the great majority of the
persons in charge of library learning resource centers had traditional
training. Everett L. Moore, who collected the data for his study in the
summer of 1970, found that over 90 percent of the head librarians had
at least a year of library training in graduate school; there were a few
who, in addition, held a Ph.D. degree or were engaged in work leading
towards the Ph.D. Several held a subject master's in addition to the
Ph.D.[3]

Elizabeth W. Matthews, who assembled her data about two years
later, used as the generic term the title Director of Library Learning
Resource Center rather than Librarian or Director of the Library.
Analyzing the background of the directors of these centers, she found
that those holding degrees in library science represented 84.6 percent
of the sample. About 25 percent of this group also had done advanced
work in other fields, with education predominating. Of those who
did not hold graduate degrees in library science, the majority—about
9 percent—had degrees in education; of the remaining small group, a few
each had pursued their graduate studies in the audio-visual area and the
instructional materials area, as well as in fields not related to education
or library science.[4]

The majority of the directors had had previous experience; only
2 percent came direct from graduate school. Nearly a third had their
previous experience in a secondary school, about a fourth were previously
employed in a junior college, and another fourth had been employed in a

senior college or university; the remaining directors came from elementary school, the public library, and other fields of employment, usually in the educational sphere.[5]

While the percentage of those coming from the elementary and secondary schools decreased if compared with the findings of an earlier study,[6] it is noteworthy that the schools are still a major training field for prospective community college learning resource center staff members.

Community colleges are today no longer generally considered components of secondary education but rather a part of the higher education system. For this reason it may be expected that the number of job applicants with experience in senior colleges and universities will increase. The number of those with previous experience in community colleges should also increase because there are many more community colleges than a decade ago, and there is greater opportunity to obtain one's first experience in a community college.

Titles

There has always been a great variety of titles for the heads of learning resource centers.

Several years ago when the scope of the library was more narrow, when its resources consisted nearly exclusively of books, and when libraries were either not at all or only peripherally concerned with nongraphic media, the designation of librarian was practically the only title used for the person professionally attached to the junior college library.

As an earlier study shows, the individual in charge of the library used the plain title librarian in about two-thirds of the cases, followed by head librarian in 2 percent of the cases.[7] In a few instances such titles as director of library services, director of the library, chairman of the division of the library, chairman of the department of the library, and chief librarian were also found. Until about 1970, head librarian remained a favorite title. But by that time director of library services, library director, and chief librarian, in that sequence, were found in over one-fourth of the cases. Librarian was still used in about one-fourth of the cases, which is a considerable reduction from the former two-thirds. In over 11 percent of the cases a title relating to learning resources had appeared.[8]

Matthews' study shows a much greater diversity in 1972, when her data was gathered.[9] There is a very large increase in the percentage of

designations having a learning resources connotation. Here 41.2 percent
of the titles indicated a connection with learning resources, director of
learning resources being the most frequent. About 35 other variants are
enumerated by Matthews, among them, dean of learning resources, coordinator of learning resources, chairman of learning resources, and
department chairman of learning resources. A designation containing
the term library was used in 58.2 percent of the cases, with director of
library services appearing most frequently, namely, in nearly one-third
of the total.

The diversity in titles is also found to occur at the levels below chief
administrative officer. An examination of learning resource center handbooks, college catalogs, and organization charts shows that learning
resource centers still use the designation *librarian* extensively not only
for staff members engaged in traditional library activities, but also for
staff whose work has come to be concerned with nonbook media.
However, some institutions have chosen more inclusive titles to indicate
that a staff member is responsible for all or at least many kinds of media.

A case in point is the choice of the titles resources consultant or
materials reference consultant instead of reference librarian. In some
learning resource centers different persons are responsible for book and
nonbook media, respectively. Persons responsible for nonbook media
may be called A-V librarian but they are frequently termed A-V specialist
(or consultant or coordinator) and media specialist (or consultant or
coordinator).

Often production is in a separate unit headed by a media production
coordinator (or director or specialist). Production may again be split
into several units, and there may be a TV production specialist, an A-V
production specialist, and a graphic materials production specialist. Also
found are such titles as individualized learning services director, director
of study skills center, instructional services coordinator (or specialist),
and developmental learning laboratory director. The title computer
specialist identifies the person who is in charge of computer applications
to library work.

It should be strongly emphasized that the titles listed represent only
a few examples of the many different designations which have either
replaced or been added to the time-honored title librarian. The practices
vary greatly. There is lack of uniformity, and in certain cases it may be
necessary to have a particular learning resource center define its usage
of a specific job title.

Faculty Status

Faculty status entitles the holder to a set of privileges to which faculty members have traditionally been entitled. Faculty status also obligates the holder to the meeting of certain customary obligations.

Both the 1960 Standards[10] and the 1972 Guidelines[11] stipulate that the professional librarian or other professional members of the learning resource center (LRC) be accorded faculty status as well as rank, whenever rank is accorded to faculty members.

These are some of the major privileges which LRC staff members acquire by having faculty status: They are compensated in accordance with the same pay scale as those involved in classroom teaching. They are given sabbatical leaves if such leaves are granted to the classroom teacher. They are permitted, or even encouraged, to attend professional meetings and (if funds are available) are given an allowance on the same basis as other faculty members. They have the same vacation time as other faculty members. They are eligible to membership in faculty committees. They receive tenure after fulfilling the necessary academic and performanc requirements. And they acquire pension benefits under the same conditions as do other faculty members.

On the side of obligations, librarians and other professional LRC staff members with faculty status must meet the same academic requirements as other faculty members. Parenthetically, it may be mentioned that on the community college level professional LRC staff members usually do have academic preparation equal to or more advanced than that of the teaching staff.

The two recent studies that dealt with the heads of learning resource centers found a relatively satisfactory situation. Moore found that as a group the head librarians were granted practically all of the privileges of faculty status except for some variations in the salary scale, which was lower in certain cases and higher in others.[12] In Matthews' sample over 80 percent reported having faculty status while the others stated they did not.[13]

An earlier study also showed a very favorable picture, with practically all heads of libraries as well as the great majority of the other library staff members accorded faculty status.[14]

Since the professional LRC staff member may be involved with teaching, sometimes as a team member, and sometimes independently as a resource person for individualized learning or instruction, it is logical to view him in the same perspective as the classroom teacher. The evidence in support of faculty status is so clear that one might not expect to hear any dissenting voice. But a few administrators and a few colleagues in teaching departments would place professional staffs of learning resource centers into a different category—usually with fewer privileges. Fortunately these persons can often be shown that faculty status produces the highest degree of satisfaction on the part of the LRC staff and brings them into the academic mainstream as equal partners, a situation in which they can be most effective. All LRC staff members—not only its chief administrator—must have this full opportunity of interaction, and consequently all professional LRC members must be accorded faculty status on equal terms with other faculty members. Since the learning resource center needs persons with backgrounds appropriate to their respective assignments, training and degrees in one specialty must be given the same weight as comparable appropriate training and degrees in another specialty.

The term *faculty status* is sometimes used broadly to encompass situations where learning resource center staff share only some of the privileges of faculty status enjoyed by faculty members engaged in classroom teaching.

To characterize such a modification, which confers less than full faculty status, the term academic status is used by some. Others, however, use academic status and faculty status synonymously.[15] To remove any possible ambiguity, it would seem preferable in such situations to qualify faculty status by the adjective "limited," or by an explanatory note whenever less than full faculty status is meant. We would still recommend the use of the term faculty status without qualification if only nonessential elements were lacking, as, for instance, reimbursement of expenditures for attending a conference. In reviewing briefly the community college situation in New York, one writer makes a statement which may illustrate this discussion: "While most community colleges in the State have given librarians faculty ranks, only a minority have given them full faculty status and treat them as equal to the teaching staff in terms of compensation, leaves, promotion, tenure, and other faculty perquisites."[16]

Rank

Traditionally rank has been deemed to add prestige to a faculty and to encourage its members to grow professionally, since academic advancement is (or is supposed to be) rewarded by promotion to higher rank.

Quite clearly, academic rank brings a faculty into the sphere of higher education.

While faculty rank is common and well nigh universal at universities and senior colleges, there are still many community colleges that have not (or not yet) adopted a scheme of ranking the faculty. The number of institutions adopting rank is increasing.[17] To argue whether or not a scheme of ranking is or is not proper for a community college is not our purpose. However, we do strongly contend that the learning resources staff be included in the ranking scheme should it be adopted by a community college. This view is also recorded in the 1960 Standards and in the 1972 Guidelines.[18]

A recent study revealed that 38 percent of the colleges from whom data were obtained had rank. In these instances (ninety-five cases) head librarians could be found on all levels of the ranking scale, the majority, however, occupying the two top levels—professor and associate professor.[19]

Since ranking takes into account academic background and experience and since the directors frequently exceed the average levels in academic attainment and/or experience, it may be assumed that there would have been a larger representation of the two lower ranks—assistant professor and instructor—if all learning resource center staff members had been included.

Professional Preparation

If a learning resource center assumes the comprehensiveness in scope which the new Guidelines envisage, the centers will need a staff whose members have diversified preparation. We will deal with the director and the other staff members separately, although in many aspects requirements for their positions overlap.

The director of the center should be a generalist. He may well have in-depth training in a specialty, but he must have an understanding of the whole configuration of the center. What kind of professional preparation would be most suitable for a director? In her investigation Matthews polled the directors with the request that they recommend, in descending order of preference, courses they deem useful.[20] It is evident that the directors consider the core courses offered in library school of greatest importance. These are courses in reference, book selection, library administration, and cataloging. But the directors consider many other courses also essential—courses that have been usually lacking from the first-year graduate curriculum. A partial list of these courses reads: the community college, junior (community) college libraries, general communication, psychology of learning, nonbook cataloging, college and university libraries, curriculum design, and electronic data processing.

A future administrator would find it difficult to take courses in all of the areas that contribute to a fuller understanding of the tasks to be performed. In some instances he may get an overview by independent reading; in other areas he may consider it necessary to enroll in a college or university for formal course work. The director should be familiar with the community college and its unique characteristics; he must also be familiar with the principles and elements of administration, a familiarity he can obtain in a general course or in a course geared to college and university library administration or junior college library administration. In addition, he should understand the psychology of learning, new techniques of instruction, and types of nonbook materials.

It would seem to be inadvisable to insist on identical preparation for all directors. Each learning resource center has its own emphasis. However, all directors of centers must go beyond their own specialty and recognize their responsibility towards the center's total operation. A person trained primarily in traditional librarianship must give full attention to nonbook media; a person who had his principal training in nonbook media must give books and periodicals their rightful emphasis.

PROFESSIONAL STAFF MEMBERS

Depending on the size of the learning resource center and the philosophy that governs its operations, staff members may need to be either generalists or specialists.

If an institution is small and has only one professional staff member in addition to the director, this staff member should probably be a generalist. Assuming that an institution has several staff members besides the director, there are alternatives. If an institution expects to have all of its staff members involved with all media, each would need to be a generalist. In such a situation the staff member performing reference functions would be responsible for reference work covering all media. Another institution might prefer to have different employees for each of the different media. In the reference area it would not have a general consultant, but rather a librarian for the traditional kind of library work and an audio-visual specialist for nonbook media.

In the first situation, where the staff member has responsibility for a wide range of media, he would need correspondingly broad training. In the second instance the training would emphasize the specialty. In a number of centers there are specialists in television producton, in design of audio-visual materials, or in the direction of a learning laboratory. Each of these persons should not only have preparation in depth in his particular area of responsibility, but also an acquaintance with the other aspects of the LRC's work.

In many respects the academic background of the LRC staff members should be similar to that of the director. In addition to graduate work in librarianship or graduate work in a specialty appropriate to the specific assignment, an LRC staff member should have a grasp of the history of the junior college and its place in American higher education. He should have preparation in the psychology of learning and in the psychology of students of the various age groups that make up the LRC users. If a staff member has obtained his education in a graduate library school, he may require further study to familiarize himself with the types and characteristics of nonbook media. An employee whose graduate training has been devoted exclusively to a specialty outside of the traditional library field might be encouraged to also study cataloging, classification, and perhaps general reference tools and procedures subsequent to his specialist's training. In sum, the aim should be to have a staff each of whose members is expert in some one area and in addition has a generalized understanding of the other areas.

The vast majority of LRC heads are library trained. This is also true for the staff as a whole. In the statistics issued by the U.S. Office of Education most of the staff members are identified as librarians.[21] Only a small percentage appears in the category "Other Professional Staff": "persons who though not librarians are in positions normally requiring at least a Bachelor's degree."[22] Many institutions have only librarians on their staff. As the scope of many libraries widens, more staff members with specialized skills will be needed, but persons trained in librarianship are likely to form the largest group for many years to come.

The question arises as to where the staff members of the LRCs will obtain the background particularly suited to their needs. An inquiry made several years ago regarding the training of junior college librarians revealed that the graduate library schools did not have any courses specifically designed for junior college librarians.[23] Some of the schools did not offer education by type of library. These schools expect all of

their students to enroll in the same core curriculum. Other schools that
did offer education by type of library encouraged students interested
in junior college librarianship to take the course which might be entitled
academic library, or college and university library. This was suggested on
the assumption that junior college librarianship is a type of academic
librarianship and that its problems are embraced in the course dealing
with academic libraries. Several of the heads of the library schools who
responded to the inquiry were, however, quick to point out that their
school takes into account particular interests of students and encourages
those interested in the junior college to prepare papers and reports dealing
with the junior college. A few schools advised students who intended to
become junior college librarians to choose pertinent electives in other
academic departments such as education. Popular courses bear such titles
as junior college, development and organization of higher education, and
improvement of college teaching.

At the time the inquiry was made, only one school offered a seminar
in junior college libraries. In accredited graduate library schools there
is virtually no opportunity to follow a special first-year program in community college librarianship.

Since the graduate library schools are not likely to introduce within
the first-year graduate program a specialized curriculum for the future
junior college librarian, he must seek other avenues of additional post-
graduate training. The sixth-year post-master's program lends itself very
well to specialization in community college librarianship. This work,
characterized as lying "between MLS and Ph.D.,"[24] usually leads to a
specialist's diploma such as Ed.S. For instance, at Western Michigan
University, where such a program is offered, a student does not draw
only on courses from the library field. His work is enriched and deepened
by courses such as characteristics of the college student, curriculum trends,
and the community college.

The seminar which has been offered by Rosary College, River Forest,
Illinois since the late 1960s formed an exception to the general rule that
special emphasis is not given to community college librarianship within
the first year curriculum. At Rosary both students in the master's program and in the post-master's program may enroll in the seminar. A
prerequisite for registration in the seminar is a course in college and
university libraries or extensive college library experience. The seminar
gives participants the opportunity to study in depth two or three topics of

their choice. Since some of the reports are presented in class, all students share in extended discussion of perhaps eight to ten broad topics that are of particular concern to the community college librarian. Areas on which students have reported include: book selection in the community college with special emphasis on book selection tools in the vocational-technical area, the training of the junior college librarian, newer media in the community college, comparison between the traditional junior college library and the community college learning resource center, and physical facilities for the center.

The program designed for an Institute conducted by the Graduate Library School, Indiana University[25] is noteworthy because it might serve as a model for community college library education at accredited library schools. This federally-funded Institute, "Education for Librarianship in Urban Community Colleges," is of 12 months duration, extending from August 1973 to August 1974. Participants who complete the program will receive the master of library science degree.

The Institute has adopted an interdisciplinary approach for the training of its enrollees—eighteen college graduates from minority backgrounds (thirteen Blacks, four Mexican-Americans, and one South American). The Institute stresses individual counseling and guidance. It provides for workshops and seminars dealing with topics which are of particular concern to the administrator of the urban two-year college learning resources program: LRC management, learning theories, curriculum development, industrial technology, library automation, and characteristics of the population groups which often constitute the urban LRC's clientele. The curriculum also includes the courses usually covered in the general master's program, such as reference, library services and collections, cataloging, and introduction to information sciences. Field trips offer students the opportunity to see urban two-year colleges in operation.

In program planning and development, implementation and evaluation, the Institute's director is assisted by an advisory committee which includes student representatives. The committee's faculty members are drawn from Indiana University's Graduate Library School and from the university's departments of Instructional Systems Technology, Afro-American Affairs, and Higher Education.

It should also be noted that work in junior college librarianship has been offered at several non-ALA accredited schools. Deserving of special mention is the institute offered by Appalachian University, devoted

specifically to the learning resource center of the two-year college.[26]
This institute was intended to improve the academic background of
students who had been employed as librarians. Those attending the entire program and having the necessary prerequisites were expected to be
able to obtain an M.A. degree in library science. This institute gave
students an exceptional opportunity to obtain a thorough understanding
of community college library problems since the institute attracted a
group of lecturers and consultants of national reputation.

It is important to be familiar with training opportunities that exist
outside the confines of the ALA-accredited library schools, because some
community colleges do not insist on graduation from ALA-accredited
schools as a condition for employment. Some colleges accept persons with
school library degrees that are often acquired in departments of education.
Since in the school library programs stress is laid on materials needed at
the primary and secondary school level and on administrative problems
encountered at this level, it is highly desirable that holders of school
library degrees acquire additional training that will familiarize them with
materials and problems particular to the community college level.

Other important opportunities for the study of community college
library problems are offered at conferences such as the three-day conferences which have been held annually in Illinois during the past seven
years under the auspices of the Illinois Library Association and one of
the Illinois universities or colleges. Of comparable importance are conferences held in connection with American Library Association meetings,
such as the outstanding conference of 1967 whose proceedings were
published by the ALA.[27]

PROFESSIONAL AND SUPPORTIVE STAFF: SIZE, SEX, AND CONTRACT STATUS

Before discussing in some detail the supportive staff category we will
introduce two tables and a chart which give statistical data relating both
to the professional and the supportive staff. In the tables and the chart,
based on the U.S. Office of Education, *Library Statistics for Colleges
and Universities,* Fall 1971, the term *clerical* is broadly used to mean
supportive. In our brief analysis of the tables and chart, we follow U.S.
Office of Education terminology. In the next section, however, the
term clerical is used in a more narrow sense and applies only to a segment
of the supportive staff.

Table 1 shows that the staff increases as the size of the institution increases. Also, the percentage of clerical in relation to total staff increases as the total staff becomes larger.

Table 1

Median, 25-Percentile, and 75-Percentile for Staff of Library in Full-time Equivalents (FTE) of Public Two-year Institutions: Aggregate United States, Fall 1971

Enrollment Size	Total Number	25-Percentile	Median	75-Percentile
1	2	3	4	5
	Professional Staff			
Two-year Institutions	2,408.4	2.0	3.0	4.2
10,000 or more	535.4	6.0	7.2	12.0
5,000 to 9,999	487.5	4.0	5.0	7.5
1,000 to 4,999	1,117.6	2.0	3.0	4.0
500 to 999	209.7	1.0	1.5	2.0
Fewer than 500	58.2	1.0	1.0	2.0
	Clerical and Other Regular Staff			
Two-year Institutions	2,762.8	1.0	2.6	5.0
10,000 or more	777.3	7.4	11.0	17.0
5,000 to 9,999	635.6	4.7	7.0	11.0
1,000 to 4,999	1,161.0	2.0	3.0	4.5
500 to 999	145.6	0.5	1.0	2.0
Fewer than 500	43.3	—	1.0	2.0

SOURCE: U.S. Office of Education, National Center for Educational Statistics, *Library Statistics of Colleges and Universities,* Fall 1971, Analytic Report (Part C), Washington, D.C., 1973, p. 50 (Table C-13).

Table 2 gives the ratio of men to women employees for three staff categories: librarians, other professional staff, and clerical and other regular staff. It is obvious that men hold a much higher percentage of the positions in the librarian group than in the clerical group. To be exact, only 11 percent of the clerical employees are men while the women represent 89 percent. In the librarian category the corresponding ratio is 38 percent to 62 percent. The percentage of men in other professional staff is still higher; they account for 52 percent of the positions, while women occupy 48 percent. To bring this picture into clear focus and to allow comparisons with other kinds of institutions of higher learning, Figure 2 is reproduced here. The percentages for the other kinds

Table 2

Number and Percent of Librarians, Other Professional Staff, and Clerical and Other Regular Staff, in Full-time Equivalents, of Public Two-year Institutions, by Contract Status and Sex: Aggregate United States, Fall 1971

Enrollment Size	Employed 11-12 Months						Employed 9-10 Months				
	Total Number	Men		Women		Total Number	Men		Women		
		Number	Percent of Total	Number	Percent of Total		Number	Percent of Total	Number	Percent of Total	
1	2	3	4	5	6	7	8	9	10	11	
					Librarians						
Two-year Institutions	1,250.1	524.8	42.0	725.3	58.0	834.9	274.6	32.9	560.3	67.1	
10,000 or more	221.9	107.4	48.4	114.5	51.6	259.5	111.1	42.8	148.4	57.2	
5,000 to 9,999	267.5	115.5	43.2	152.0	56.8	139.3	53.5	38.4	85.8	61.6	
1,000 to 4,999	628.7	259.9	41.3	368.8	58.7	331.4	91.2	27.5	240.2	72.5	
500 to 999	107.2	36.0	33.6	71.2	66.4	76.6	14.6	19.1	62.0	80.9	
Fewer than 500	24.8	6.0	24.2	18.8	75.8	28.1	4.2	14.9	23.9	85.1	

	Professional Staff Other Than Librarians									
Two-year Institutions	235.4	119.9	50.5	115.5	49.1	88.0	46.8	53.2	41.2	46.8
10,000 or more	45.4	25.0	55.1	20.4	44.9	8.6	7.2	83.7	1.4	16.3
5,000 to 9,999	73.6	39.6	53.8	34.0	46.2	7.1	6.1	85.9	1.0	14.1
1,000 to 4,999	101.5	50.3	49.6	51.2	50.4	56.0	25.2	45.0	30.8	55.0
500 to 999	10.9	3.0	27.5	7.9	72.5	15.0	7.0	46.7	8.0	53.3
Fewer than 500	4.0	2.0	50.0	2.0	50.0	1.3	1.3	100.0	—	—

	Clerical and Other Regular Staff									
Two-year Institutions	2,414.1	285.7	11.8	2,128.4	88.2	347.7	27.4	7.9	320.3	92.1
10,000 or more	724.8	107.6	14.8	617.2	85.2	52.5	4.0	7.6	48.5	92.4
5,000 to 9,999	578.6	66.3	11.5	511.8	88.5	57.0	5.0	8.8	52.0	91.2
1,000 to 4,999	983.4	104.8	10.7	878.6	89.3	177.6	14.0	7.9	163.6	92.1
500 to 999	95.0	6.5	6.8	88.5	93.2	49.6	3.4	6.9	46.2	93.1
Fewer than 500	32.3	—	—	32.3	100.0	11.0	1.0	9.1	10.0	90.9

SOURCE: U.S. Office of Education, National Center for Educational Statistics, *Library Statistics for Colleges and Universities*, Fall 1971, Analytic Report (Part C), Washington, D.C., 1973, pp. 51, 52, 53 (Tables C-14, C15, and C16).

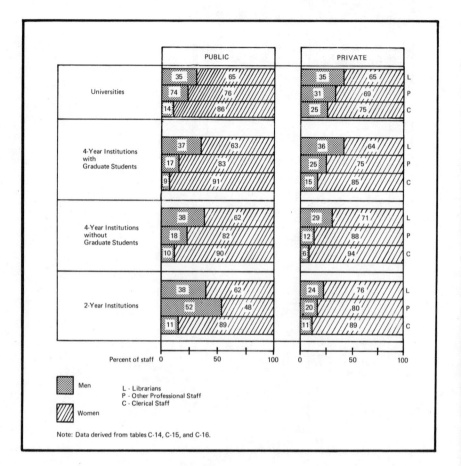

Figure 2

**Percent Distribution of College and University Library
Staff in Full-Time Equivalents (FTE), by Control of
Institution, Type of Position, and Sex of Staff:
Aggregate United States, Fall 1971**

SOURCE: U. S. Office of Eduction, National Center for Educational Statistics, *Library
Statistics for Colleges and Universities,* Fall 1971, Analytic Report (Part C), Washington,
D.C., 1973, p. 13 (Chart 8).

of public and private institutions of higher learning are very similar to
those obtained for two-year colleges. In all types of institutions men

occupy a much higher percentage of librarian and other professional
positions than clerical positions. There is a notable variation in employment ratios of men to women between two-year institutions and all the
other types; the two-year institutions have a markedly higher percentage
of men in the other professional staff category. This difference can
probably be explained by the greater need of the comprehensive community college learning resource center for more media production and
utilization staff. Such positions are at present—but not necessarily in
the future—more frequently occupied by men than by women.

If the staffs are classified by contract status, we find that about
40 percent of the librarians hold an 11-12-month contract and about
60 percent are on duty 9-10 months. The corresponding figures for
other professional staff are 30 percent and 70 percent. In the clerical
category about 88 percent of the employees work 11-12 months and only
about 12 percent work 9-10 months. If the ratio of men to women in the 11-12-
month contract status is compared with this ratio in the 9-10-month
contract period, we find considerable differences. In the 11-12-month
group, male librarians represent 42 percent of the librarian category; other
professional male staff members number 50.9 percent; male clerical staff
members account for 11.8 percent. The corresponding figures in the 9-10-
month contract group are: librarians 32.9 percent, other professional
staff 53.2 percent, and clerical 7.9 percent. Inasmuch as the total for
each position level within each contract status is 100 percent, the percentage of women employees is obtained by deducting the percentages
for male staff members from 100 percent. Without explanatory data
it is not possible to determine whether those librarians and other professional staff working 9-10 months have an advantage over those working
11-12 months per year. In general, clerical staff members are paid for
work performed during the summer. Librarians and other professional
staff are frequently, but not always, paid for summer assignments. In
some institutions their salary (not higher than that received by faculty
during the academic year) is spread over a twelve-month period. In such
instances the persons on 11-12-month assignments would be receiving
less pay for work performed than those on 9-10-month assignments.
Many of those who receive additional pay for summer work welcome
the opportunity to be gainfully employed; others, however, opt for
time off rather than for extra income. It should be emphasized that one
of the essential features of full faculty status for librarians is that they
are compensated at the same rate of pay as classroom instructors.

SUPPORTIVE STAFF

A term frequently used for this category is clerical staff. U.S. Office of Education statistics designate employees in nonprofessional supportive positions as clerical.[28] We prefer the term supportive because at some institutions the nonprofessional staff has become stratified and, in addition to clerks, we find an in-between category variously called library technicians, media technicians, or technical assistants. Technicians are higher than clerks but not fully professional; they are therefore also designated as semi-professional.

For decades library literature has stressed the urgency to include nonprofessional staff members, and it is generally accepted today that it is necessary for library staffs to include supportive personnel. It is clear that the professional librarian has to devote much of his attention to routine tasks unless he is aided by persons with clerical and semi-professional backgrounds. While the vast majority of libraries now have supportive staff, there are still a number who lack them.[29] Based on the experience of many libraries it has been suggested, and even stipulated by several state agencies, that the ratio of professional to nonprofessional should be 1:2. Recent statistics, however, indicate that there is no uniform application of this formula. Very often this ratio is not reached; there are often fewer nonacademic workers than this formula would indicate as desirable. In some instances, on the other hand, there are more nonacademic workers than a strict application of the formula would yield. This formula should not be rigidly applied. The ratio will be influenced by the conditions at individual institutions. For instance, if an institution has all processing done by an outside firm or agency, or if it is highly mechanized, it may need fewer nonacademic staff members than another institution with approximately the same student body and a collection of about the same size.

Also, in an institution with a broad learning resources program there is likely to be need for a larger number of supportive staff members with diversified backgrounds than at another institution of similar size but more limited scope. The Guidelines express this well: "The number and kind of supportive staff needed will be determined by the size of the college and the services provided. The educational background and experiences of such supportive staff should be appropriate to the tasks assigned."[30]

In a learning resource center that still deals mainly with books there is need for clerical workers who circulate books, read shelves, mark books, type, file, handle correspondence, and perform other office operations. This type of LRC will also need supportive staff to assist with cataloging tasks (such as cataloging from Library of Congress copy), bibliographic checking, and answering information-type reference questions.

An organization that embraces many learning resource functions requires staff members who can service various kinds of equipment, some of it quite intricate. It is evident that many kinds of proficiencies are needed, at the higher ranges verging on the professional level.

In the library technical assistant (LTA) category, as has been stressed before,[31] we should not be misled by the adjective "technical" in the position title library technical assistant or by the noun "technician" in the position title library technician (these two position titles are interchangeably used). Technical or technician indicates a level of performance. Library technical assistants are not limited to assignment in a library's technical services department. They may work in any department; they may be assigned any kind of library work. Library technical assistants may work in the catalog, order, circulation, and reference departments, or in a department or unit devoted to nongraphic media. They may work in any type of library: community college, senior college, university, public library, school library, or special library. The LTA stands between the professional librarian and the clerk. A professional librarian must be familiar with the bases of his profession; he must know the interrelationships between the components of the whole learning resources configuration. He must be able to devise policies and work independently in planning work. The technical assistant must also have a good knowledge of the field, but he is not expected to be fully familiar with the theoretical foundations of the field. He is rather expected to know the practical applications, and his assignments would be more narrowly circumscribed and less intricate. In some assignments LTAs might be expected to supervise other LTAs or clerks.

How is the LTA distinguished from the clerk? The library clerk usually performs tasks of lesser difficulty; frequently—but not always—such tasks are repetitive or of a routine nature. His assignments are often more narrow in scope, and usually he is more closely supervised.

So far the title library technical assistant or library technician has only been sporadically used in community college LRCs or in any of the other categories of libraries. Often the term clerk or library clerk is used for all supportive staff members who assist with library tasks. Usually several steps are provided in the clerical category, and persons who have been placed on the highest level, or on the level next to the highest, often carry out work which may be identical with the level of performance expected of LTAs in other institutions. An examination of numerous handbooks and organization charts revealed, however, widespread use of the term technician for staff working in the nonbook media field.

The term "media technician" often denotes a nonprofessional or semi-professional staff member whose concern is nonbook media exclusively. But this practice is not uniform since some learning resource centers use media technician to mean library technical assistant— a staff member who can be involved in the whole range of media—book and nonbook.

The term technician or technical assistant also appears with a more narrow meaning. For instance, we encountered the term audio-visual technician being used for a nonacademic staff member who had audio-visual responsibilities within the learning resource center, or individualized learning center technician for a staff member stationed in the individualized learning center. Other examples which stress the specialty or the department are electronics technician and television technician.

Supportive staff employees who perform largely clerical functions and who are usually designated as clerks would come to the learning resource center with a general clerical background involving familiarity with such skills as typing and filing.

The library technical assistant (or library technician) may be appointed on the basis of courses taken, or of experience, or by the successful completion of specially designed examinations or a combination of any of these.

The Community College as Training Agency for LTAs

Since with few exceptions the community college provides the formal training for prospective LTAs, we shall examine its role as a training agency.

The technician who wishes to acquire familiarity with the new media of learning can obtain this in some of the LTA curricula. A number of programs include one or more courses providing orientation to nonbook media and sometimes also to the equipment needed for the utilization of the media. Most of these nonbook courses are identified as aspects of audio-visual media. Some course titles are broad, as for instance, audio-visual services, audio-visual techniques, audio-visual clerical techniques, audio-visual methods and materials, audio-visual materials and equipment. We also encounter such titles as nonbook materials and equipment, and media materials and equipment. These two titles are used as synonyms of audio-visual materials and equipment. Other titles indicate a more limited scope and denote that a course deals only with certain aspects of the audio-visual field. Examples of this category are audio-visual production, audio-visual production skills, production of projected A-V materials, and production of nonprojected A-V materials.

Some institutions have a completely integrated approach. Rather than separately presenting books, nonbook media, and the equipment needed to utilize the media, all media are included for consideration in such courses as introduction to media, production and classification, and media technology. The curriculum, in this instance, is labeled media technology rather than library technology.

The library technical assistant (LTA) programs are of the same nature as are the numerous other technician programs offered by community colleges in other fields. It is therefore in keeping with community college policy to provide library technician training. Community colleges felt impelled to enter the LTA training field because graduate library schools did not offer training—even in a separate program—on the vocational level. To provide such a program would have meant a complete reorientation of the graduate library schools and possibly the need for two different faculties, one for the graduate and one for the vocational program.

While a few programs for the training of the nonprofessional library aide were offered as early as the 1950s, the movement to establish an intermediate level gained momentum when in the 1960s measures had to be taken to meet the library manpower shortage. Most of the programs in existence today were established between 1967 and 1970.[32]

Many librarians were apprehensive that graduates of these programs might not only be employed in supportive positions but might compete with librarians for professional assignments. However, opposition against LTA programs disappeared gradually. The ALA, reflecting this changed mood, has made positive statements in favor of supportive staff categories and has urged that curricula and standards for their training be developed

and, where already in existence, LTA programs be strengthened.[33] To
assist persons who intend to establish programs and to aid in the evaluation of already existing programs, the Library Education Division of the
ALA adopted a report entitled "Criteria For Programs to Prepare Library
Technical Assistants." This report represents a statement of policy of
the Library Education Division.[34] This statement, following prevailing
practice, considers the community or junior college the agency which
should offer formal training.

The director of the library is deeply involved in this program. Without
his initiative most library technical assistant curricula would never have
seen the light. If an institution is small it may be necessary that the library
director also take over the active direction of the LTA program.[35] The
Criteria, however, do not condone that the library director hold joint
responsibility including both the administration of the resource center
and the active direction of the LTA program. However, an organization
that places the head of the teaching program within the learning resources
division would seem to be in compliance with the Criteria, if the main
condition of a separate coordinator or director of the program has been
met. Both the director of the LRC and the head of the LTA program are
expected to be ex-officio members of the advisory committee for the
LTA program.

It is of course quite proper for the director either to teach a formal
course or assume some other teaching responsibility in the LTA program.
The teaching program would usually be strengthened by the director's
participation in the program. He could, e.g., give occasional lectures on
selected topics, or he could be one of the resource persons in a seminar.

The close connection of the program with the library is not only
evidenced by advice and general support received from the director of
the LRC; the program relies heavily on the book collection and the other
resources of the library. In fact, the latter element is considered so crucial
that LTA programs should not be started unless there is adequate provision in terms of space, collection, and organization of materials.

A recent study has surveyed to what extent the LTA programs meet
the Criteria.[36] The survey has shown that many of the Criteria are met
by only some of the institutions offering LTA programs. The investigator,
Bill Hensley, cites as a mitigating circumstance the fact that a good number
of the programs had been adopted before the Criteria were established.
It may be assumed that some of the institutions that are not fully in
compliance with the Criteria will attempt to meet them as soon as feasible.

While we have noted a phenomenal growth in the number of programs, especially in the period between 1967 and 1970, we must also record that twenty-nine programs were discontinued in the period 1968 to 1971.[37] Hensley's study shows that many of the programs were on shaky ground from their inception. In some instances, funds needed for their operation were not made available. Lack of student enrollment and lack of job opportunity were cited as the principal causes for the demise of these programs.[38]

While the LTA category has been recognized in some jurisdictions and included in some civil service schemes, such recognition is far from general. As long as the persons who obtain formal training as LTAs do not receive rewards in terms of compensation and identification in position titles, this category cannot develop as rapidly, as widely, and as fully as the intrinsic personnel needs of the nation's libraries demand.

The prospects for the LTA as a viable staff category were quite bleak some ten years ago, and the uphill battle promised to be heavy.[39] In certain states civil service commissions still fail to include LTAs as a category in their classification schemes. However, in spite of roadblocks and setbacks the library technical assistant has come of age,[40] and it is certain that he will receive ever-wider recognition and become more and more firmly anchored in the broad field of librarianship.

A graduate of an LTA program should be qualified to fill most of the supportive positions in the community college learning resource centers, especially if he has become familiar during the training program not only with books but also with nonbook media and equipment. However, in some LRCs there will be need for supportive staff with specialized training, just as there is need for nonlibrarians on the professional level. Supportive staff with specialized assignments, e.g., electronics technicians and television technicians, may acquire the necessary background in the appropriate areas either by following specialized curricula or by pertinent experience in commerce and industry.

Student Assistants

Students are a most important category of assistants. They are used for many tasks since they bring to their work a wide variety of skills and experiences. They may be found in any unit of the LRC in technical and in public services. Usually they perform work of a routine nature. In practically all libraries they are either responsible for or assist with shelving. They may be found at circulation counters issuing books; they may be stationed in catalog and order departments assisting with typing or marking books; they may assist in bibliographic checking; they are often responsible for transporting A-V equipment and for operating various kinds of projectors and other devices. They may act as messengers.

While the Guidelines are emphatic in stating that student assistants should not replace provision for adequate full-time staff,[41] there are in actuality quite a number of instances where students are being used in lieu of full-time workers. This is especially true when the full-time LRC staff consists of one person; this LRC staff member may use his student assistants for tasks that in more adequately financed libraries would have been assigned to full-time staff members.

It is important to know how many hours per week students work, because the supervisor's span of control—the number of people he has to supervise—is wide if quite a number of students work only a few hours per week. It is more narrow when fewer persons have to be supervised. For instance, if the college uses 200 hours of student help per week and each student works 8 hours, the total allotment would be distributed among twenty-five students. If the average work week per student were increased to 15 hours, only thirteen students would be involved. A recent questionnaire inquiry submitted to about fifty libraries revealed that over half of the student assistants worked 15 hours on the average, one quarter worked 10 hours, and the remainder—except for two—between 10 and 15 hours. At only two institutions did students work less than 10 hours per week.[42] A survey undertaken about ten years ago, showed that very few students in junior college libraries worked as many as 15 hours; the average work week was much smaller, over half being in the 6 to 10 hour per week group.[43]

If present-day pay is compared with pay received ten years ago, we of course find considerable increases. Since pay rates are continuously subject to change, it would not seem useful to give exact figures. In general, then, increases of student aid compensation did keep pace with other pay increases. Again, as had been shown in earlier surveys, there are considerable variations in pay rates.

More institutions provide a fixed amount of pay than a graduated scheme. The former gives the same compensation to all student assistants without considering proficiency, skill, experience, or length of service; the graduated scheme takes these and/or other factors into account in establishing the rates for the individual students. The current preference for fixed amounts is in agreement with the findings of the earlier survey.

In recent years the federal government has made available funds to employ students on the work-study program. Many colleges have taken advantage of this opportunity, which usually makes it possible to employ many more aides than would have been the case without such financial assistance.

There are certain disadvantages connected with employing student aides. Aides may be tempted to stay away from work at exam time or on other occasions that appear emergencies to the student; the period of employment is relatively short, since a student usually does not continue as an aide after graduation. In spite of these disadvantages, students should be employed. They can contribute in many areas to the successful operation of the LRC. Students are assets as library aides in other ways than the help they can provide in many library activities. They are also likely to attract fellow students to the library. They may view their involvement with the library in such a positive fashion that they may wish to make librarianship their career and become either professional or supportive staff members.

NOTES

1. Association of College and Research Libraries, Committee on Standards, "Standards for Junior College Libraries," *College & Research Libraries* 21, no. 3 (May 1960):202 (hereafter cited as 1960 Standards).

2. American Library Association (Association of College and Research Libraries), et al., "Guidelines for Two-Year College Learning Resources Programs," *College & Research Libraries News* no. 11 (Dec. 1972):311 (hereafter cited as 1972 Guidelines).

3. Everett LeRoy Moore, "The Library in the Administrative and Organizational Structure of the American Public Community College" (Ph.D. diss., University of Southern California, 1973), pp. 216-7.

4. Elizabeth W. Matthews, "Characteristics and Academic Preparation of Directors of Library-Learning Resource Centers in Selected Community Junior Colleges" (Ph.D. diss., College of Education, Southern Illinois University, 1973), pp. 134-6, 138-9, 141.

5. *Ibid.*, pp. 93-94.

6. Fritz Veit, "Personnel," in *Library Services for Junior Colleges,* ed. Charles L. Trinkner (Northport, Ala.: American Southern Pub. Co., 1964), pp. 86-87.

7. *Ibid.*, p. 83.

8. Moore, *op. cit.*, pp. 219-21.

9. Matthews, *op. cit.*, pp. 84-90.

10. 1960 Standards, p. 202.

11. 1972 Guidelines, p. 311.

12. Moore, *op. cit.*, pp. 210-1.

13. Matthews, *op. cit.*, p. 102.

14. Veit, *op. cit.*, pp. 81-82.

15. Robert B. Downs, "The Current Status of University Library Staffs," in *The Status of College and University Librarians*, ACRL Monographs, no. 22 (Chicago: American Library Association, 1958), p. 14.

16. Leonard Grundt, "Community Colleges in New York State and Their Libraries," *The Bookmark* (January-February 1972): 70.

17. Leland L. Medsker and Dale Tillery, *Breaking the Access Barriers: A Profile of Two-Year Colleges* (New York: McGraw-Hill, 1971), pp. 96-97.

18. 1960 Standards, p. 202, and 1972 Guidelines, p. 311.

19. Moore, *op. cit.*, pp. 207-8.

20. Matthews, *op. cit.*, pp. 150-62.

21. U.S. Office of Education, National Center for Educational Statistics, *Library Statistics for Colleges and Universities Institutional Data. Part A, Fall 1971,* DHEW Publication No. (OE) 72-103 (Washington, D.C.: U.S. Office of Education, 1972).

22. *Ibid.*, p. 243.

23. Fritz Veit, "Training the Junior College Librarian," *Journal of Education for Librarianship* 9, no. 2 (Fall 1968): 108-15.

24. J. Periam Danton, *Between M.L.S. and Ph.D.* (Chicago: American Library Association, 1970).

25. Indiana University, Graduate Library School, *The Graduate Library School, Indiana University Presents: "Education for Librarianship in Urban Community Colleges,"* folder (Bloomington, Ind.: Indiana University. Graduate Library School, 1973?); and Charles E. Hale, Director of Institute, Interview, March 15, 1974.

26. Appalachian University, Department of Library Science, "An Institute for Training in Librarianship: The Learning Resource Center of the Two-Year College . . . Academic Year 1969-1970," folder (Boone, N.C.: Appalachian University, 1970).

27. Everett L. Moore, ed., *Junior College Libraries: Development, Needs, and Perspectives,* ACRL Monograph no. 30 (Chicago: American Library Association, 1969).

28. U.S. Office of Education, *op. cit.*, p. 243.

29. Ibid., pp. 190-235.

30. 1972 Guidelines, p. 311.

31. Fritz Veit, "The Library Technical Assistant: Some General Observations," *Illinois LIbraries* 52, no. 7 (September 1970): 711-4.

32. Noel Grego, ed., *1971 Directory of Institutions Offering or Planning Programs for the Training of Library Technical Assistants* (Chicago: Council on Library Technology, 1971).

33. A.L.A., Interdivisional Ad Hoc Committee of the Library Education Division and the Library Administration Division, "The Subprofessional or Technical Assistant: A Statement of Definition," *A.L.A. Bulletin* 62, no. 4 (April 1968): 387-97.

34. A.L.A., Library Education Division, "Criteria for Programs to Prepare Library Technical Assistants," *A.L.A. Bulletin* 63, no. 6 (June 1969): 787-94.

35. Duane R. Paulsen, "The Program Coordinator's Job," in *LTA'S in the Library Manpower Picture,* Richard L. Taylor, ed. (Chicago: Council on Library Technology, 1972), pp. 28-38.

36. Billy N. Hensley, "A Survey of Programs for the Training of Library Technical Assistants" (M.A. thesis, Graduate Library School, University of Chicago, 1971); see also: Billy N. Hensley, "Status Quo," in Richard L. Taylor, ed., *op. cit.,* pp. 4-16.

37. Grego, *op. cit.,* pp. 1-2.

38. *Ibid.,* p. 2.

39. William G. Dwyer, "End of an Experiment," *Library Journal* 87, no. 18 (October 15, 1962): 3619-22.

40. Adapted from the title *Coming of Age of LTA's,* ed. Sister Mary Chrysantha Rudnik (Chicago: Council on Library Technology, 1971).

41. 1972 Guidelines, p. 312.

42. By Sharon L. Grieder and Marvin Licht, graduate students at Rosary College, Fall 1972.

43. Veit, "Personnel," pp. 102-8.

3

ADMINISTRATIVE ORGANIZATION

The administrative organization of the learning resource center depends on many factors. There is the impact of history, or differently expressed, the persistence of an established pattern even after the basis for its continued existence has disappeared. There is the general administrative college pattern into which the learning resource center must fit. There is the size of the institution; generally, the larger the institution the more administrative levels are necessary. There is the preferred administrative style of the persons or groups who are in policy-setting positions. There is the inclination to adopt a pattern that has been successfully used in other institutions.

There is the impact of state laws or regulations that may establish an organizational framework or may prescribe curricular offerings. There is the educational role the center is expected to play, and the conviction that a certain administrative pattern is most suitable for carrying out this role. Also of importance is the question whether in a district consisting of several units, the units are free to determine their organizational pattern, or whether the pattern is set by a central office. Of great significance for the form of administrative organization is the scope of the LRC. As has been stressed repeatedly, today the majority of libraries are broader in scope than they were one or two decades ago, or even just a few years ago. An ever-increasing number of libraries are no longer concerned exclusively with print, but encompass all media—or at least a wide range.

There are several ways of dealing with nonbook resources. Each instructor can acquire and handle them on his own. This is the procedure that was widely followed when use of these nonbook resources was not common and when their acquisition depended on an individual instructor's initiative. As increasing numbers of instructors or whole teaching departments became users of these media, centralized handling was indicated. Often a separate audio-visual department was established that would be in charge of ordering, inventorying, and overseeing the college-wide utilization. Sometimes—even after an audio-visual center was established—individual instructors or departments were permitted to remain in charge of a portion of the nonbook media, for instance, films or slides.

In some colleges the library extended its role and became either totally responsible for nonbook media, or partially, by sharing this responsibility with individual instructors or with an audio-visual center. A survey by Fleming Bennett shows to what extent the various interested parties have provided audio-visual services in the mid-fifties.[1]

Librarians who assumed responsibility for both book and nonbook media followed the leadership of Louis Shores, B. Lamar Johnson, and others, who years ago pleaded for the unified treatment of all communication materials.[2] In recent years an ever-increasing number of librarians accepted such broadened responsibility.[3] The 1960 Standards had already urged that the library order, house, and administer audio-visual materials, unless another college department already handled them effectively.[4] By the time the new Guidelines were published, the unified approach was envisaged as the usual and prevailing form.[5]

Audio-visual, or more broadly speaking, nonbook media, were originally relatively small in number and unsophisticated in kind. They usually included films, filmstrips, slides, records, and the tools needed for their utilization, such as projectors. Some older nonbook media have been refined, and newer media have been devised, such as various forms of television and computer-assisted instruction.

When all media are included within one unified center or one unified institutional program, the scope of the center or program is comprehensive.

We are interested in two different aspects of administrative organization: the internal organization of the LRC and the place of the LRC within the total college structure. The difference between these two aspects can perhaps be made clear when we state that in the first instance we are largely concerned with the scope of the center, the functional units into which the center is divided, and the hierarchical staff arrangements within the center. In the second instance, we are primarily concerned with the official to whom the head of the center reports and also with his administrative position in relation to other college personnel.

INTERNAL ORGANIZATION

The internal organization of services and facilities is not complex if the learning resource center is small and consists of one person only. In such instances it may be considered preferable not to divide the job into distinct functional segments.

Since there are many small learning resource centers, it is not surprising that in his investigation Everett L. Moore found that about 34 percent of those community colleges responding to his questionnaire had practically no internal organization. Over 60 percent had the traditional forms of functional organization with departments of cataloging, circulation, and reference, and only 6.3 percent had other forms.[6]

Moore, who uses the traditional term audio-visual for nonbook services, notes that in his sample of 255 institutions, the library administered this service in 58 percent of the cases, that it was assigned to a separate audio-visual department in 20 percent of the cases, and that academic departments of the college administered it in 2 percent of the cases. In 20 percent of the cases both the library and other units of the college provided separate audio-visual services—9 percent were complementary to each other and 11 percent duplicated each other.[7] Table 3, derived from U.S. Office of Education data, which were collected about a year later than Moore's and are based on a larger sample (660 institutions), shows a higher percentage of library-connected audio-visual collections (74.4 percent) and a smaller percentage of independent audio-visual units (17.3 percent). The percentage of nonprint collections administered by other academic units, while still small (8.3 percent), is larger than in Moore's sample. Table 3 does not record separately, as Moore did, the cases where library-connected and separately administered audio-visual units exist side by side. The findings of Table 3 would probably have been still closer to those of Moore if both tabulations had used identical categories.

As already mentioned, nonbook services may be integrated in various ways with book services. It is possible to leave the whole range of nonbook services as a distinct entity that would be under the control of the same official who supervises the unit concerned with graphic media—books, periodicals, etc. Or at the opposite end of the range of possible configurations, one may have specialists responsible for all media within their area of specialization. An example where this complete integration has taken place is the College of DuPage. This philosophy is reflected by the designations given to the organizational areas and by the titles given the staff members.[8]

The areas are materials utilization, materials production, materials distribution and technical processes, and developmental learning laboratory. The term materials includes all communication media. In the

Table 3

Number and Percent of Public Two-year Institutions with Centralized Organized Collections of Audio-visual and/or Other Nonprint Materials: Aggregate United States, Fall 1971

Enrollment Size	Number of Institutions	Total Responses	Administration of Organized Collection of AV and/or Other Nonprint Materials					
			Part of Library		Independent Unit Other Than Library		Other Academic or Service Unit of Institution	
			Number	Percent	Number	Percent	Number	Percent
1	2	3	4	5	6	7	8	9
Two-year Institutions	660	618	460	74.4	107	17.3	51	8.3
10,000 or more	55	54	29	53.7	20	37.0	5	9.3
5,000 to 9,999	80	78	55	70.5	17	21.8	6	7.7
1,000 to 4,999	357	329	248	75.4	52	15.8	29	8.8
500 to 999	123	117	97	82.9	12	10.3	8	6.8
Fewer than 500	45	40	31	77.5	6	15.0	3	7.5

SOURCE: U.S. Office of Education, National Center for Educational Statistics, *Library Statistics for Colleges and Universities*, Fall 1971, Analytic Report (Part C), Washington, D.C., 1973, p. 60 (Table C-23).

Learning Resources Center Handbook the patron is advised regarding
the materials utilization area: "Use this area for help with reference
problems, for the location and use of all LRC personnel, materials, equipment and services. . . ."[9] With regard to materials distribution and technical processes, it is noted that "this area orders and receives all materials,
equipment and supplies for the LRC and also prepares and catalogs for
use all materials. . . ."[10]

It may be mentioned that at a recent reorganization of the DuPage
LRC administrative structure the two areas, materials utilization and
materials production, were combined to form one unit[11] (See Figure 15.)*

In many other learning resource centers it is assumed that specialists
are needed to deal with book and nonbook media separately; and different staff members are in charge of book and nonbook media, respectively. There are also numerous instances where hardware—the
equipment required for the utilization of the media: projectors for
movies, projectors for filmstrips, etc.—is in the charge of specially trained
persons, while the software is with the print materials. It is also possible
that most nonbook materials and the necessary equipment are integrated
with graphic media but that certain media, in particular those that require treatment of a highly technical nature, form a distinct unit; an
example would be a television unit.

There are numerous possible forms of organization for which examples can be found in practice. Even if the nonbook materials are administered as a unit within the LRC, it is not unusual that the technical
services department catalogs the software. Also quite often the order
department (or acquisitions department), which orders books and
periodicals, also orders nonbook materials. For instance, at Macomb County Community College, South Campus, Warren, Michigan, the learning
media center consists of three units: library, audio-visual, and programmed
learning. The technical services department, which is part of the library
unit, handles the acquisition of materials and the other technical processes
for all three units of the learning media center. (See Figure 6.)

As we have mentioned previously, a considerable number of institutions
have altered the designation library to learning resource center or to an
equivalent term that reflects the concern for many media rather than for
print only. However, such title changes have not been carried through
everywhere. Many comprehensive resource centers are still called libraries.
In some cases this may be ascribed exclusively to the desire to retain a

* For all figures in this chapter, see pages 55-73.

well-known designation; in other instances it may conform to widespread usage in a state.

An examination of organizational patterns of over 100 institutions from all over the United States shows great variety. We will reproduce a few of the charts that seemed representative of the principal forms.

It has already been stressed that the smaller the institution the simpler the organization is likely to be. In fact, if there should be only one staff member, he would have to handle all work himself. However, if he analyzes the whole range of duties and puts related tasks together into activity groupings, he may be able to perform his job more efficiently. Such analyses, of course, become more purposeful and more urgent when larger staffs are involved.

Fortunately, most community college learning resource staffs today consist of more than one member (professional and nonprofessional members combined). The head of the learning resource center should then introduce division of labor and select the staff member most suitable for the task or cluster of tasks to be performed. If there are only a few staff members, each may have to assume responsibility for several activity areas; if the staff is large, greater specialization is indicated. Arrangement and grouping of activities can rest on a variety of bases. We will mention just four: function, clientele, geography, and subject.

Arrangement by function is the division of work by activity, such as acquisition, cataloging, and reference.

The criterion of clientele is applied, for example, if different collections and staffs are used for transfer students and for terminal students.

Geography is the essential decisive element if activities and services must be determined by location, as would be the case with satellite, departmental, or branch libraries.

Subject refers to the arrangement of library functions and materials on the basis of a subject field; for instance, the establishment of separate libraries for art or music or psychology.

TO WHOM SHOULD THE HEAD
OF THE CENTER REPORT?

As a matter of principle it is desirable that the LRC head report to the highest official possible; this will vary with the situation in each institution. In the past it has been advocated that the librarian report to the chief administrative officer of the college. In fact, the 1960 Standards state flatly that the librarian is usually appointed by the chief administrative officer of the college and that he should be directly responsible to him for the management of the library.[12] This is no longer expressed in such an unequivocal way. Today there are many large community colleges with enrollments of several thousand students and a correspondingly large faculty and nonacademic support staff. To administer such an aggregate of students, faculty, and civil service employees necessitates a complex administrative machinery. The chief administrator requires the aid of assistants who are in charge of day-to-day administration. The chief administrator is usually called president, but he may also be known by other designations, such as chancellor. Typically the chief administrative officer of a large college is assisted by three to four second-level aides who may be called vice-president, vice-chancellor, or dean. The term vice-president (or vice-chancellor) is usually used by the larger institutions, and the term dean by the smaller colleges. The three most commonly found second-level officials are vice-president or dean of student affairs, vice-president or dean of academic affairs, and vice-president or dean of business affairs. Additional second-level officials are appointed with titles such as vice-president or dean for special services, and vice-president or dean for development. Not usual on the community college level is the pattern which places an executive vice-president on the second level and the other vice-presidents on the third level. In rather small organizations the administrative setup is very simple and may consist of only the president and one dean on the second level.

It should also be mentioned that in former years the chief administrative officer of the college was more frequently called dean, or occasionally executive dean. This was especially true where junior colleges were part of the common school system, and where the general superintendent of schools was also president of the college. When the highest official of a college is called dean, second level officials usually are called assistant deans.

To whom should the head of the learning resource center report if he does not report to the chief administrator directly? It is generally recommended that the LRC head report to the officer in overall charge of academic affairs. This trend is also reflected in the new Guidelines, which prescribe that the chief administrator of a learning resources program report to that official who is responsible for the college's instructional program.[13] This officer may be called academic vice-president or academic dean. In a small institution where there is only one dean, his title would not be particularized by an adjective.

In increasing numbers, heads of learning resource centers report through an academic vice-president or dean or other intermediate officer; this trend has been noted by Moore[14] and others. Only 14.2 percent of Moore's sample of 254 reported directly to the president, while Helen Wheeler[15] noted in her study (which preceded Moore's by several years) that 58 percent of those responding reported directly to the chief administrative officer. Moore considers that the differences between the findings of his study and Wheeler's might have been somewhat less if each questionnaire had not been so different in several respects.

Our investigation confirms that in most instances the director of learning resources reports to the college official who is in charge of academic affairs. However, occasionally the director is assigned to another division. In a specific situation this administrative organization may work out satisfactorily; however, there is some risk that the learning resources program may not achieve the necessary close contact and interaction with the instructional program.

The instances of direct reporting to the head of the institution have been further reduced in recent times and gradually have become the exception. Discussions with heads of library resource centers disclosed that the pattern as it is established on charts does not always reflect the actual situation, or does not reflect it completely. In such discussions heads of centers have occasionally stated that informal relationships exist between the chief administrative officer of the college and the head of the resource center. The chief administrative officer often makes himself accessible and sometimes functions in practice as the official with whom direct administrative contacts could or should be maintained.

FLUIDITY OF ORGANIZATIONAL ARRANGEMENTS

Many institutions of higher learning review their curricula and organizational patterns at stated or irregular intervals. Such reviews often entail organizational changes. What may have been a correct representation when the chart was developed may no longer be correct at the time an outsider examines it.

For instance, in an article that appeared in 1967 Fred F. Harcleroad[16] introduced the organization of Brevard Junior College as an example of the integration in one division of media of all kinds. This division—the division of educational services—included the following seven units: 1) office of instructional resources; 2) office of data processing and technical resources; 3) library; 4) TV and radio center; 5) A-V resource center; 6) study skills clinic; and 7) language laboratory.

Upon inquiry as to whether any changes had occurred within a five-year span, the writer was informed[17] that the old division of educational services had been completely reorganized into a learning resources operation under a dean of learning resources. The learning resources division consists of the following areas: Cocoa campus library, Melbourne campus library, media services, and engineering. It is noted that within the learning resources division libraries perform the traditional library functions, and that media services handles the traditional A-V functions as well as audio and video productions, and procurement of materials and related equipment for both Cocoa and Melbourne campuses. Engineering services handles the maintenance and repair of media services equipment and also electronic requirements of both Cocoa and Melbourne campuses.

The fluidity of organizational arrangements is well illustrated by the case history reported by Alice Griffith, who describes the changes her own institution, Mohawk Valley Community College Library, has undergone.[18] At four successive periods the charts reflect the changes that have resulted from additions to staff and consequent redistribution of duties. Mrs. Griffith states that she found it necessary to have at least two professional associates before she could devote a sizable amount of her time to administration. The case history of her library illustrates typical library developmental processes. At first the staff consisted of one professional and one clerk (1956); three years later a secretary as well as an A-V assistant were added; two years later another secretary was added; the following year the professional staff was increased by one person. Only then could the head librarian withdraw from such non-administrative functions as reference and circulation work. The most recent chart (1972) shows, in addition to the library director, five professional staff members—four librarians and an A-V specialist. This chart is reproduced as Figure 3.

Another and more recent example of change may be observed by comparing a set of charts for William Rainey Harper College, Palatine,

Illinois (Figures 11-14). The pattern that appeared in the staff booklet for 1971-1972 shows a director of library services responsible for book services only and a director of instructional services responsible for all nonbook functions. The organizational pattern dated 5/3/72 reveals that the resource center has abandoned the division into book and nonbook resources. The new system makes one official responsible for all media in the public service area and another official responsible for all media in the processing area. The production services that formerly were part of the instructional services unit were assigned to a separate division.

VARIOUS PATTERNS

At this point we shall introduce a number of additional charts that give a few of the many possible configurations. We are interested in the LRC internal organization: in differences among them in scope, in arrangement of the functions, and in the units or divisions into which the functions fall. We are also interested in the the hierarchical level assigned to the head of the center.

Some charts give only the position of the head of the resource center in the total college hierarchy. Some give the internal organization of the resource center only. Some charts give both kinds of information. We will move from the more simple to the more complex.

Traditionally, community college libraries, like other libraries, have performed the functions of ordering, cataloging, reference, and circulation; frequently they have also had the responsibility for nonbook materials. If the organization was small, the one-person library was not broken down into departments or divisions. Differentiation set in with the increase in number of staff members. A library with several staff members frequently showed the kind of pattern that developed in the Mohawk Community College Library (Figure 3). There is considerable interaction among personnel and mutual use of records. Therefore, order work, cataloging, and related technical activities were combined by some LRCs into a technical services division. Likewise, reference, circulation, and other aspects of service to the public were combined into a public services division. This arrangement has the advantage of reducing the number of prsons with whom the chief administrator of the LRC must maintain direct contact. Such an arrangement is illustrated by Chaffey College (Figure 4). At Chaffey the library is not in charge of audio-visual activities. The arrangement for Clayton Junior College is similar, except that here nonbook media are the responsibility of the library and the staff is increased by a media services librarian (Figure 5).

As illustrated by Figure 8, at Portland Community College, Portland, Oregon, the official in charge of the media center is called head librarian rather than director of media center. He heads two units: library and learning center. The head librarian reports to the coordinator, instructional support services who, in turn, is responsible to the college services director.

An examination of the organization chart for Monroe Community College (Figure 9) reveals that the head is called director of libraries and instructional services; the chairman of instructional services is therefore responsible to him. However, the vice-president for faculty affairs, who is the superior of the director of libraries, maintains a direct non-supervisory relationship with the chairman of instructional services.

At Central Piedmont Community College the learning resources area, which is headed by a vice-president, comprises six units (Figure 10). As may be seen on this chart, the media service department is in charge of A-V hardware only. The library services department is responsible for the acquisition and cataloging of all A-V software as well as for the ordering of materials for preview and rental. The A-V librarian is attached to the library's technical serivces department. William Rainey Harper Community College is represented by Figures 11-14, with Figure 11 giving the total college setup, Figures 12 and 13 reflecting the situation of the learning resource center, before reorganization, and Figure 14 giving the learning resource center pattern as created by the reorganization of May 1972. Like the revised chart for Harper (11) and the chart for DuPage (15) the chart for Reading Area Community College (16) shows the full integration of book and nonbook resources and services.[19]

The charts for two colleges of the junior college district of St. Louis—Florissant (Figure 17) and Meramec (Figure 18)—are introduced to show that institutions under the jurisdiction of the same board of control may have patterns that are different from each other. This is more likely to happen if the units are treated as individual colleges rather than as campuses. Many examples could be cited from all over the nation to illustrate this point. In the Los Angeles community college district, for instance, there is considerable variety among the eight colleges regarding the scope of the library. Hal C. Stone informed the writer that the practices at the eight colleges of the district vary with regard to responsibility for audio-visual services.[20] In some colleges A-V is connected administratively with the library, in other colleges it is not. Only at LACC are all areas under one coordinator. Stone also noted that there is a considerable degree of cooperation among the library coordinators of the colleges. They meet regularly to discuss policies and procedures as well as actual problems. There is some cooperation in interlibrary loan. The eight colleges jointly share a bindery contract and a purchasing and processing contract, but book selection and internal organization are autonomous.

Betty Duvall noted that there has been no need for formal cooperative agreements among the three colleges of the junior college district of St. Louis, since all three operate under the umbrella of the district.[21] The cooperation is informal, yet very close, and in Mrs. Duvall's view works to the advantage of everyone involved. The catalog for the district, being a union catalog, facilitates interlibrary loan and other cooperative endeavors.

On the other hand, there may be central direction of the LRCs of several colleges maintained by the same district. The Tarrant County junior college district is a clear example of a multi-unit organization with central direction.[22] The college currently includes the south campus (Fort Worth, Texas) and the northeast campus (Hurst, Texas); the addition of a third campus and possibly a fourth is anticipated.

The office of dean of learning resources provides central leadership and sets overall policies. The technical services, including all automation activities, are performed centrally. It is the intention of the central office to relieve the campus librarians of "routine and mundane" tasks in order that they can make their more specialized services fully available to students, faculty, and other staff. The Tarrant County junior college district operational model contains numerous charts illustrating organization and flow of work. The chart which is reproduced below (Figure 19) reflects the organization of the learning resources area.[23] It also shows that the dean of learning resources reports directly to the college president. This places him on the same hierarchical level as the dean of instruction.

Figure 21 is a detailed model developed by Janiece F. Fusaro.[24] It is built on the library-college concept and therefore illustrates the integration of all media under unified administration. Special attention is given to innovative practices by the provision of an innovations and curriculum design center. This center, part of the learning resources program, is headed by an educational development officer—or, to use B. Lamar Johnson's only half-facetious term, "Vice-President in Charge of Heresy" (VPCH).[25] At the time the model was prepared, the Guidelines for two-year college learning resources programs had not yet been issued. However, the Standards for school media programs were already in force and could be utilized by Mrs. Fusaro.

Branch Libraries

These are units of service provided by a college—frequently, but not necessarily, at locations different from the main campus. Branch libraries are generally considered integral parts of the main library. Usually the main library orders the materials for a branch library. However, occasionally it may be more practical to authorize a branch library to order and catalog its own materials, particularly if these materials are specialized and need not also be represented in the main library.

It would seem advisable not to base decisions on ordering and cataloging responsibilities on abstract principles, but on practicality. Within the City University of New York, the Borough of Manhattan Community College, the Bronx Community College, and the New York City Community College have branch campuses, each with its own library. New York City Community College has two branch libraries: Livingston Street, serving business and graphic arts students, and Voorhees (formerly an independent technical institute). At New York City Community College the main library orders and processes the materials for the branches. Figure 20 shows that the branch librarians report to the head of public services of the main library.

The branch library under the jurisdiction of Bronx Community College is unique. It is the branch nursing library, located in the nursing center of the Bronx Municipal Hospital Center. It is near classrooms, laboratories, and the living quarters of the nurses. Here it has been deemed advisable that the branch order and catalog materials directly.[26]

Departmental Libraries

In university libraries, and to a lesser extent, in senior college libraries, departmental libraries can still be found though not as numerously as one or two decades ago. The outstanding example is Harvard where the library facilities are highly decentralized. Harvard consists of over 90 units: departmental libraries, branch libraries, and other entities with varying degrees of independence from the main library. Following the European example, university departments formed their own collections, often more extensive than the main collection in their respective fields.

Figure 3

Mohawk Valley Community College Library

Reproduced by permission of Mohawk Valley Community College.

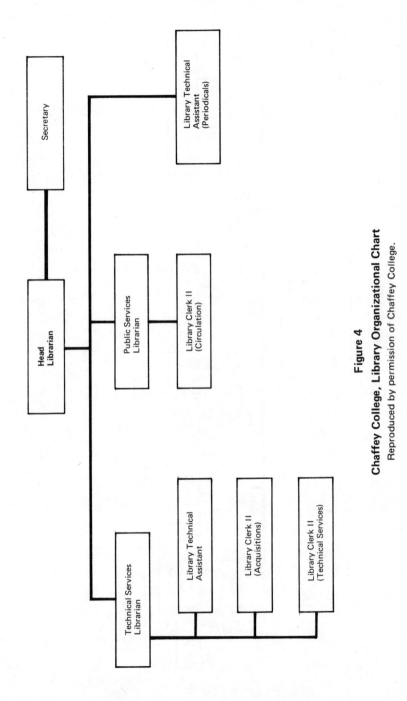

Figure 4
Chaffey College, Library Organizational Chart
Reproduced by permission of Chaffey College.

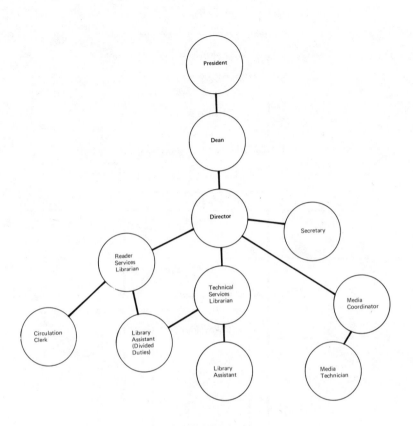

Figure 5
Clayton Junior College Library
Reproduced by permission of Clayton Junior College.

Cost of duplication and inconvenience to nondepartmental members are some of the reasons that militate against departmental collections and favor the centralization of resources. When increasing enrollments and growing collections made it necessary for large institutions to erect new buildings, the resources were usually gathered together and placed into central libraries. However, in many institutions a few of the departmental libraries survived, either because they served a highly specialized field, or because they served departments at faraway corners of the campus.

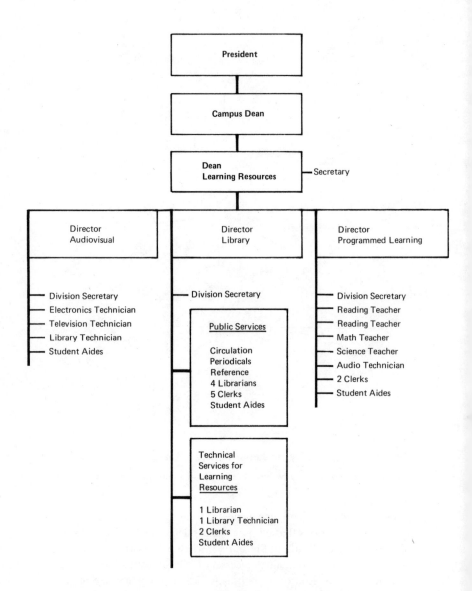

Figure 6

**Macomb County Community College, South Campus,
Learning Media Center**

Reproduced by permission of Macomb County Community College.

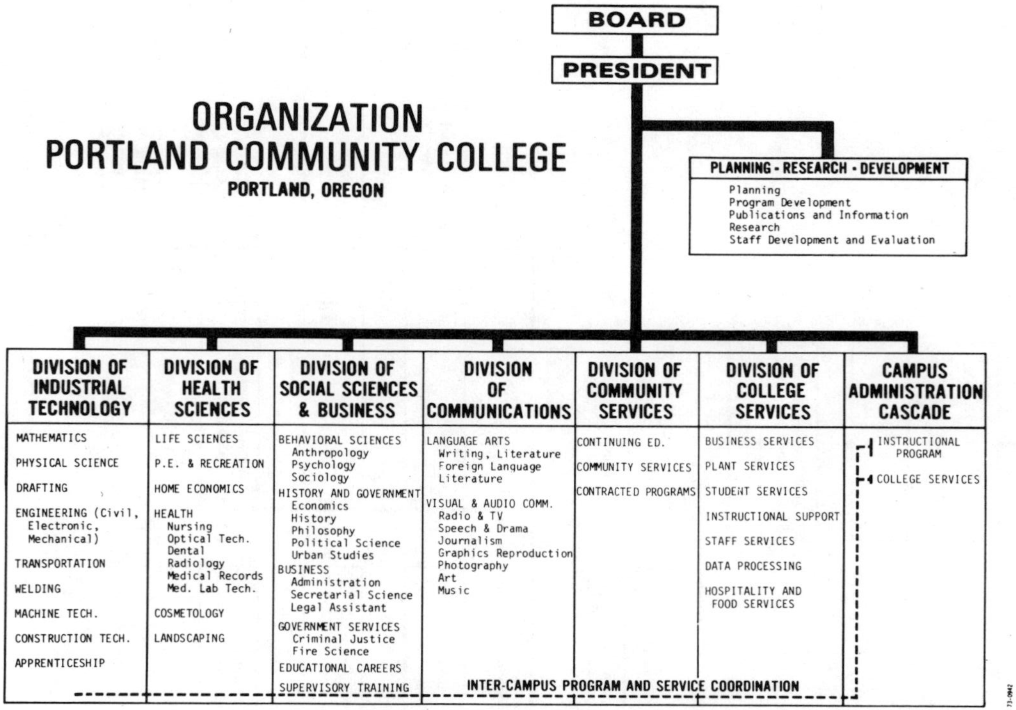

ORGANIZATION
PORTLAND COMMUNITY COLLEGE
PORTLAND, OREGON

BOARD

PRESIDENT

PLANNING - RESEARCH - DEVELOPMENT
Planning
Program Development
Publications and Information
Research
Staff Development and Evaluation

DIVISION OF INDUSTRIAL TECHNOLOGY	DIVISION OF HEALTH SCIENCES	DIVISION OF SOCIAL SCIENCES & BUSINESS	DIVISION OF COMMUNICATIONS	DIVISION OF COMMUNITY SERVICES	DIVISION OF COLLEGE SERVICES	CAMPUS ADMINISTRATION CASCADE
MATHEMATICS	LIFE SCIENCES	BEHAVIORAL SCIENCES	LANGUAGE ARTS	CONTINUING ED.	BUSINESS SERVICES	INSTRUCTIONAL PROGRAM
PHYSICAL SCIENCE	P.E. & RECREATION	Anthropology	Writing, Literature	COMMUNITY SERVICES	PLANT SERVICES	COLLEGE SERVICES
DRAFTING	HOME ECONOMICS	Psychology	Foreign Language	CONTRACTED PROGRAMS	STUDENT SERVICES	
ENGINEERING (Civil, Electronic, Mechanical)	HEALTH	Sociology	Literature		INSTRUCTIONAL SUPPORT	
TRANSPORTATION	Nursing	HISTORY AND GOVERNMENT	VISUAL & AUDIO COMM.		STAFF SERVICES	
WELDING	Optical Tech.	Economics	Radio & TV		DATA PROCESSING	
MACHINE TECH.	Dental	History	Speech & Drama		HOSPITALITY AND FOOD SERVICES	
CONSTRUCTION TECH.	Radiology	Philosophy	Journalism			
APPRENTICESHIP	Medical Records	Political Science	Graphics Reproduction			
	Med. Lab Tech.	Urban Studies	Photography			
	COSMETOLOGY	BUSINESS	Art			
	LANDSCAPING	Administration	Music			
		Secretarial Science				
		Legal Assistant				
		GOVERNMENT SERVICES				
		Criminal Justice				
		Fire Science				
		EDUCATIONAL CAREERS				
		SUPERVISORY TRAINING				

INTER-CAMPUS PROGRAM AND SERVICE COORDINATION

Figure 7

Portland Community College, Organization
Reproduced by permission of Portland Community College.

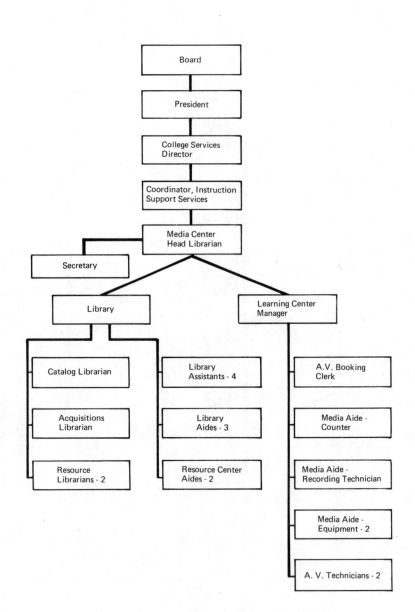

Figure 8

Portland Community College, Media Center

Reproduced by permission of Portland Community College.

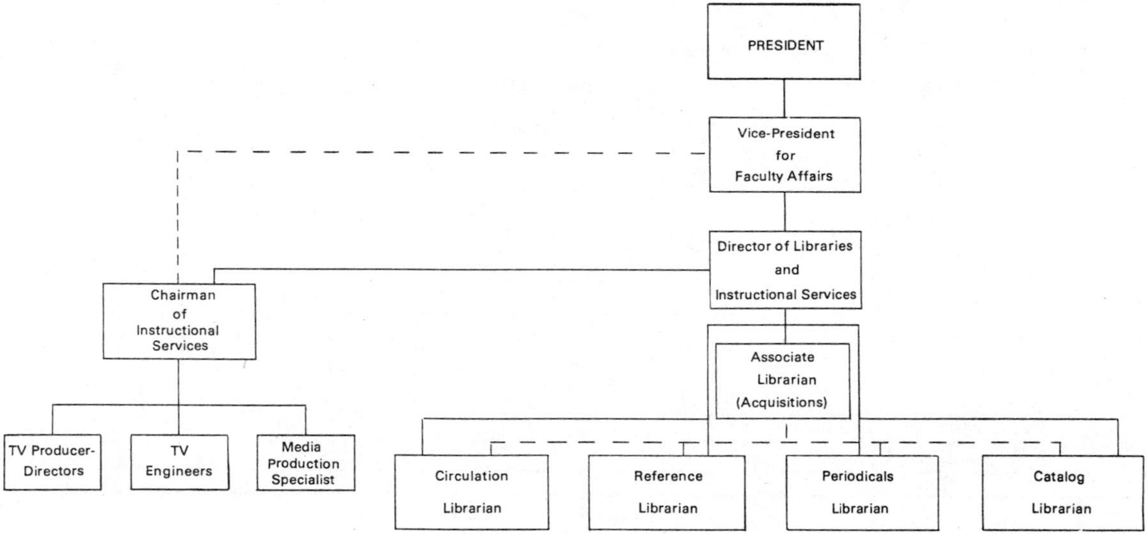

Figure 9

Monroe Community College
Library and Instructional Services Organization Chart, 1970-1971

Reproduced by permission of Monroe Community College.

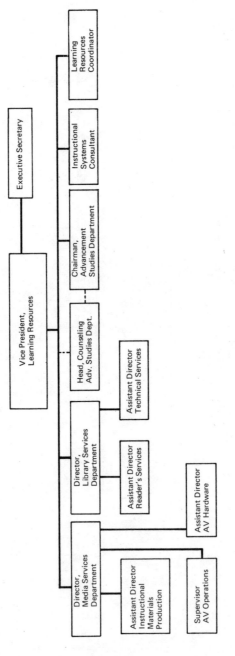

Figure 10

Central Piedmont Community College, Learning Resources Division

Reproduced by permission of Central Piedmont Community College.

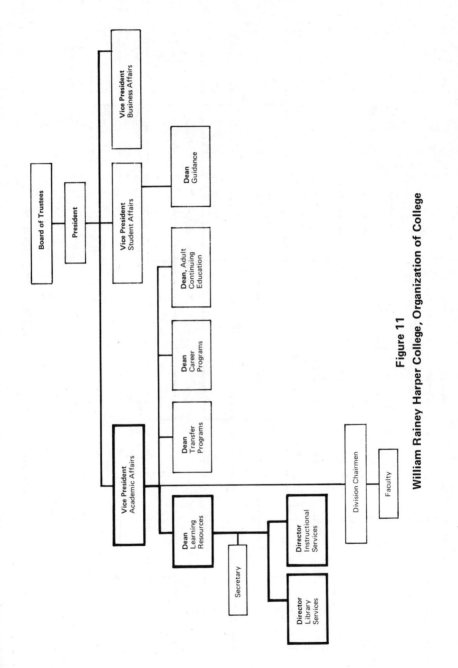

Figure 11

William Rainey Harper College, Organization of College

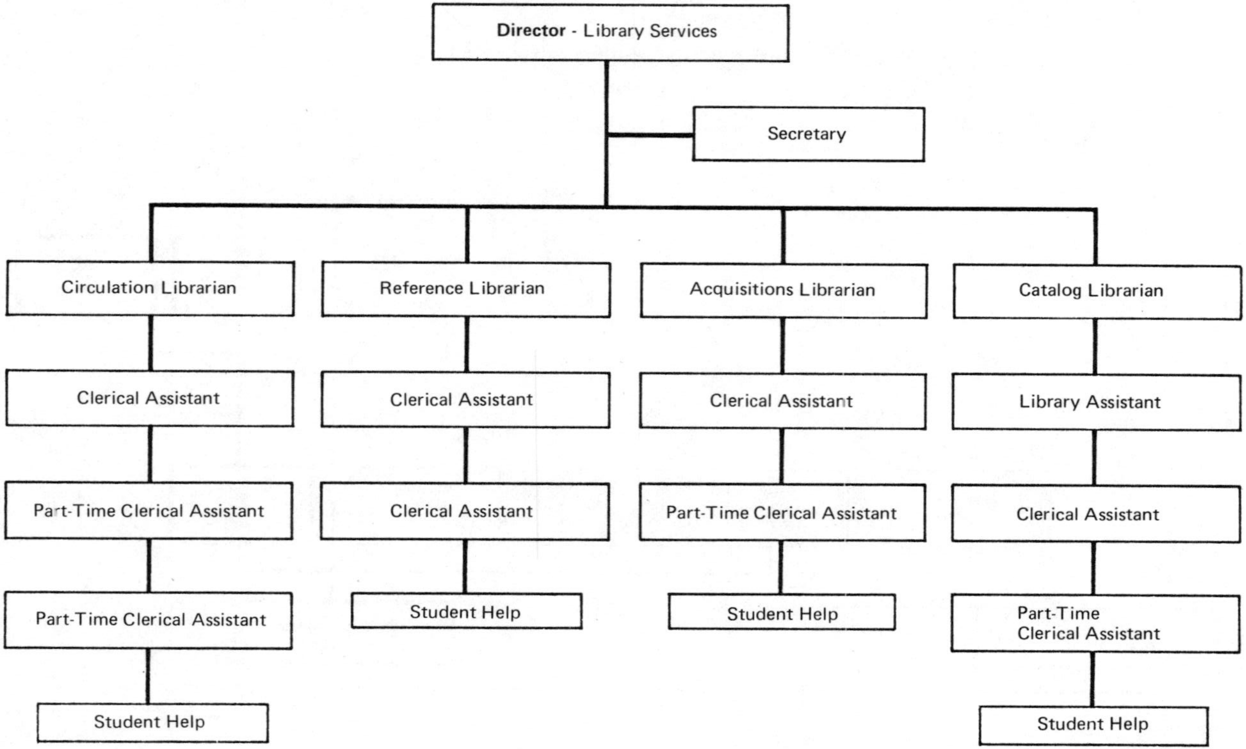

Figure 12
William Rainey Harper College, LRC Library Services

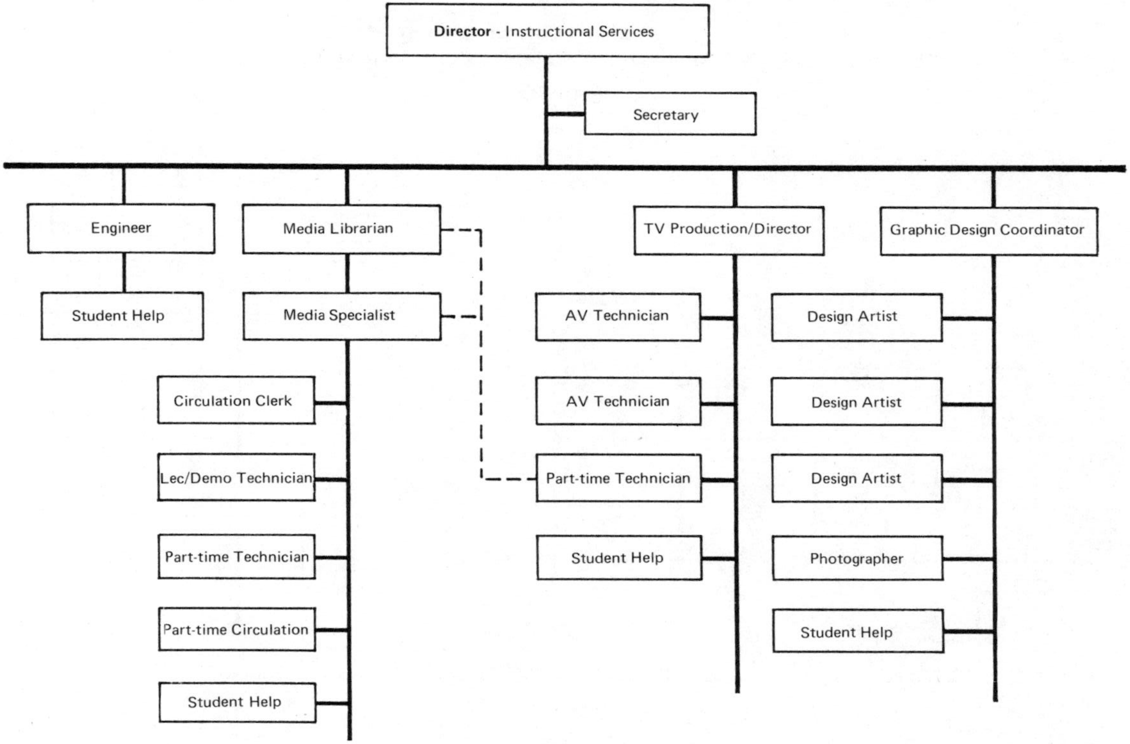

Figure 13
William Rainey Harper College, LRC Instructional Services

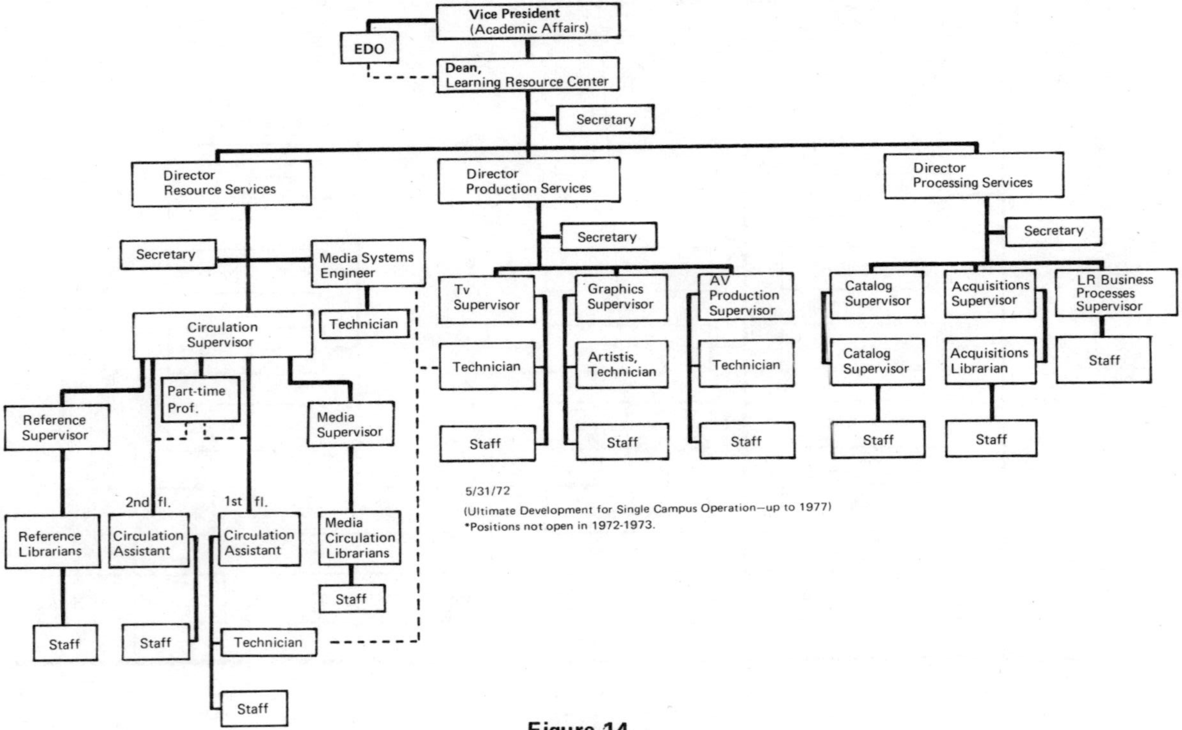

Figure 14

William Rainey Harper College, Learning Resource Center, Reorganization Dated 5/31/72

Figures 11 throuth 14 reproduced by permission of William Rainey Harper College.

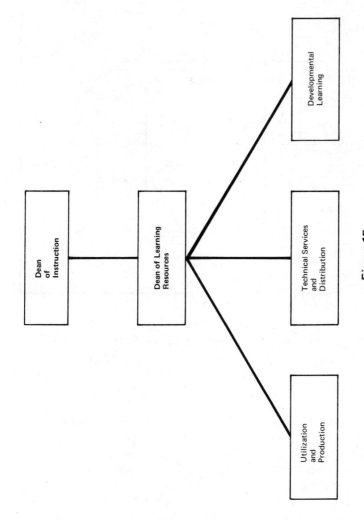

Figure 15

College of DuPage, Learning Resources Center

Reproduced by permission of College of DuPage.

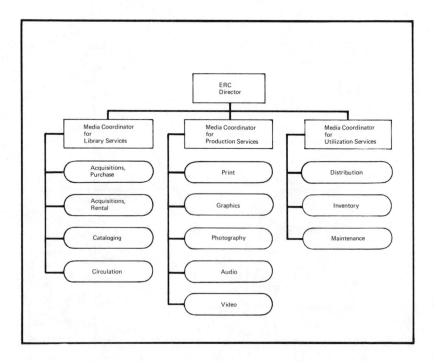

Figure 16

Reading Area Community College, Educational Resources Center

SOURCE: Jeanne M. Douglas, "Media Library Integration in Practice,"
Audio-Visual Instruction 18, no. 3 (March 1973): 84. Reproduced by permission
of Jeanne M. Douglas.

In the community college field the facilities of a campus usually are located
within a smaller geographical area. Moreover, from the outset it was
generally understood that the book and periodical resources would be
kept in the college library. Therefore, we find that only a few community
colleges have departmental libraries. However, as community colleges
grow in size and occupy ever larger acreage, pressure for providing service
at various locations on the campus will become strong. The demand will
probably not be for the traditional kind of departmental libraries, which
by definition are limited to a narrow field. Departmental libraries would
then consist of collections with selections from all fields represented in

the main library or of micro-collections formed from an aggregate of several fields. The demands would differ from institution to institution, depending on the respective curricular requirements. In the community college field these secondary resource locations are usually designated as satellite libraries or satellite centers.

Institutions in the process of assessing their future resources requirements have been concerned with this problem. For instance, in discussing resource projections for the Tarrant County junior college district this observation has been made: "The growing need for satellite centers to

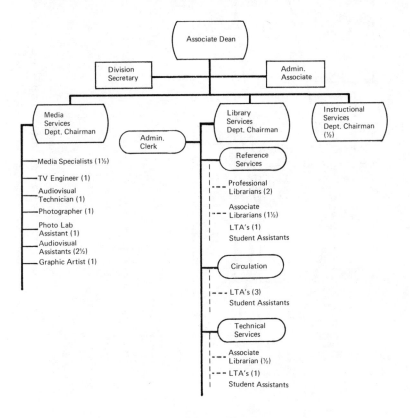

Figure 17

Florissant Valley Community College, Instructional Resources
Reproduced by permission of Florissant Valley Community College.

ORGANIZATION CHART
Levels of Authority and Decision Making

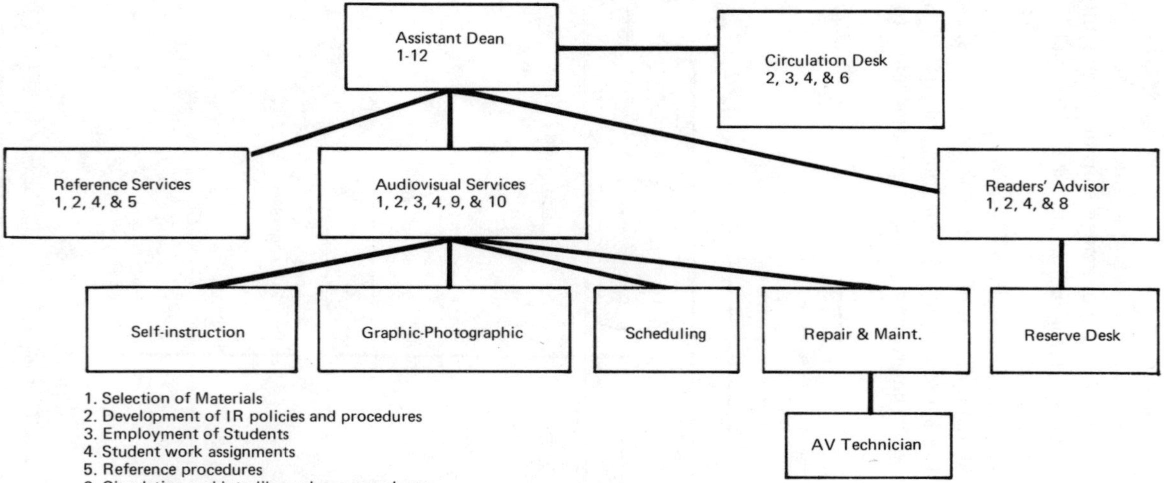

Assistant Dean
1-12

Circulation Desk
2, 3, 4, & 6

Readers' Advisor
1, 2, 4, & 8

Reference Services
1, 2, 4, & 5

Audiovisual Services
1, 2, 3, 4, 9, & 10

Reserve Desk

Repair & Maint.

Scheduling

Graphic-Photographic

Self-instruction

AV Technician

1. Selection of Materials
2. Development of IR policies and procedures
3. Employment of Students
4. Student work assignments
5. Reference procedures
6. Circulation and interlibrary loan procedures
7. Procedures pertaining to acquisition of books, periodicals and microfilm
8. Reserve procedures
9. Audiovisual procedures pertaining to media production, repair and
   maintenance, and equipment distribution
10. Audiovisual procedures pertaining to acquisition of filmstrips, records,
    slides, tapes, etc.
11. Budget and purchasing
12. Staff recommendations

Figure 18

Meramec Community College, Instructional Resources Division

Reproduced by permission of Meramec Community College

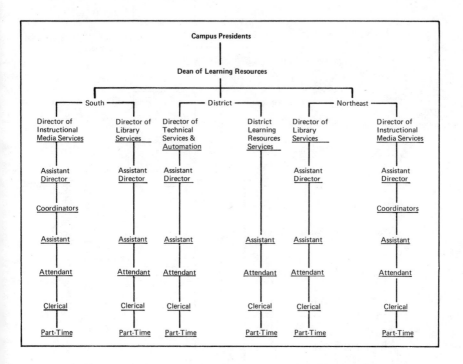

Figure 19

Tarrant County Junior College District, Learning Resources

Reproduced by permission of Tarrant County Junior College District, South Campus.

support instruction is another area demanding careful attention because of the requirements for staff and resources inherent in this type of service...."[27] At DuPage the matter of establishing satellite centers was considered when the college was subdivided into six cluster colleges of varying sizes. However, it was decided that all services offered by the learning resource center and the developmental learning laboratory should remain centralized, with the option that facilities and resources could be decentralized into small resource laboratories as individual college needs might demand. Further possibilities considered were that each college might have a browsing room and/or a reading shelf of important books and periodicals relating to the college, as well as basic A-V materials.[28]

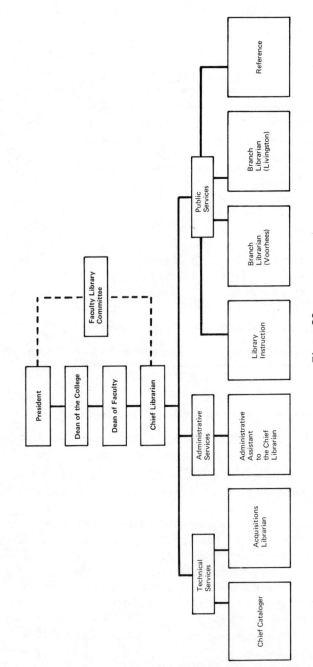

Figure 20

New York City Community College, Library Department

Reproduced by permission of New York City Community College, Brooklyn, New York.

LIBRARY-COLLEGE MEDIA CENTER

Dean, Associate Dean
or
STRUCTURE AND SERVICES   Director

Media Services (print and nonprint)

Study Skills Center & Learning Labs.	Public Services	Technical Services	Instructional Services	Innovations and Curriculum Design Center
Reading Lab. Independent Study Labs. CAI, Dial Access, and other educational technology	Reader's Services SDI Current Awareness Circulation Periodicals Reserve	Acquisition Cataloging Processing Duplicating Services	Educational Media Services: Materials Production Art and Photography Printing Television Booking and Scheduling Previewing	Professional and Innovations Library Research and Development Faculty Conference Rooms Experimental Classrooms

STAFFING NEEDS

| 1 Reading Specialist 1 Learning Specialist Counselors & Faculty ad lib Clerk Typist Student Help Other Technical Help as needed | 1 Media Specialist 1 Media Technician 1 Media Aide | 1 Media Specialist 2 Media Technicians 1 Media Aide | 1 Media Specialist Teacher Aides 1 Media Technician 1 Media Aide Other Technical Help as needed | EDO (VPCH) 1 Curriculum Specialist 1 Media Aide |

Titles Suggested: Dean, Associate Dean, or Director of Learning Media Center, Study Skills Center Coordinator; Media Services Coordinator; Instructional Services Coordinator; Educational Development Officer (VPCH)

TOTAL STAFFING NEEDS

4 Media Specialists (Standards* call for 1 professor per 250 students; diagram is for 1,000 students)
4 Media Technicians (Standards call for 1 media technician per media specialist)
4 Media Aides (Standards call for 1 media aide per media specialist)
1 Reading Specialist
2 Learning Specialists or Curriculum Specialists (professor and technical staff as needed)
1 Educational Development Officer
*Standards for School Media Programs.

Figure 21
Library-College Media Center

SOURCE: Janiece Fusaro, "Toward Library-College Media Centers; A Proposal for the Nation's Community Colleges," *Junior College Journal* 40, no. 7 (April 1970): 44. Reproduced with permission of Janiece Fusaro.

At DuPage all of the clusters are in close proximity to the learning resource center. Satellite centers were therefore not found necessary, especially since each cluster college has been assigned a member of the LRC staff as a special consultant. These consultants have been able to act as expediters of many of the special requirements cluster colleges may have.

The pressure for establishing satellite resource centers may also come in an indirect fashion. In a number of institutions, carrels with dial access to a central originating source have been distributed over many buildings.

Since these carrels usually are under the jurisdiction of the LRC, the LRC
may possibly be approached with the request to provide more comprehensive satellite service, i.e., to add graphic resources to the information
obtained through electronic channels.

Divisional Libraries

This arrangement, which should be distinguished from the departmental
arrangement, occurs relatively infrequently at the community college
level. The departmental form deals with small segments of knowledge.
There are, e.g., departmental libraries in physics, chemistry, mathematics,
economics, German, psychology, and music. However, if we combine
related departments into larger units we form divisions. Following the
example of some large public libraries, some larger college and university libraries have divided their holdings into two, three, four, or even
five large divisions. Favored divisions are social sciences, humanities,
and natural sciences. In the sciences division, e.g., the holdings in
physics, chemistry, biology, mathematics, and all the other disciplines
in science would be combined. Such divisions are not practical if the
collection is relatively small. This is why the divisional arrangement is
infrequently found on the community college level.

The decision to split the library into divisions may be made at the
time a building is planned, or it may be chosen because the layout of an
already existing campus makes the divisional pattern the most practical
arrangement. Probably the best-known example of a divisional arrangement is that of Mt. San Antonio College, Walnut, California. The library
is divided into two large areas, each of which contains two divisions:
social sciences—humanities form one area; and biological sciences-
physical sciences, including technology, form the second area. To
interpret the collection, subject specialists are assigned to each of the
four divisions. The subject specialists also assist in the building of the
collections in their respective divisions. Also part of the Mt. San Antonio
College Library are the audio-visual facilities and the developmental
laboratory, each of which form a separate unit.

While the broad subject areas into which the library at Mt. San Antonio
is divided are along traditional lines, the arrangement of the Lansing
Community College LRC is tailored to fit a local situation. The learning
resources division of Lansing Community College consists of two libraries,
two instructional media centers, and the planetarium. One collection and

one instructional media center are in the liberal arts college building in which arts, sciences, and health careers instruction takes place; another collection and another instructional media center are in the business-technology college building. In general each library has the materials that are related to the work of the teaching departments housed in the building. Since the libraries are in different buildings, and since some of the same materials are needed in both areas, a certain amount of duplication could not be avoided.[29]

Brookdale Community College consists of four physically separated institutes that offer different options to the student. These institutes, which might also be termed cluster colleges, are the institute of applied humanities, the institute of human affairs, the institute of business and management, and the institute of natural and applied sciences. Each institute has a unit of the learning resource center that contains the materials needed by that institute. The resource areas of the several institutes are interconnected so that they form a continuous learning resource area and offer to the user unhampered access to the total resources.[30]

NOTES

1. Fleming Bennett, "Audio-Visual Services in Colleges and Universities in the United States," *College & Research Libraries* 16, no. 1 (January 1955): 11-19.

2. Louis Shores, "The Junior College Impact on Academic Librarianship," *College & Research Libraries* 30, no. 3 (May 1969): 214-21; B. Lamar Johnson, *Vitalizing the College Library* (Chicago: American Library Association, 1939); and B. Lamar Johnson, "Vitalizing a College Library; A Quarter Century Later," in his *Junior College Library* (Los Angeles: University of California, 1966), pp. 23-29.

3. Ruth M. Christensen, "The Junior College Library as an Audio-Visual Center," *College & Research Libraries* 26, no. 2 (March 1965): 121-8.

4. Association of College and Research Libraries, Committee on Standards, "Standards for Junior College Libraries," *College & Research Libraries* 21, no. 3 (May 1960): 204.

5. American Library Association (Association of College and Research Libraries), et al., "Guidelines for Two-Year College Learning Resources Programs," *College & Research Libraries News* no. 11 (December 1972): 305-6.

6. Everett LeRoy Moore, "The Library in the Administrative and

Organizational Structure of the American Public Community College"
(Ph.D. diss., University of Southern California, 1973), pp. 148-9.

7. *Ibid.,* pp. 150-2.

8. College of DuPage, Glen Ellyn, Ill., *Learning Resources Center
Handbook 72-73.* (Glen Ellyn, Ill.: College of DuPage, 1972), pp. 6-9.

9. *Ibid.,* p. 6.

10. *Ibid.,* p. 8.

11. Interview, September 21, 1973.

12. Association of College and Research Libraries, Committee on
Standards, *op. cit.,* p. 200.

13. American Library Association (Association of College and Research
Libraries), *op. cit.,* p. 308.

14. Moore, *op. cit.,* p. 199.

15. Helen R. Wheeler, "The Community College Library: An Appraisal
of Current Practice" (Ed. D. project, Columbia University, Teachers
College, 1964), p. 185 (as cited by Everett L. Moore, *op. cit.,* pp. 200-1).

16. Fred F. Harcleroad, "Learning Resources Approach to College and
University Development," *Library Trends* 16, no. 2 (October 1967): 228-40.

17. J. J. Gilliam, Dean of Learning Resources, Brevard Junior College,
letter dated March 4, 1971.

18. Alice B. Griffith, "Organization," in *Library Services for Junior
Colleges,* ed. Charles L. Trinkner (Northport, Ala.: American Southern
Pub. Co., 1964), pp. 41-42. Brought up to date by charts supplied by
Mrs. Griffith in communication dated January 22, 1972.

19. Jeanne M. Douglas, "Media Library Integration in Practice," *Audio-
Visual Instruction* 18, no. 3 (March 1973): 84.

20. Hal C. Stone, Coordinator Instructional Resources, Los Angeles
City College, letters dated February 15 and March 14, 1972.

21. Betty Duvall, Associate Dean, Instructional Resources, Florissant
Valley Community College, letter dated January 25, 1972.

22. Tarrant County Junior College, "Learning Resources Operational
Model" (Fort Worth, Tex.: May 1971), esp. pp. 1-7.

23. Tarrant County Junior College, *op. cit.,* Revised April 1972, p. 6.

24. Janiece F. Fusaro, "Toward Library-College Media Centers; a
Proposal for the Nation's Community Colleges," *Junior College Journal*
40, no. 7 (April 1970): 40-44.

25. The full-scale staffing plan for ultimate single campus development
of William Rainey Harper College (Figure 14) provides for an EDO. George
H. Voegel, Dean of Learning Resources of the College, states that there is
considerable interest in this officer and in his position within the learning
resources organization. Voegel observes further that ". . . the west coast

people feel that it belongs 'down' in the design/production area, while some southern colleges and some eastern colleges have an EDO reporting to the Dean (VP) of Instruction. I feel this is where such a position belongs and it should be tied into the ongoing support services of the LRC." Letter dated April 26, 1974.

26. Alice B. Griffith, "Report on a Study of Selected Community College Libraries in New York State" (Typewritten, July 1972), pp. 2-3.

27. Tarrant County Junior College, *op. cit.*, May 1971, p. 5.

28. College of DuPage, "Model for Reorganization," January 15, 1971, Glen Ellyn, College of DuPage, 1971, p. 6.

29. Lansing Community College, Learning Resource Division, *Library Handbook, Fall 1971.*

30. Brookdale Community College, Lincroft, N.J., *An Environment for Learning* [1970?], pp. 13-19; Brookdale Community College, *Newsletter* vol. 2, no. 1 (April 1972).

The author wishes to express his appreciation to the chief administrative officers of learning resource centers (or libraries) who supplied the organization charts and who granted permission to reproduce them here. In two instances (Figures 16 and 21) the charts appeared in periodical articles; in these two cases the sources are given in notes accompanying the charts.

4

TECHNICAL SERVICES

SELECTION AND ACQUISITION OF MATERIALS

As far as could be discovered, all librarians invite and encourage the
faculty to participate in the selection of materials. In some institutions
the faculty has the major, nearly exclusive, responsibility for this task.
In other institutions it is truly shared between faculty and library staff.
In still others the library staff assumes the major role in building the
collection.

Some institutions place the whole amount earmarked for book purchases under the direct control of the librarian, and departments do not
receive specific allotments on which they could draw. The departments
simply submit their requests, and the librarian then acquires the titles
as long as funds are available. It is the librarian's responsibility to maintain a well-balanced collection. This may mean that he must establish an
order of priority among the requests or even discourage or refuse the
acquisition of certain items.

In other institutions, however, the library allots the major portion of
the book fund to the various departments and retains a certain percentage
in a general fund. The percentage of the total placed in the general fund
varies from institution to institution. Usually it ranges between 15 percent
and 30 percent of the total book fund, but it may be higher or lower. The
general fund is used for materials that are within the purview of more
than one department or division. Usually the library draws on this fund
to purchase general reference materials and general periodicals. In some
institutions it may be used for all periodical purchases since these institutions feel that continuity can be best maintained if the library staff,
rather than a teaching department, assesses the pros and cons of continuing a subscription.

There are various modes of arriving at a decision regarding the distribution of the book fund.[1] The decision may be supported by a formula that is based on the number of publications in a field, the number of students taking courses in a field, the number of faculty members in a department, and the condition of the collection in a particular area. The allocations may be pragmatically determined by a library committee, by the director of the library, by the official to whom the director reports, or by some other designated official. Whatever procedure is chosen, the librarian should always be involved in establishing the formula for the distribution of funds to the departments. Whatever formula is being applied, it should be flexible, and the librarian and his staff should be not only free to but expected to obtain materials in a field if the affected department itself fails to participate in the selection process. Some writers and practitioners would go beyond this still somewhat limited role of the library staff in book selection and would give the librarian and his staff the sole responsibility for selection.[2]

The library staff must be helpful to the various departments engaged in book selection and forward suggestions and recommendations for purchases to faculty members either through their department chairman or directly, depending on the practices in the institution. Recommendations might include such items as reviews, publishers' announcements, pertinent sections of bibliographies, etc. It is probably optimally fruitful to send materials directly to the most interested faculty member, as has been suggested in an article dealing with book selection and acquisition procedures in an inner-city college.[3]

Procedures regarding the selection and acquisition of materials should be in writing and made available to the college community as an official publication.[4]

Some libraries have detailed written book selection policies; sometimes the policies are more broadly conceived and apply also to other media of communication. Typically these statements note the kinds of materials that are within the scope of the particular community college's concerns, establish categories, and indicate which materials should have priority in case of limited funds.

The book selection policy statement usually stresses that the learning resource center is host to all opinions and persuasions and that truth and adherence to fact and quality of writing should be the only criteria for acceptance or rejection. Usually it is stated that the college supports the position taken by the ALA and that censorship may not be exercised. The statement also usually indicates the procedure to be followed if a problem arises regarding the acceptability of an item. Officials to whom appeals of decisions are to be directed within institutions vary. The decision regarding a disputed item may be referred to the library committee, the official to whom the director of the LRC reports, the president of the college, the board of trustees, or possibly to other officials.

One may question the need for a lengthy book selection policy statement. All that is necessary is a brief statement noting that all books required for the curriculum and for general cultural enrichment should have a place in the LRC. One could establish a priority list as a guide in case funds are limited. It might be noted, for instance, that books required to meet curricular needs should be ordered ahead of books for cultural enrichment. Then the procedure should be detailed for instances in which the acquisition of a title is challenged. The statement should also endorse the "Library Bill of Rights," the document which advocates freedom in book selection and freedom from censorship.[5]

Not all libraries have written book selection policy statements. Much more common are written directions specifying how order requests are to be prepared and submitted by faculty members. These directions are frequently made part of an LRC faculty handbook, where such a handbook is issued; sometimes they are noted on individual direction sheets or in separate pamphlets. In some institutions that deal with both book and nonbook media, separate procedures for each category have been issued. However, some other institutions with responsibility for book and nonbook media have presented the order procedures for all media in one unified document.

Selection Tools

The need for selection tools had already become evident several decades ago, and comprehensive aids for book selection specifically tailored to the needs of the junior college were published as early as 1930. Since that time a number of lists have been issued. Several have been produced within the past few years. The principles that have governed the preparation of these tools may help in the evaluation of existing lists and those that may be published in the future.

The selection of titles for these book selection aids may be based on curricular offerings. In that case courses taught by community colleges across the country are surveyed and books suitable for these courses are selected for inclusion in the book selection volume. Another procedure would be to ask outstanding librarians and professors to recommend titles they consider valuable for a typical junior college library. A third procedure would combine three or four shelf lists of junior college libraries that are known to have excellent collections and consider the resulting combined list as the basis for the book selection tool.

It is also possible to base the collection on *Books in Print* and have experts select from this source items suitable for a junior college library. In all methods noted, the compiler or editor usually enlists the assistance of colleagues, but there are occasions when a compiler will proceed alone and largely rely on his own judgment. It is possible, and rather usual, to combine features of the several methods.

As a rule the prefaces or introductions to the various tools indicate the methodology followed. The list may include books only, or books and periodicals, or graphic media and nonbook materials, such as films and filmstrips. It may include current materials only, or it may be a source for both current and noncurrent materials. It may be restricted to liberal arts topics or to vocational technical fields, or it may embrace the whole range of junior college subjects.

For historic reasons—and as examples of methodology and types just discussed—we will not only introduce the most recent lists but also briefly mention several of the earlier lists, all of which have gained wide recognition.

Eugene Hilton's compilation appeared as early as 1930, and the subjects selected were based on courses taught in junior colleges. The compiler submitted the bibliography to instructors in junior colleges and universities throughout the country. He relied greatly on their judgment in establishing orders of priority among the titles[6] Another list appeared only one year later. The procedure used by its compiler, Edna Hester, was rather informal, but she seems to have succeeded in enlisting the help of knowledgeable individuals.[7] Hester and Hilton both classified books on the basis of their suitability for junior college courses, but Hester included sections of general readings as well as periodicals and reference books.

Of great importance and used over an extended period was Foster E. Mohrhardt's compilation, which he undertook on behalf of the Carnegie Corporation.[8] His *List of Books for Junior College Libraries* followed a pattern established by Charles B. Shaw.[9] The compiler first drew up a list of items he considered appropriate for the junior college level. It was about twice as long as the projected final list. He sent participating evaluators the sections pertaining to their specialty. A university and a junior college instructor acted as consultants for each section. Mohrhardt's book had to fulfill a double purpose: as a measuring stick—a standard against which the Carnegie Corporation could compare the holdings of the junior college libraries—and as a buying guide. Since this latter function was considered major, the Mohrhardt list included only current items.

This list needed to be brought up to date and supplemented. The ALA and the AAJC commissioned Frank J. Bertalan[10] to prepare a compilation to fulfill this function. The titles in Bertalan's list—about 4,000—did not duplicate those in Mohrhardt unless they had been revised.

The basic Bertalan list was derived from suggestions of over 100 junior college libraries. These suggestions were combined and arranged by frequency of nomination and sent to cooperating junior college faculty members for further evaluation. This evaluated list was the basis of Bertalan's final compilation. Bertalan's work is noteworthy for including not only books but also audio-visual materials.

Charles A. Trinkner produced a list that included 20,000 titles.[11] According to the 1960 Standards, this is the minimum number of items a junior college library should contain. Theoretically, then, a junior college library could have met the minimum book requirements by ordering all titles listed in Trinkner. Apart from the fact that it would never be desirable to base one's library selections on just one source—however excellent it might be—there were criticisms of Trinkner's volume, concerned with largely the manner of compilation, which created some unevenness.

Designed as a source for the first five thousand titles a college might acquire, Helen Wheeler assembled a list that included both liberal arts, technical, and vocational books.[12] However, two more comprehensive lists by other authors followed its publication, and, being more inclusive, found wider use.

By 1968 there appeared a completely revised and enlarged edition of Bertalan.[13] The other recent comprehensive list was prepared by James Pirie under the auspices of the American Library Association.[14] Pirie's work is viewed as the successor to Mohrhardt's. Pirie's compilation was based on the collections of three outstanding junior college libraries. The catalog cards for these three collections were combined. Subject specialists—425 in all—who were reviewers for *Choice* acted as consultants in their respective areas of competence. Pirie's volume is limited to books, mainly intended to support transfer and liberal arts programs. Edmund R. Arnold[15] who acknowledges that Pirie's list is a quality product, nevertheless notes that about 70 percent of the titles—if pre-1964 titles are discounted—are duplications of titles contained in *Books for College Libraries*.[16] He asks whether there should not be more coordination between those engaged in the very arduous task of making book selection tools. Adopting a distinction introduced by Margaret Egan and Jesse H. Shera,[17] the reviewer contrasts two concepts of bibliography: the microscopic and the macroscopic. The microscopic concept implies that each bibliography is entire unto itself and is its own justification. The macroscopic concept implies that a bibliography is a "functioning part of a whole system."[18] Pirie's volume would meet the criteria of the "microscopic" concept. Arnold would prefer that future bibliographical work be undertaken within the framework of a sort of comprehensive masterplan of bibliographic needs; each bibliography would then be devoted to one specific, unique area. However, Arnold's recommendation does not take into account the fact that libraries without the funds to acquire many book selection aids, may find it much more convenient and economical to have a list assembled for them in accordance with the microscopic concept.

The magazine *Choice* has proven one of the most popular book selection tools for the junior college.[19] Vocational books and books intended mainly for graduate study are not included. *Choice* does not stress any one level of the undergraduate curriculum, but comprises the range of interests extending from freshman through senior years. After an extensive period of preparation, *Choice* was published in 1964 and has enjoyed continued publication and practically universal acclaim ever since. In addition to the magazine format there has been an edition on cards since March 1968, especially helpful inasmuch as the cards may serve as book request forms, as outstanding order cards, and subsequently as temporary catalog cards.

A large number of specialists drawn from the undergraduate faculties of the nation, including librarians if they are also subject specialists, are the unpaid *Choice* reviewers. Reviews are not graded by college level, and there is no notation as to a title's particular suitability for a community college. The person selecting books for the community college must base his decision on the reviewer's overall evaluation. An analysis of the runs of several years of *Choice* reveals that in general the reviews evaluate the books succinctly and clearly so that a selector can easily determine the suitability

of an item for his particular library. As a particular aid to libraries that are
in the process of establishment, the editors of *Choice* have prepared an
"Opening-Day" collection. It first appeared in sections in the 1965
September through December issues of *Choice,* consisting of 1,400 to
1,500 titles that were suitable for liberal arts or transfer curricula. Vocational technical titles were excluded. The "Opening-Day" collection was
reprinted in revised form in the October 1969 to January 1970 issues of
Choice. To satisfy continuing demand, the editors of *Choice* have compiled a new completely revised edition of the "Opening-Day" collection.
It consists again of about 1,500 titles in the various subject categories
reviewed in *Choice.* It will first appear in four installments during the
period December 1973 to March 1974. After completion of the in-issue
publication, the entire collection will also become available as a separate
volume.[20]

Many junior colleges now cover vocational subjects in their curricula.
While some of the book-selection tools did include materials for vocational
areas, this coverage was not sufficiently extensive for most of the community colleges that had enlarged their vocational and technical coverage.
Responding to the need for selection aids in the vocational-technical areas,
several titles were prepared. Bruce Reinhart compiled the *Vocational-
Technical Library Collection.*[21] This list contains books, periodicals, and
items such as shop and laboratory manuals. It is meant to serve the student,
but it has also sections specifically intended for use by the educator. Because
the field of technical and vocational education is so extensive, Reinhart
stresses only a few areas, among them business, home economics, and
health. The book is designed to appeal to a diversified group of users from
high school to college—this reduces its usefulness at the college level.
Another list in the vocational area was prepared by Edward Mapp and
includes only books.[22] All titles are from 1960 or later years. The subjects covered include the standard curricula of community colleges and
career-technical-vocational institutes. It should prove particularly useful
in the forming of new technical-vocational collections.

More recent and of different emphasis is the title prepared by Patricia
G. Schuman.[23] It is a unique guide, a first in its field. Rather than a list
of the materials, it leads to sources of materials. Along with the sources
are noted the kinds of materials obtainable from each source—books,
periodicals, pamphlets, films, or other media. The guide lists about 600
sources and covers over 60 instructional areas. An even later aid in this

area is the listing of vocational/technical periodicals that appeared as a special feature in the October 1973 issue of *Choice*.[24]

Questionnaires were sent out to about seventy libraries in the fall of 1972 to elicit information on what tools specifically geared to the junior college they used.[25] About one fourth of the group noted that they did not use any of the special tools but only the general tools that were not directed to the community college specifically. Most of those who did use specialized tools mentioned Pirie and Bertalan. In a few instances respondents noted that they had also consulted Wheeler and Trinkner. The tools for the selection of vocational materials were not mentioned by any of the respondents, perhaps because these were too recent to have come to the attention of the junior college librarians.

Judging by the questionnaire returns, numerous personal interviews, and various studies, it is evident that the general book selection media are very important to the community colleges.These media help the community college librarian keep his collection up to date. *Choice* was ranked highest in all surveys. Other journal and newspaper selection sources frequently utilized are: *Library Journal, Book List, The New York Times Book Review, The New York Review of Books, Publishers' Weekly, Saturday Review,* and *Wilson Library Bulletin.* These findings are, on the whole, corroborated by Reeves.[26]

With the change of many libraries from book centers to multi-media centers the need for multi-selection tools has emerged. *Books in Print* lists almost every book published in the U.S.; however, there is no such comprehensive listing for nonbook media. The selector will need to have recourse to many sources to cover the whole nonbook field, which is still in the developmental stage. Most of the nonbook selection tools concentrate on specific kinds of nonbook media and are frequently limited to one medium or related categories. We shall not attempt to evaluate the various selection media for nonbooks but rather refer to listings and evaluations found elsewhere. Warren B. Hicks and Alma M. Tillin, for instance, have provided such listings in their volume entitled *Developing Multi-Media Libraries.*[27] Selection sources and buying guides appear at appropriate locations throughout this volume.

Hicks and Tillin stress that, as of now, reviewing media for nonbooks are not available to the same extent as for books. It is quite often necessary to preview a nonbook item before purchasing it. Hicks and Tillin emphasize that the criteria for selection fo nonbook media are basically the same as for books. Such traditional evaluation criteria as authenticity, appropriateness, scope, interest, and organization also apply to nonbooks. But evaluation of the visual product involves additional factors like effective composition, proper focus, and proper use of color. Tonal quality and clarity become considerations in evaluating the audio product.[28] Much more attention may have to be paid to the cost of acquiring a nonbook item, since materials are often very expensive in this field. A nonbook item may be highly suitable, yet its acquisition may be impossible, because the college may not have a sufficiently large budget. A film, for instance, may cost several hundred dollars, and it may therefore be necessary to borrow rather than purchase. Even if a film is of moderate cost, it may be preferable to rent rather than to buy if only infrequent use is likely to be made of it.[29]

Methods of Ordering Materials

The times at which orders can be placed by librarians are a very important consideration. When many of the junior colleges were part of a city's common school system, they were often obliged to follow the order procedures established for the public schools. In quite a number of instances this meant that orders could be placed only at certain stated periods—two or three periods within the academic year. Such restrictions apparently are no longer operative. All librarians to whom inquiries were sent stated that they could order books and other materials at any time during the year. This change is indicative of the progress the junior college has made in becoming an institution with its own identity and specific needs. In order to satisfy requests for materials (which may emerge any time throughout the year) and allow a library to keep its processing staff efficiently engaged during the whole year, a college must have flexible order arrangements.

Some learning resource centers have integrated all media and have formed the corresponding administrative organization. They may have one public services department and one technical services department dealing with all media. Production may remain a separate entity or be included in either the public or technical services department. Other learning resource centers have chosen to maintain separate units for book and nonbook resources; they have a library, an audio-visual department (or division or center), and possibly some other units under the coordinating umbrella of the learning resources director. But even if this second arrangement prevails, we find quite frequently that the acquistions department acquires not only books and periodicals but also the resource materials for the other units of the center. Likewise, as we shall see later on, the catalog department frequently catalogs the materials for all units of the LRC. These two departments then become the order department and the catalog department, respectively, for learning resources. Or, if catalog and order work are combined in a technical services department, this department will concern itself with all learning resources.

It is evident that the time lapse between placement of an order and receipt of the ordered items will be influenced by the number of steps necessary to complete the order procedure. If the order department can order books directly from the supplier, they will usually reach the LRC more speedily than if an intermediary agency or department must be used.

The function of direct ordering should be delegated to the LRC whenever compatible with laws and regulations. In many instances restrictive requirements can be overcome if the librarian is designated the agent of the college purchasing department.[30] Should there be local provisions that college materials must be ordered from the lowest bidder, an effort should be made to exclude the purchase of books and, if possible, other learning resource materials from these provisions.[31] On the academic library level the expected financial advantage to be derived from ordering through a central purchasing department often turns out to be illusory, and the successful bidder often fails to secure items that are nonstandard or otherwise difficult to obtain. The LRC order department is then left with the time-consuming task of placing direct orders for these items.

Central purchasing may be effected on a district-wide level through the headquarter offices of a junior college (community college) district. In such instance all orders emanating from any of the colleges or campuses under the jurisdiction of the district are channeled through the central purchasing department. Centralization may also occur on a higher administrative level, as in North Carolina. Where schools must order materials bought with state funds through the Office of Library Technical Services (LTS) of the Department of Community Colleges, North Carolina Board of Education. A learning resource center has the option of processing books on its own campus or by the Office of Library Technical Services. In the first instance the vendor ships the books directly to the college; in the second instance the vendor sends them to Library Technical Services for processing. Since LTS only processes books at present, all nonbook

materials purchased through LTS are shipped direct to the college that
ordered them.[32]

Approval Plans

This acquisitions method provides that a library develop an approval plan
profile, which specifies the fields for which the library is to receive the
materials directly from the supplier. For example, if the library selects
psychology, sociology, and geography, all items published in these areas
during the life of the contract must be routinely supplied by the publisher
immediately after publication. The scope of the plan can be made less
comprehensive by omitting scholarly books or noting that books over a
certain cost should not be sent but only their availability announced. In
many approval plans the library may examine the items sent and return
any that it does not wish to retain.

Only a few of the very large LRCs can profit from subscribing to such
a plan. In the vast majority of the cases the plan would bring too many
books from the selected fields into a learning resource center. Even with
the privilege of returning unwanted items, the tendency to retain books
once they are received would probably cause many items of mere border-
line interest to be kept in the LRC.[33]

Size of the Collection

How large should the community college book collection be? The
1972 Guidelines for two-year college learning resource programs do not
offer any specific quantitative measures. The 1960 Standards, in force
until the Guidelines were adopted, prescribe 20,000 volumes as the
minimum size for an institution with an enrollment up to 1,000 and increments of 5,000 volumes for each additional group of 500 students.[34]
During the time the 1960 Standards were discussed and adopted and after
they were in force, some strongly opposing views surfaced regarding
these holdings requirements. To the proponents they seemed reasonable;
to the opponents they seemed unrealistically high.[35] In addition, there
have always been advocates of the propostion that quantitative requirements of any kind are out of place. They mention that each institution
should be evaluated in terms of its particular objectives and there should
be careful examination of the extent to which a collection can support
the institution's objectives.

In the early 1960s only a small percentage of the junior college libraries reached the Standards' minimum size of 20,000 volumes. Bach reports that in 1962 only 9 percent of the libraries met this requirement. By 1963-1964, according to Bach, this figure increased to 23.6 percent, and by 1968-1969 to about 50 percent.[36] Table 4 reveals that the trend towards larger collections has been continuous and that by 1970-1971 about 60 percent of the libraries had collections of more than 20,000 volumes. Table 4 also shows a positive relationship between size of student body and size of collection. As may be expected, the collection grows larger as the student body increases.

We must stress that size per se is not an indication of a collection's usefulness for a particular institution. In a particular situation a smaller collection may be more effective and more purposeful than a larger collection. All books included in a particular collection should be selected to meet the needs of the institution; however, even if this requirement is met at the time a collection is being formed and as it is maintained, a larger collection is bound to contain more of the great and important books than a smaller collection.[37] There should, however, be an upper limit, not to be arbitrarily set for all institutions alike, but determined by the manageability of the collection. The decision will be influenced by enrollment size and especially the kind of curriculum offered, but ultimately by the professional judgment of the library director and his staff.

The size of the book collection will be influenced by how other media are being acquired or used. The problem of microforms will be discussed in Chapter 6, but we should mention that the counting of the bibliographic entities in microform is not consistent in application. Is a title in microform equivalent to a title in original book form? Most librarians would answer this question in the affirmative.

Table 4 supported the expected situation that the size of the book collection is in a positive correlation with the size of enrollment. This is equally true for the periodicals collection, as may be deduced from Table 5 which, like Table 4, is based on U.S. Office of Education data.

CATALOGING AND CLASSIFICATION

Cataloging is still done in-house in most instances. However, increasing numbers of libraries receive books fully cataloged and provided with the

Table 4

Number of Volumes Held at End of Year by Public Two-year Institutions: Aggregate United States, 1970-1971

Enrollment Size	Total Number of Institutions	Number of Institutions, by Volumes Held at End of Year								Mean Number of Volumes
		Less than 5,000	5,000 to 9,999	10,000 to 19,999	20,000 to 29,999	30,000 to 49,999	50,000 to 99,999	100,000 to 249,999	250,000 to 499,999	
1	2	3	4	5	6	7	8	9	10	11
Two-year Institutions	660	17	74	169	178	148	66	7	1	28,132
10,000 or more	55	—	—	—	1	15	32	6	1	73,088
5,000 to 9,999	80	—	1	5	11	38	24	1	—	42,441
1,000 to 4,999	357	5	25	89	136	93	9	—	—	24,913
500 to 999	123	9	26	59	28	1	1	—	—	14,255
Fewer than 500	45	3	22	16	2	1	1	—	—	11,218

SOURCE: U.S. Office of Education, National Center for Educational Statistics, *Library Statistics for Colleges and Universities*, Fall 1971, Analytic Report (Part C), Washington, D.C., 1973, p. 38 (Table C-1).

Table 5

Median, 25-Percentile, and 75-Percentile for Periodical Titles Held by Public Two-year Institutions: Aggregate United States, 1970-1971

Enrollment Size	Total Number	25-Percentile	Median	75-Percentile
1	2	3	4	5
		Periodical Titles		
Two-year Institutions	266,618	205	305	461
10,000 or more	60,589	577	793	979
5,000 to 9,999	51,813	393	519	629
1,000 to 4,999	121,676	235	319	428
500 to 999	25,089	164	200	240
Fewer than 500	7,451	105	146	223

SOURCE: U.S. Office of Education, National Center for Educational Statistics, *Library Statistics for Colleges and Universities,* Fall 1971, Analytic Report (Part C), Washington, D.C., 1973, p. 42 (Table C-5).

necessary catalog cards and sometimes even spine labels and book pockets. Based on the replies received for her study, Matthews notes that 23 percent of the LRCs now obtain materials preprocessed from a commercial or other agency.[38] Some investigators have explored the possibility of establishing processing centers for junior colleges on a state or regionwide basis.[39] In California the community college libraries have formed a statewide network consisting of twelve regional educational resource centers, each of which coordinates certain technical services for eight to ten community colleges. The plans include cooperative purchasing, cataloging, and processing.[40] The operations of the Ohio College Library Center[41] should also be mentioned; this is an agency which supplies cataloging copy, although it does not order books for the participating libraries. This center serves all levels of academic librarianship, including the junior college. As of 1974 there are efforts to extend the Ohio College Library Center beyond its present regional limits and to form cooperative ventures with similar objectives in other parts of the country. It will be important to closely observe these developments. It may be assumed that community colleges would be welcomed as members just as they were accepted as equal partners by the Ohio College Library Center.

Dewey or Library of Congress?

A decade ago practically all junior college libraries used the Dewey classification scheme. A survey published in 1963 found Dewey in over 96 percent of the libraries.[42] By 1968 another survey revealed that a strong shift from Dewey to Library of Congress had occurred.[43] Of those responding, 13.3 percent were using LC, another 8.4 percent were in the process of changing from Dewey to LC, and another 6 percent were planning on changing from Dewey to LC. In 1968 about 22 percent of the junior college libraries were committed to Library of Congress. A study completed in 1973 shows that LC is now used by 56.4 percent of the institutions and Dewey by 42.9 percent.[44] From this development it is clear that LC is being increasingly favored by community colleges.

In the early to middle 1960s many junior college librarians were hesitant to change from Dewey to Library of Congress or, in the case of a new library, to adopt LC. The feeling that Dewey fit community college requirements particularly well was very strong. Librarians felt that Dewey would bring related materials more consistently together and that a student could browse more easily in Dewey-classified sections. Another advantage claimed for the Dewey scheme was the flexibility and ease with which it could be tailored to local needs; this, however, had the disadvantage of creating inconsistencies, exceptions to rules, and above all, caused a considerable amount of work. Many librarians saw that much time could be saved if a call number assigned to a book by LC would be accepted without modification. Librarians also saw an advantage in adopting a scheme that would be applied nationally by most academic libraries. The advocates of LC made it clear that the expected savings could be realized only if LC copy were to be accepted as is and not modified, as Dewey copy generally had been. Advocates of LC noted that technicians could be utilized to perform many cataloging functions that were formerly reserved to the professional. The professional librarian could then become a reviser, a supervisory coordinator, and the expert who catalogs materials for which LC copy is not available.[45]

Treatment of Nonbook Materials

As we have noted in other connections, an increasing number of institutions give the learning resource center responsibility for book and nonbook materials. However, the two categories of materials need not be cataloged and classified in the same way. While practically 100 percent of the centers classified print material by either Dewey or LC, only 44 percent of the centers classified nonprint materials in this way.[46] The remaining LRCs arranged nonprint items in accordance with a local scheme, or with a numbering scheme taken from a printed catalog or list (such as Schwann's catalog) or by accession number.

The author's questionnaire inquiry revealed various filing practices of catalog cards for book and nonbook materials. Most LRCs that catalog all media combine the cards for book and nonbook media into one catalog. They have created an integrated catalog, which can also be termed a mixed-media, multi-media, or omni-media catalog. A few libraries place cards for nonbook materials in both the integrated (main) catalog and in a separate nonbook catalog. Others place these cards in a separate catalog only; several respondents from this group have indicated that they intend to discontinue the separate catalogs for book and nonbook items and plan to establish an integrated catalog. Several institutions that responded affirmatively to the question, "Do you classify nonbook materials?" added the restrictive word "some"; or they specified the items they did classify. Filing the cards in an integrated catalog for all book and nonbook materials would facilitate search by a user since he has to consult just one, rather than two or more, catalogs. However, a local situation may warrant an exception to this rule. An audio-visual or media center may be at some distance from the library department (though both are units of a learning resource center). Lack of personnel may necessitate preparing just one set of cards for the nonbook materials. This set should then probably be filed in the audio-visual center, since those who use the nonbook materials need a key to the materials near at hand.

It is more difficult to maintain a multi-media catalog than separate catalogs for book and nonbook media. An effort has been made to fit nonbook cataloging into the framework established for book cataloging; however, important differences in treatment seem necessary. One of the most significant differences is the choice of the main entry: Usually the author is chosen as the main entry for books and the title as the main entry for nonbook items. This difference will frequently separate main entry cards for books from nonbooks—a cause for confusion especially when both the book and nonbook items have been produced by the same author. The problem of nonbook cataloging in relation to book cataloging has been given increasing attention, as the literature indicates.[47]

Newer Catalog Types

Most libraries, with a number of exceptions, use the traditional card catalog. It seems probable that newer forms will increase, especially if the computer finds wider application in the processing area. A few of these newer catalog types found in the community college field will be briefly described.

Book Catalogs. Such catalogs had been in wide use before they were gradually replaced by the card catalogs in the course of the last century. There has been some revival of the use of book catalogs, made possible by technological advances. Book catalogs have an advantage over card catalogs: They can be produced in multiple copies and therefore can be placed in various locations on campus or even off-campus. The disadvantage is keeping them up to date by supplements and cumulations.

Book catalogs can be produced in various ways. The Junior College District of St. Louis, one of the early users of this format, prepared the catalog by photographically reproducing catalog cards that had been arranged in the desired sequence in sheet form. From these sheets keypunching was done and transferred to the computer.[48] The present coordinator of instructional resources for the district notes that the current catalog preparation and production follows very much the same procedure as in 1967. He explains the basic differences: "1) We now perform our own data processing, 2) the catalogs are produced from artwork which has been automatically phototypeset [not produced from computer print chain printouts] , 3) we now capture more information on each catalog entry than we did in 1964, and 4) the data base is now updated weekly, and author, title, and subject indices are provided to the libraries at the same frequency."[49]

Today, most book catalogs are produced in a different way.[50] Very often the catalog is only one of the products of an automated library system that may comprise any or all of the following activities or procedures in addition to catalog production: acquisition, circulation, serials, etc. Institutions that are using book catalogs include Fullerton Junior College, Fullerton, California; Illinois Valley Community College, Oglesby, Illinois; Lorraine County Community College, Elyria, Ohio; and Los Angeles Valley Community College.

Other Forms. A library may decide to retain a card catalog where all entries give complete bibliographic information and to have, in addition, finding lists that give brief information about books in the collection. These lists would be used as finding tools and check lists and would be especially helpful at locations far away from the main catalog and the shelf list. San Antonio College, San Antonio, Texas, has created such lists—library finding lists that give brief information about books in the collection. These lists would be used as finding tools and checklists and would be especially produces limited bibliographies, i.e., listings of selected ranges of the Dewey classification, and it keeps the library users informed of new acquisition by its new holdings reports.[51]

A different form of a catalog is used by El Centro College[52] which is part of the Dallas, Texas, Junior College District. This college, which began operation in 1966, first used a computer-produced run of its holdings and then a printed book catalog. The College found this catalog to be expensive and difficult to maintain. It abandoned the book catalog and in 1969 adopted a catalog on microfilm produced by the "micromation" technique. The computer center maintains a master record of the library holdings on magnetic tape. By use of special conversion equipment a 16mm microfilm is prepared directly from this tape and installed on a special cartridge. Cartridges are then displayed in the library resource center on Datagraphix 1700 inquiry stations. The cartridges are updated every two months. In 1973 the holdings consisted of about 35,000 books and 1,500 phono discs. Their listing by author, title, and subject requires only 21 microfiches. The users, both faculty and students, seem to have accepted the scheme, but it should be stressed that the entries do not contain complete bibliographical data and that mechanical failures of the inquiry stations do occur.

In the more distant future, after availability and use of the computer will have become more widespread, some institutions may dispense with a specially prepared catalog. Inquiry stations that can be manipulated without difficulty would be placed in many locations of the community college, and the user could then command the computer to display entries on a screen; if the user should so wish, he could produce a hard copy of the displayed items.

NOTES

1. See, for instance, Norman E. Tanis, "The Departmental Allocation of Library Book Funds in the Junior College: Developing Criteria," *Library Resources and Technical Services* 5 (Fall 1961): 321-7.

2. Harry Bach, "The Junior College Library Collection," *California Librarian* 73, no. 2 (April 1972): 88-99.

3. Katherine M. Brubeck, "The Junior College," *Library Resources and Technical Services* 12, no. 2 (Spring 1968): 156.

4. American Library Association (College and Research Libraries), et al., "Guidelines for Two-Year College Learning Resources Programs," *College & Research Libraries News* no. 11 (December 1972): 313 (hereafter cited as 1972 Guidelines).

5. Originally adopted in 1939, extended to include all communication media in 1957.

6. Eugene Hilton, *Junior College Book List* (University of California Publications in Education, vol. 1, no. 1; Berkeley, Calif.: University of California Press, 1930).

7. Edna A. Hester, *Books for Junior Colleges* (Chicago: American Library Association, 1931).

8. Foster E. Mohrhardt, comp., *A List of Books for Junior College Libraries* (Chicago: American Library Association, 1937), about 5,300 titles.

9. Charles B. Shaw, *A List of Books for College Libraries* (Chicago: American Library Association, 1931), approximately 14,000 titles. Supplemented by *A List of Books for College Libraries, 1931-1938* (Chicago: American Library Association, 1940), about 3,600 titles.

10. Frank J. Bertalan, comp., *Books for Junior Colleges: A List of 4,000 Books, Periodicals, Films, and Filmstrips* (Chicago: American Library Association, 1954).

11. Charles L. Trinkner, ed., *Basic Books for Junior College Libraries: 20,000 Vital Titles* (Northport, Ala.: Colonial Press, 1963).

12. Helen R. Wheeler, *A Basic Book Collection for the Community College Library* (Hamden, Conn.: Shoe String Press, 1968), about 5,000 titles.

13. Frank J. Bertalan, ed., *The Junior College Library Collection* (Newark, N.J.: Bro-Dart Foundation, 1968).

14. James W. Pirie, comp., *Books for Junior College Libraries: A Selected List of Approximately 19,700 Titles* (Chicago: American Library Association, 1969).

15. Edmund R. Arnold, Review of *Books for Junior College Libraries,* comp., by James W. Pirie, *College & Research Libraries* 31, no. 5 (September 1970): 355-6.

16. Melvin J. Voigt and Joseph H. Treyz, *Books for College Libraries: A Selected List of Approximately 53,400 Titles* (Chicago: American Library Association, 1967).

17. Margaret Egan and Jesse H. Shera, "Toward a Foundation of a

Theory of Bibliography," *Library Quarterly* 22, no. 2 (April 1952): 125-37.

18. Arnold, *op. cit.,* p. 356.

19. *Choice* 1, no. 1–(Chicago: American Library Association, 1964–).

20. "Basic Undergraduate Collection," *American Libraries* 4, no. 11 (December 1973): 679, and 5, no. 10 (November 1974): 554.

21. Bruce Reinhart, ed., *The Vocational-Technical Library Collection: A Resource for Practical Education and Occupational Training* (Williamsport, Pa.: Bro-Dart Pub. Co., 1970).

22. Edward Mapp, *Books for Occupational Education Programs: A List for Community Colleges, Technical Institutes and Vocational Schools* (New York: R. R. Bowker, 1971).

23. Patricia G. Schuman, *Materials for Occupational Education: An Annotated Source Guide.* (New York: R. R. Bowker, 1971).

24. Association of College and Research Libraries, Community and Junior College Section, Bibliography Committee, "Vocational-Technical Periodicals for Community College Libraries," *Choice* 10, no. 8 (October 1973): 1137-51.

25. The author had the assistance of Sharon Grieder and Marvin Light, graduate students at Rosary College, in administering and analyzing this questionnaire.

26. Pamela Reeves, "Junior College Libraries Enter the Seventies," *College & Research Libraries* 34, no. 1 (January 1973): 9-10.

27. Warren B. Hicks and Alma M. Trillin, *Developing Multi-Media Libraries* (New York: R. R. Bowker, 1970).

28. *Ibid.,* pp. 14-18.

29. *Ibid.,* p. 42.

30. Daniel Melcher, *Melcher on Acquisitions* (Chicago: American Library Association, 1971), pp. 4-8, 117-20.

31. *Ibid.,* see also 1972 Guidelines, p. 310.

32. Carol V. Andrews, Assistant Director, Libraries and Learning Laboratories, letter dated October 19, 1973.

33. Peter Spyers-Duran and Daniel Gore, eds., *Economics of Approval Plans: Proceedings of the Third International Seminar on Approval and Gathering Plans in Large and Medium Size Academic Libraries* (Westport, Conn.: Greenwood Press, 1972); see also Bach, *op. cit.,* pp. 94-95.

34. 1960 Standards, p. 203.

35. B. Lamar Johnson, "The New Junior College Library Standards: An Analysis and Critique," *ALA Bulletin* 55, no. 2 (February 1961): 155-60. Reply by Felix E. Hirsch, "How High Should We Aim?" *ALA Bulletin* 55, no. 2 (February 1961): 160-62.

36. Bach, *op. cit.,* p. 95.

98   THE COMMUNITY COLLEGE LIBRARY

37. Robert H. Muller, "The Undergraduate Library Trend at Large Universities," in *Advances in Librarianship*, ed. Melvin Voigt, vol. 1, (New York: Academic Press, 1970) pp. 116-7.
38. Matthews, *op. cit.*, pp. 97-98.
39. Everett L. Moore, "Processing Center for California Junior College Libraries: A Preliminary Study," *Library Resources and Technical Services* 9, no. 3 (Summer 1965): 303-17.
40. "Community College Libraries Form Network in California," *Library Journal* 97, no. 12 (June 15, 1972): 2140-1.
41. The operations of the Ohio College Library Center have been described in a number of articles. For instance see: Frederick G. Kilgour, "Evolving, Computerizing, Personalizing," *American Libraries* 3, no. 2 (February 1972): 141-7; and the more technical presentation: Frederick G. Kilgour, et al., "The Shared Cataloging System of the Ohio College Library Center," *Journal of Library Automation* 5, no. 3 (September 1972): 157-83.
42. Arthur R. Rowland, "Cataloging and Classification in Junior College Libraries," *Library Resources and Technical Services* 7, no. 3 (Summer 1963): 256.
43. Desmond Taylor, "Classification Trends in Junior College Libraries," *College & Research Libraries* 29, no. 5 (September 1968): 351-6.
44. Matthews, *op. cit.*, p. 129.
45. For an extensive discussion in favor of adopting LC, see: Elton E. Shell, "Rationale for Using the Library of Congress System in Reclassification," in *Conference in Reclassification, 1968* (University of Maryland, School of Library and Information Service, 1968), pp. 30-55.
46. Matthews, *op. cit.*, p. 130.
47. See for instance: Jean R. Weihs, "The Standardizing of Cataloging Rules for Nonbook Materials: A Progress Report—April 1972," *Library Resources and Technical Services* 16, no. 3 (Summer 1972): 305-14; Suzanne Massonneau, "Cataloging Nonbook Materials: Mountain or Molehill?" *Library Resources and Technical Services* 16, no. 3 (Summer 1972): 294-304; Warren B. Hicks and Alma Trillin, *op. cit.*, pp. 66-190; and Jean R. Weihs, et al., *Nonbook Materials: The Organization of Integrated Collections* (Ottawa, Ont.: Canadian Library Association, 1973).
48. Robert C. Jones, "St. Louis-St. Louis County Junior College District," *Pioneer* 29, no. 2 (Fall 1967): 4-7.
49. Grant E. MacLaren, Coordinator-Instructional Resources, letter dated January 10, 1974.
50. General Research Corporation, Library Systems, *Computer Book Catalog System for Libraries* (Santa Barbara, Calif.: General Research Corporation, [n.d.]) [8 p.].

51. Paul E. Dumont, "San Antonio College's Computer Augmented Resources System (CARS). A Tape/Slide Presentation to SLICE/MARC Institute. January 14, 1972 (San Antonio, Texas, 1972), [Processed] " pp. 6-8.

52. Lawrence Di Pietro and Shula Schwartz, "A Micromation Catalog System for Library Holdings," *Texas Library Journal* 46, no. 2 (Summer 1970): 77-79; see also: Mickey M. Sparkman, Letter to Editor, *College & Research Libraries* 34, no. 3 (May 1973): 225.

5

LEARNING MATERIALS
AND EQUIPMENT

In the preceding chapter we have dealt with methods used in collection building, giving special attention to selection tools. We have noted great variations in the size of collections; as to be expected, large institutions usually have more extensive holdings than the smaller ones. The objectives of a specific college generally have proved the most important factor both in determining the general character of its collection and of priorities in acquisition of the various learning materials. Among other elements that have an impact on size and character of the collection are availability of funds, nearness to other available collections, and cooperative efforts among learning resource centers.

It would go beyond the scope of our investigation to undertake a detailed analysis of learning resource center holdings in book and nonbook media. However, we shall enlarge to some extent upon the discussion in the preceding chapter by presenting additional data for book and nonbook resources. In the first section we shall deal with book media, in the second with nonbook media except for microforms, which will be treated separately in the following chapter.

BOOK MEDIA

The curricula of most community colleges have in common the offering of a number of core courses. Books and other materials suitable for these courses will therefore be found in most LRCs. Beyond meeting these basic requirements, many LRCs also include the objective of meeting the special needs of the community they serve. It is not surprising that we find special collections in quite a number of community colleges. We shall first deal with such specialized holdings and then direct our attention to government documents and paperbacks.

100

Special Collections[1]

There are many examples of institutions that have assembled collections
to support unique curricula ŏr curricula of only local concern. For instance,
the New York Fashion Institute of Technology in New York City has collections on fashion, fashion designers, the apparel industry, and textile
science, and collections of swatch books and sketches of original Paris imports.
Southern Maine Technical Institute at South Portland, Maine, maintains
a collection of marine science publications in support of a marine science
program. Charles County Community College at LaPlata, Maryland, emphasizes a pollution abatement technology program and therefore concen-
trates on building a collection in this field. Similarly, Luzerne County
Community College at Wilkes-Barre, Pennsylvania, describes hotel management as one of its successful programs, and the library strengthens
it with a specialized collection in the hotel management areas.

Other special collections reflect ethnic concerns; examples include the
Dr. Martin Luther King Afro-American collection of the T. A. Lawson
State Junior College at Birmingham, Alabama; the special collections of
Mexican-American and Afro-American materials of East Los Angeles
College and Los Angeles Harbor College; the records of contributions of
ethnic minorities to United States and world civilization, with emphasis on
Black and Chicano thought, at Merritt College at Oakland, California.

A rather large number of LRCs collect materials relating to the com-
munity which they serve. Some learning resource centers have included
in their sphere of interest the state or the region of which they are a part.
A few of the many available instances will be cited to illustrate this point.
Cisco Junior College, Laredo Junior College, San Jacinto College (at
Pasadena), Texas Southmost College (at Brownsville), and Wharton County
Junior College, all in Texas, report a Texana collection as a special
feature. North Idaho Junior College at Coeur d'Alene has assembled a
collection in Western and Pacific Northwest history. Northwestern
Michigan College at Traverse City notes the availability of microfilm
archives of Northwestern Michigan.

Several colleges provide services or collections ordinarily offered only
by senior and research institutions. Norwalk Community College at
Norwalk, Connecticut, holds membership in the Consortium, which has
assembled and organized highly indexed files, primarily of an ethno-
graphic nature, intended for comparative and area studies. Fullerton

Junior College at Fullerton, California, and Moraine Valley Community College at Palos Hills, Illinois, are among several institutions that report that they subscribe to the ERIC (Educational Resources Information Center) files. These files contain educational data in microfiche; most of these data are not available in any other form. The ERIC files yield source materials for many kinds of research in education. In a community college the data should prove helpful both in research undertaken by individual faculty members and in institutional research. At Corning Community College, Corning, New York, friends of its Houghton Library have gathered a collection of books and manuscripts which illustrate the history of the written word from Babylonian cuneiform tablets to early printed books. Corning also has a collection of selected original autographed documents of British rulers since James I, of Presidents of the United States, and of other important Anglo-American personages.

To further appreciation and understanding of art, a number of LRCs have set aside art collections for home use. In this group are Mercer College at Trenton, New Jersey, and El Centro College at Dallas, Texas. To facilitate selection by prospective borrowers, El Centro College has prepared a full, visible catalog of the circulating items. The Houghton Library of Corning Community College explains that it maintains two art collections, one of which is on display in the library's exhibit area on a rotating basis. The other is the lending collection available for home loan. The lending collection consists of the picture collection, numbering more than 200 framed selections, and of the sculpture collection, a selection of sculpture reproductions.

Government Documents

Several community colleges in various parts of the country are federal government publications depositories. As a rule an institution desiring to become a depository seeks nomination through a member of Congress in whose district the institution is located. A representative or a senator usually gives preference to the larger research institutions or to the larger public libraries, should there be competition among larger and smaller libraries for obtaining this privilege. (A representative may designate two institutions in his congressional district; a senator, two in the state.)

There are two kinds of depositories. The complete depository includes all depository publications. The partial depository includes only the subjects selected by the depository library. Whether it is a complete or a

partial depository, the library must agree to make its deposited government publications available for use by outsiders. In a number of cases
community college LRCs are depositories for federal government publications and for the government publications of their own states. Northwestern Michigan College at Traverse City, for instance, receives the
publications of the federal government and those of the state of Michigan.
Ocean County College at Toms River, New Jersey, is a depository for
federal documents and for those of the state of New Jersey.

A community college should very closely consider the implications of
becoming a government publications depository, especially a federal
depository. The federal government issues a large number of publications
each year. There is the responsibility for housing all the materials, arranging
them, and making them accessible not only to the college community but
to anyone else who may wish to consult them. For the purposes of a
community college it would usually suffice to become a selective depository. Even as a selective depository the learning resource center is likely
to receive more materials in the selected fields than it needs for its students.
Still, it may be advisable for a community college LRC to seek federal
government depository status. There may not be another library—academic
or public—in the district that can and will assume this function.

Paperbacks

If a title is meant for the permanent collection, it is obtained in hard
cover by most libraries, even if it also is available much less expensively
in paperback form. In hard cover the book will, of course, be much more
wear-resistant and last through many more circulations. However, certain
books—and this has been happening more frequently in recent years—are
issued in paper cover only. An LRC that needs the title for its permanent
collection will then have to acquire it in paperback form. Many libraries
have adopted the policy of having such paperbacks rebound in hard cover
before making them available for circulation.

Paperbacks may also be obtained for a special paperback collection of
books of general interest. The LRC would usually set these books apart
from the general collection and display them prominently. In most libraries
these books do not appear in the main catalog but in separate files. The
practices regarding their circulation vary. They may be governed by the
same circulation rules as the regular library materials, but more frequently
the circulation procedures are less formal. Often there is an honor system

allowing withdrawal of books without any record of the transaction. It is assumed that most borrowers will return the items.

Another use made of paperbacks affects the LRC, even though the center is usually not involved in acquisition of the items. Many instructors in English, the social sciences, and to a somewhat lesser extent in other disciplines, require students to purchase paperbacks either as principal or as collateral readings. This has reduced the students' dependence on the library. The library, in turn, does not have to acquire for reserve use titles that now can be in every student's possession.

Loan Collections

A number of libraries subscribe to services such as the McNaughton Plan, which supply a revolving basic collection of current high-demand fiction and nonfiction titles.[2] As titles diminish in popularity, they are returned to the supplier's offices and replaced by other titles of bestseller status.

Each college establishes a profile based on its own selection policies. Therefore, the collections sent to the various colleges are not identical but conform in each instance to a specific profile.

Since the books are sent on loan only, they are usually not listed in the library's catalog but in a separate file kept with or near the loan collection. The books may be circulated in any way the library desires— either according to the regulations that govern the circulation of library-owned books, or for shorter or longer periods.

MULTI-MEDIA PACKAGES

It seems appropriate that multi-media packages, also called kits or learning resources packages, be discussed here, between the sections dealing with books and nonbook media, since multi-media packages may include both. They often contain a large variety of self-teaching and self-testing materials, such as booklets, filmstrips, tape recordings, study prints, slides, overhead transparencies, identification charts, and flat pictures.[3] Descriptions of kits from two different community colleges are introduced here to get a clearer picture of the characteristics of such packages.

The faculty of Fullerton Junior College, Fullerton, California, has prepared a package for use in precalculus mathematics courses.[4] These packages, which consist of filmstrips, tapes, and worksheets, have been well received by Fullerton College students and have been responsible for a drop in student withdrawals from mathematics classes at Fullerton.

The learning resources packages assembled by the division of instructional media of the Des Moines Area Community College are designed for students who need fuller understanding of certain concepts in a course.[5] The intent is to make it possible for the students to acquire specific information and/or skills. For instance, Des Moines Area College students enrolled in the physical science survey course may avail themselves of the learning resources package entitled "Mathematics Review for Science." This package offers in self-instructional format brief segments of the course, such as figuring square roots or changing fractions to decimals. The learning resources packages may be used for either remedial or supplemental purposes.

In his *Dateline '79* Arthur M. Cohen predicts that the college of the future will be a decentralized institution operating by means of a number of branch centers each enrolling around 900 to 1500 students.[6] Each of these branch centers will have a library. (Had Cohen written his book only a few years later, he would probably have chosen the term "learning resource center" in lieu of "library.") He anticipates that in this community college library of the future, media of all sorts will be arranged in kits corresponding to units of the core courses. Cohen believes that there will be many media patterns. He suggests, for instance, that the kit for a unit of a course might contain a closed-loop, single-concept film, a tape, and reprints of selected portions of books. The units would be reexamined from time to time, and outdated or otherwise superseded materials would be replaced by more current materials that might or might not be in different form.

Cohen's community college library of the future would not stock hard-cover books, only paperbacks. Students would have the option of either borrowing such paperbacks or purchasing them through the college bookstore, which would be managed by the library. Under Cohen's proposal the library would not attempt to assemble a large collection, since the student would be expected to obtain his general readings from the public library.

NONBOOK MEDIA

The United States Office of Education has provided statistics by individual institutions and national aggregates for books, periodicals, documents, and microforms. Although microforms belong in the nonbook category, they have been treated by most libraries as if they were books since practically without exception the microforms received by libraries and LRCs are microreproductions of periodicals, books, and documents. Federal library statistics do not provide data for nonbook materials other than microforms, nor do they provide data for equipment needed for media operation and media production.

Sources of Information

Probably the most comprehensive source of information on nonbook holdings of community colleges is the volume entitled *American Junior Colleges.*[7] The data for this volume were gathered in the summer of 1970 and are for the year 1969-1970.[8] This national directory gives figures for each institution under the entry "Special Facilities." Listed are the institutions' holdings of book media and of films, filmstrips, slides, records, audio tapes, and video tapes. Also indicated is the possession by institutions of language laboratories, learning laboratories, or other types of laboratories; closed circuit television; dial access information retrieval systems (DAIRS); and any other special kind of facility or equipment. Institutions vary in their administrative arrangements as to the scope of their library or learning resource center. Therefore, the same facility may be listed in one institution as part of the learning resource center; in another it may be independent or part of another administrative unit.

Other sources of information on nonbook media and equipment are collections of statistics that have been assembled in a number of states by state authorities or professional associations. As a rule, these statistics cover only the institutions within their respective jurisdictions. From state to state the statistics vary as to comprehensiveness. As an example of a state with a comprehensive reporting policy we shall refer to the statistics issued by the Washington State Library. These statistics provide figures on all kinds of learning resources, including equipment held by the community colleges located in the State of Washington. The statistical reports appear in the annual statistical issue and certain other issues of the *Library News Bulletin* of the Washington State Library.[9] The statistical reports include nearly all items specifically mentioned in the Washington Standards. The list of equipment for campus-wide use comprises 16mm sound projectors; 8mm projectors (these may be silent single concept [standard or super], sound cartridge, reel to reel, or any combination of these); slide and/or filmstrip projectors (these may be slide projectors, filmstrip projectors, slide/filmstrip or sound filmstrip projectors, or any combination of these); overhead projectors; opaque projectors; projection screens; audio tape recorders; cassette tape recorders and/or players; tape duplicators; video recorders; television receivers; filmstrip viewers and slide viewers; and portable audio lecterns and/or public address systems.

The statistical reports also give data on equipment for materials production. Here, too, the categories included in the checklist correspond to the items enumerated in the Washington Standards.[10] The statistical reports issued by the Washington State Library indicate which of the items each community college holds, but the reports do not indicate quantities.[11] The checklist items are recorded here because they are representative of equipment generally considered standard for LRC production units. (It must be kept in mind that the minimum quantitative standards for Washington community colleges were adopted in 1970 and that they therefore do not include items developed since.) Included in the list of production equipment are 8mm, 16mm, and 35mm cameras; rapid process cameras; equipment for darkrooms; polaroid cameras; copy cameras and stands; film rewind, cleaning, and inspection equipment; film splicers; slide reproducers; audio and video recording equipment; transparency production equipment; light tables; dry mount presses and tacking irons; and laminating material. This list represents minimum requirements, and it is assumed that in order to meet particular needs and learning objectives the various community colleges will have additional appropriate items of equipment.

The tables and charts reproduced in the *Library News Bulletin* show great variations in holdings of nonbook materials among the community colleges of the State of Washington.[12] Some institutions lack certain learning materials or items of equipment necessary to meet the minimum requirements stipulated in the Washington Standards. Other institutions, however, exceed the requirements for some or most categories. The findings for Washington State are not unusual; in other jurisdictions there are also great variations among the institutions in LRC holdings of nonbook media.

The Washington Standards include also "Items for Special Consideration"[13]: Large group (multi-media) instruction areas; television installations; 3¼ x 4 projectors (where still used by college instructors); and telelectures. Specifications are presented for each of these "items." For instance, the television installation should be a complete distribution system of at least six channels so that it can receive broadcast TV 2500 MHz, UHF, or VHF. It should also be possible to distribute signals to each room from the central TV reception area and/or a central TV studio and to feed signals into the system from any classroom. It should be further possible to produce video tapes and "live" broadcasts. If the college has a television technician program among its vocational offerings, the TV installation should be available to the students for training purposes.

Only a few state library agencies or state library associations publish data on nonbook media and equipment comparable in completeness to those of Washington (State). To obtain information about nonbook holdings or equipment of an institution located in another state, it may therefore be necessary to secure data directly from the institution. In published documents such as handbooks and manuals, institutions often list their equipment only by type without noting the exact number of each type available for use. It is frequently indicated whether carrels are "dry" or "wet." In the first instance they are merely individual study facilities, in the second, they are equipped with electronic or electronic-mechanical devices for the transmission of sound and/or video information.

Media Production

Practically without exception, learning resource centers throughout the nation play an important part in the production of learning materials. This work is most fruitful if LRC staffs, instructional specialists (who may or may not be members of the LRC), and classroom instructors work together. The classroom instructor as subject specialist usually decides on the content of the media being developed. The LRC staff has the primary responsibility for translating ideas into concrete form and for effective arrangement of the subject matter. The instructional development specialist assists in tne development of objectives, tests, and media evaluation.

A single small task often involves only the classroom instructor and one, or perhaps two, members of the LRC staff. Regardless of the size or complexity of the job, the aim is always to produce learning materials that can best satisfy local needs. Before undertaking local production the LRC staff and the subject specialist should have ascertained that satisfactory learning materials are not commercially available. As a rule these items are less expensive than similar items that are locally produced.

Copyright Protection. When learning materials are created, it is sometimes desirable to incorporate materials produced by another individual or another agency. In this connection it should be observed that not only books and periodicals and other printed materials enjoy copyright protection. Copyright covers works such as recordings, plays, music compositions, and broadcasts unless they are in the public domain: a TV address by the President of the United States, or a fuel conservation message from the Director of the Federal Energy Office. If the amount and kind of copying is covered by the Fair Use doctrine, an individual need not obtain the copyright owner's authorization. Otherwise no copyrighted item may be reproduced without the permission of the copyright holder.

Some LRCs are very conscientious about observing the copyright law and have established procedures governing the reproduction of nonbook materials. For instance, Portland Community College has adopted an "Audio and Video Tape Policy Statement."[14] If an instructor wishes to have copyrighted material audiotaped, he must first obtain a written release from the holder of the copyright. Similarly, if an instructor wishes to have a television program videotaped, he must submit to the LRC the written permission from the network or the local station, whichever has control of the production.

Range of Production Capacity

There is great variety in production capacity among the various community colleges across the country. Some colleges may only have the facilities to prepare illustrations, others may have special cameras, others may be able to produce or reproduce cassettes, and still others may be equipped to operate in all or nearly all production areas. Increasing numbers of institutions now offer an extensive range of production services. As an example, the production services provided by Orange Coast Community College are described here. The description is based on the statements contained in the handbook of its instructional media center.[15] Production is divided into these categories: audio services, graphic services, reprographic services, microfilm services, photographic services, and video services. Below are noted briefly the kinds of services included within each of these categories.

1) Audio services—Tape transcription; audio tape duplication, reel to reel, reel to cartridge, reel to cassette; audio narration (student voices); and professional narration (on a contract basis).

2) Graphic services—Original art work; instructors' ideas, diagrams, or sketches converted into finished drawings by student or professional

illustrators. Production art work: layout of material; organization of printed and illustrated information; conversion of drawings into other formats. Miscellaneous work: lamination; preparation of various kinds of transparencies.

3) Microfilm services—Conversion of printed items into microforms. (It should be noted that it is unusual for the average community college LRC to have microform processing equipment. Most items in microform an average community college LRC needs are available from commercial firms. In the instances where microforms must be specially produced for an LRC, this can often be done at lower cost by a firm specializing in this work.)

4) Reprographic services—Typing, composing, printing, and compiling of instructional materials for faculty and administrative staff.

5) Photographic services—Photocopy, photoduplication, and original photography.

6) Video services—The system consists of a three-camera studio with synchronization, switching, lighting, audio, intercom, and mixing. The video system also has a film chain that allows the introduction of film and slides into the presentation. A student support crew and staff support are available.

A faculty member may use the television medium for observation, student evaluation, and microteaching. Arrangements may be made for off-air recording for delayed playback. The studios can be used as projection studios for off-the-air and videotape programs.

Remote Access Information Retrieval Systems

These systems are designed to distribute to students and faculty audio and video programs that have been produced locally or commercially. Production and distribution are often inseparable. These systems are therefore discussed here; however, they could also have been properly dealt with in Chapter 7.

We will discuss briefly five remote access information retrieval installations.[16] Four of these are similar in type. The one that is different is limited to video and could have been treated with equal justification in the next section, which describes television installations; it is being included here on account of its remote access feature.

Florissant Valley Community College in St. Louis, Missouri, reports that it has 450 recorded and audio tapes for scheduling in its Chester Dialog

Dial Access System.[17] The tapes represent all instructional areas. The
system has 40 tape decks and each has 4 tracks. In this way 160 programs
can be scheduled at the same time. The second example, described by
David J. Slaybaugh, is the installation at Lakeland Community College at
Mentor, Ohio, with an enrollment of about 2,500 students.[18] There are
provisions for audio and video programs. Nearly all programs are prepared by local instructors. The author observes: "Using the dial access
information retrieval system (or DAIRS, as it is called at Lakeland)
probably seems somewhat magical to students who can sit down at a
carrel, consult the program schedule, and just punch some buttons to
hear or see a supplementary lesson or missed lecture. It's certainly a
distinct improvement over the language lab arrangement I suffered
through in college: stand in line to get a tape, try to thread it on a reel,
take it back and get the right one, call for help when the tape breaks,
stand in line to return the tape."[19] At Lakeland, as is the case in most
other institutions, the carrels are spread over several locations and some
are equipped with more devices than others; for instance, some have
only audio reception while other carrels have built-in television receivers.

The Dial Access Information Retrieval System (DAIRS) at Central
Piedmont College, Charlotte, North Carolina, has the capability of 79
audio and 8 video programs. Student positions are spread over the building. The video provisions include both commercial and educational
(off-the-air) television. The film chain, which is part of the system, makes
it possible to convert a 16mm film or a slide program to a video program.
The film chain also allows the injection of 16mm film or slide programs
into the Dial Access system.[20]

A report by Joseph Konecny on a three-year experience with the
DAIRS at Wesley College, Dover, Delaware, notes limitations that have
made the system less useful than anticipated by its planners.[21] The Wesley
DAIR system consists of 28 audio and 2 video programs and is provided
with 84 carrels wired for audio reception and 4 with TV monitors for
both video and audio programs.

Konecny had found the Wesley system's usefulness limited: An individual cannot really control a program even if he is its only user. The
Wesley system does not allow pacing or playback. If a program is already
in use, a second or third user has to enter at the point the first user has
reached. The system's capacity is limited by the number of playback
devices available.

At Wesley the audio cassette was found to be a much more adaptable device, largely because it offered a greater opportunity for individualized instruction. Only an inexpensive player, headsets, and a cassette tape are needed for activating a program, which a student can start at will and rewind and review as he wishes.

Since a high-speed duplicator can produce duplicate tapes rapidly and inexpensively, individual requests for tapes can be met immediately. Konecny is convinced that the DAIR system of the future must offer a student the same degree of control over a program as does the audio cassette; otherwise, he feels, it will be replaced by more versatile devices, as has been the case at Wesley.

Shirley E. Bosen, the librarian of Fullerton Junior College, reports that by 1968 when the library building was completed plans had been underway to install closed-circuit television.[22] The library staff and faculty members cooperated in the search for the most purposeful application of this form of television. The aim was to find a way to utilize the proposed video installation in much the same way as the audio-tutorial installation already in place. (The audio-tutorial installation consisted of 40 carrels equipped with tape decks and filmstrip projectors that were student-controlled and allowed self-pacing.) The video installation that was selected consists of 32 individual carrels equipped with 14-inch Setchell Carlson monitors and 10 conference rooms equipped with ten 19-inch Setchell Carlson monitors. The carrels and conference rooms are connected through a distribution system and switching matrix to a potential of 10 program sources. The Valtec solid-state video/audio distribution switcher affords the kind of random accessibility that faculty and students had found so highly desirable in the audio-tutorial system.

The Fullerton Junior College video installation allows several alternative viewing procedures. All 42 stations can receive the same program, or as many as 10 programs could be operated simultaneously and viewed by individuals in carrels or groups in conference rooms, as desired. The student can view a program in a "monitor" mode or in an "active" mode. In the first instance he tunes in and views a lesson at a scheduled time. In the second instance he uses a key on the control in his carrel and switches from "monitor" to "active." The active mode provides controls for stop, play reverse, and forward (but not frame). The student completely controls the program.

The instructor is concerned only with the content of the lessons and the manner in which the content is to be presented. The audio-visual department prepares the graphics and operates the production and play-back system. The reference department aids in the location of materials to be used in the lessons, and the library office prepares the weekly master schedule.

Television Operations—Examples

Chapter 11 describes in the section dealing with newer media that television may function as either an open- or a closed-circuit operation. Throughout the country there are numerous examples of closed-circuit television installations, ranging from simple to very elaborate and sophisticated. In preceding sections of this chapter we mentioned those at Orange Coast College and Fullerton Junior College. Some institutions are equipped to offer both kinds of television. B. Lamar Johnson reports that KCSM-TV, the station owned by the College of San Mateo, provides instructional material for closed- and open-circuit broadcasting.[23]

In 1972 California's Coast Community College District began operation of the district's first television station, KOCE-TV (UHF-50).[24] We refer to this station when we discuss the expanding role of the community colleges in community involvement (Chapter 8). It should be noted that this college will share in the use of the cable television network which the five cities of the community college district have been authorized to develop.

Probably the best-known community college educational open-circuit television operation is that of the City Colleges of Chicago. The program was instituted in 1956, supported by a grant of the Ford Foundation.[25] From its inception to the end of 1973 over 150,000 individuals enrolled in televised courses, most of the enrollees taking no more than one course. Of the total group about 80,000 enrolled for credit, and about 70,000 enrolled unofficially as noncredit students.[26] The vast majority of the students have taken only a few of their courses via television, but a limited number enrolled in the television program for all courses necessary for graduation. Students are encouraged, however, to take part of their work on campus because interaction with fellow students and faculty is considered highly important. In certain exceptional cases students cannot attend classes on campus. (About 300 inmates of three Illinois correctional institutions obtained the A.A. degree solely by enrolling for credit in TV courses.)[27]

As discussed in Chapter 8, the City Colleges of Chicago and the Chicago Public Library have cooperated in further extending the accessibility of college study. By joint action they created "Study Unlimited," which provides for study centers at the Chicago Public Library main building and at several public library branches. At these centers the student has access to video cassettes of the courses first offered through open-circuit TV. He can view these cassettes by arranging for viewing time at the "Study Unlimited" center of his choice. At these centers the student will find, in addition to the video cassettes and the TV receivers, the recommended books, study guides, and other learning materials related to each of the courses.

Cooperation in Media Production and Media Use

In the nonbook area, especially in media production, cooperation among LRCs is at least as important as it is in the traditional library field. While local production is usually undertaken to satisfy a specific local need, the product may have wider application and possibly serve another institution equally well. An institution may make locally produced items directly available to others and/or it may send them to a distribution agency for handling.

A major distribution agency for audio tapes is the National Center for Audio Tapes (NCAT) at the University of Colorado (Boulder).[28] This agency is associated cooperatively with the Association for Educational Communications and Technology (AECT) and the National Association of Educational Broadcasters (NAEB). The NCAT collection consists of tapes contributed from many sources—colleges, universities, state departments of education, public schools, government agencies, and commercial establishments. The tapes are classified and cataloged; they are duplicated when requested by educational institutions. Although the emphasis in the NCAT collection is on materials designed for the elementary and secondary school, many items are also suitable for the community college.

The Northern Illinois Learning Resources Cooperative, which in the spring of 1974 was still in the process of development, promises to be of considerable importance.[29] Eight northern Illinois two-year colleges have joined together to form this Cooperative, whose members will exchange noncopyrighted, mainly locally produced, learning materials of any kind. The requesting institution is entitled to reproduce a borrowed item and retain the copy in its own collection.

The City Colleges of Chicago have released recordings in videotape or videocassettes for use outside of Chicago. The Great Plains National Instructional Television Library of the University of Nebraska (a national distribution center) handles course rentals and purchases. Since 1973 courses have also been released directly to members of the Illinois Community College Cooperative.[30]

In Chicago television courses have usually been prepared by the members of the City Colleges faculty; in other situations faculty members from several institutions have been involved. This latter method might become the prevailing pattern when a program is made immediately available to a group of participating colleges. Colleges that pursue such an enterprise as equal partners might first cooperate in a rather informal fashion, but they would probably arrive at a more even sharing of the privileges and burdens by entering into formal agreements.

Conferences at which there is an opportunity to explore the host institution's production methods and resulting learning materials may also prove highly valuable to conference attendants. For instance at The Ninth Annual Conference of Junior College Libraries, Waubonsee College at Sugar Grove, Illinois, opened its several individualized learning laboratories to the participants and displayed the media, mostly college-prepared, which a student would need to consult to attain the course objectives.[31] Moreover, the LRC staff member and the instructor who had jointly developed the learning materials appeared at one of the conference sessions to share with the group their experiences in producing the media.

NOTES

1. The information relating to special collections and government documents was drawn from the institutions' library handbooks and from *American Junior Colleges,* 8th ed., ed. Edmund J. Gleazer, Jr. (Washington: American Council on Education, c. 1971).

2. *The McNaughton Plan . . . May Come in Handy* (Williamsport, Pa.: McNaughton Book Service, Division of Bro-Dart, Inc., 1972).

3. James W. Brown, et al., *A V Instruction: Technology, Media and Methods,* 4th ed. (New York: McGraw-Hill, 1973), pp. 410-5.

4. Arthur M. Cohen, *Case Studies in Multi-Media Instruction.* Topical Papers, no. 13 (Los Angeles, Cal.: ERIC Clearinghouse for Junior Colleges, October 1970), pp. 40-42; as reported in Brown, *op. cit.,* pp. 412-3.

5. Harold D. Sartain, "Emphasis on Learning Packages for Developmental and Supplemental Instruction," *Audio-Visual Instruction* 18, no. 9 (November 1973): 12-13.

6. Arthur M. Cohen, *Dateline '79: Heretical Concepts for the Community College* (Beverly Hills, Cal.: Glencoe Press, 1969), pp. 9-10.

7. *American Junior Colleges, cit.*

8. *Ibid.*, p. x.

9. See for instance: Washington State Library, *Library News Bulletin* 38, no. 2 (April-June 1971): 142-7, "Annual Statistical Issue"; Washington State Library, *Library News Bulletin* 39, no. 4 (October-December 1972): 410-3; see also: Washington State Association of Community College Librarians and Media Specialists, "Minimum Quantitative Standards for Washington Community Colleges' Learning Resources Programs," Washington State Library, *Library News Bulletin* 37, no. 4 (October-December 1970): 267-71.

10. *Ibid.*, pp. 272-4.

11. Washington State Library, *Library News Bulletin* 38, no. 2 (April-June 1971): 148-9; and *Ibid.* 39, no. 4 (October-December 1972): 414-5.

12. Washington State Library, *Library News Bulletin* 38, no. 2 (April-June 1971): 142-9; and *Ibid.* 39, no. 4 (October-December 1972): 410-5.

13. Washington State Association of Community College Librarians and Media Specialists, *op. cit.*, 273-4.

14. Portland Community College, Portland, Oregon, "Audio and Video Tape Policy Statement" (An Inter-Department Communication, Approved by President's Cabinet, April 1, 1971) (Processed).

15. Orange Coast Community College, Costa Mesa, California, "Instructional Media Center: IMC" [Handbook] [n.d.] (Processed).

16. For several additional listings see: B. Lamar Johnson, *Islands of Innovation Expanding: Changes in the Community College* (Beverly Hills, Cal.: Glencoe Press, 1969), pp. 143-4; for background information on remote access information retrieval systems: see Chapter 11, "Newer Media " section.

17. Betty Duval, "Innovative Programs Mark Library Services at Florissant Valley College," *Show-Me Libraries* 21, no. 8 (May 1970): 1, 11-13.

18. David J. Slaybaugh, "Dial Access System Adds Information Retrieval Capability to Community College," *School Product News* 12, no. 6 (June 1973): 1, 7-8.

19. *Ibid.*, p. 7.

20. Central Piedmont Community College, Charlotte, North Carolina, "The Media Services Department Information Booklet." Charlotte, N. C. p. [6] (Processed).

21. Joseph Konecny, "And Innovation at Wesley," *Community and Junior College Journal* 43, no. 9 (June-July 1973): 15; note also the general observations by William J. Quinly, "Carrels for Learning," *Library Trends* 19, no. 4 (April 1971): 470.

22. Shirley E. Bosen, "A Video Dial Select System that Works," *Educa-*

tional Television 3, no. 9 (September 1971): 9-11; and Fullerton Junior College Library, "Media Installations," Fact Sheet (1970) (Processed).

23. Johnson, *op. cit.*, p. 130.

24. Norman E. Watson and Bernard J. Luskin, "Cables, Cassettes, and Computers at Coast," *Community and Junior College Journal* 43, no. 3 (December 1972): 12-13.

In response to a request for a follow-up statement, Hayden R. Williams, Director of Learning Resources of Golden West College, provided the following information in a letter dated March 26, 1974: ". . . We do not have a closed circuit TV system at the College because our teachers do not want someone else determining the time at which a learning experience will take place. We use video cassettes for the distribution of TV throughout the campus. All lessons broadcast over KOCE-TV are also available in the Learning Resources Center . . . ."

25. James F. Zigerell and Hymen M. Chausow, *Chicago's TV College: A Fifth Report* (A Publication of the Learning Resources Laboratory, CCC) (Chicago: City Colleges of Chicago, 1974), p. 3.

26. *Ibid.*, p. 11.

27. *Ibid.*, p. 14.

28. Brown, *op. cit.*, pp. 210-1.

29. Pete Vander Haeghen, Director of Television, William R. Harper College, Palatine, Ill., interview May 5, 1974.

30. Zigerell, *op. cit.*, p. 18.

31. Ninth Annual Conference on Junior College Libraries, held March 14-16, 1974 at Waubonsee College, Sugar Grove, Illinois.

6

MICROFORMS

Microforms are nonprint media. However, since the microforms used in community colleges are nearly always microreproductions of books, periodicals, and bibliographical records, they are usually not handled by such nonbook units as the media center or the audio-visual center, if the center is maintained separately from the library. In such instances the library is practically always in charge of microforms. The library would, however, avail itself of technical assistance from media center staff in microform equipment selection and maintenance.

We shall first present the various kinds of microforms and also refer to equipment needed for their utilization. Then we shall discuss microform use in the community college.

Microreproductions appear in various forms and at various reduction ratios in relation to the original. Currently, the 35mm microfilm is the most widely used size. However, an increasing number of materials have begun to appear in the 16mm size. Film can be used in either roll or sheet form. Film in sheet form is called fiche and appears in a number of sizes, the 4 inch by 6 inch size being the size adopted by the various United States government agencies. The same size fiche may contain a varying number of images (pages) depending on the manufacturer. For instance, Bell & Howell fiche provides up to seventy-two images per fiche (six rows of twelve images each) and a COSATI (Committee on Scientific and Technical Information) fiche of the same size provides up to sixty images (five rows of twelve images).

Of the other microforms two will be mentioned only briefly since they are rarely, if at all, found in community college learning resource centers. There are microfiches that are placed in aperture cards, the usual pattern being a single film frame in a window-like opening of an IBM card. Aperture cards are mainly used for the microreproduction of engineering drawings. Microcards, on paper or other opaque material, also in varying sizes, were originally favored by some government agencies but have now been largely displaced by microfilm.

Books, periodicals, reports, and other documents may be reproduced at varying reduction ratios of the original. Until fairly recently the reduction ratio of items used in libraries was at 20x or below. Higher reduction ratios are increasingly utilized. Generally if the reduction ratio exceeds 50x or 60x, we speak of ultra-micro-miniaturization. Sets of materials found in some community colleges have been filmed at these high reduction ratios. An example is the *Library of American Civilization,* which will be described later in this section.

The information carried in microform generally cannot be read with the naked eye. Libraries must acquire equipment that enlarges the microform message to its original size, or to a size somewhat larger or smaller, but in any case to an eye-legible size. Within the framework of our discussion we cannot evaluate the various types of equipment available nor present in detail or evaluate thoroughly the various types of microforms nor the various kinds of readers and reader-printers needed for utilization of the microforms. There are a number of publications that should help the user to obtain an overview of the field and become familiar with criteria employed in evaluating microforms and microform equipment.[1] Several are issued by microfilm producers and may serve as clearly written introductions to the field. Publications that deserve to be singled out have been prepared by Franklin D. Crawford of the Princeton Microfilm Corporation[2] and E. Stevens Rice of University Microfilm,[3] respectively. Guidance for the selection of the proper kind of equipment can be found in articles included in the *Library Technology Reports,* issued by the American Library Association.[4]

A handbook prepared by Dale Gaddy is specially designed for the community college audience.[5] This handbook includes among its topics the following: overview of the micrographics field; description of microform software; description of microform hardware; and formulating, implementing, and evaluating microform systems. This handbook was one of the products of the American Association of Junior Colleges Microform Project, a project which we will describe briefly later in this chapter.

A handbook by Allen B. Veaner, written to serve as a manual for reviewers of microforms for *Choice* magazine, was made generally available because of its perceived usefulness to a much wider group.[6] The handbook, in Veaner's words, "will be concerned with the evaluation of all aspects of micro-publications except their subject content. The evaluation of subject content is a matter of literary or intellectual judgment and subject competence, and since micro-publications range over the entire spectrum of time and subject, subject content evaluation is beyond the scope of this handbook."[7]

Statistics reveal that during the past several years microform holdings of academic libraries have generally increased at a higher rate than holdings in books and periodicals in their original form. While a heavy increase in microforms may be seen in all types of academic libraries, it has been especially pronounced in two-year institutions. This trend is very clear from an inspection of Table 6, which gives data for the time span 1968-1971. In this table data for public and private institutions are combined. The mean number of microfilms per two-year institution has grown from 521 to 1,064, and the mean number of other microforms from 144 to 1,215. Tables 7 and 8 are introduced for 1968 and 1971, respectively, to provide separate figures for the public two-year institutions. While the trend towards large increases in microform holdings is obvious if Table 8 is compared with Table 7, it should be noted that perfect comparison is

Table 6

Mean Number of Reels of Microfilm and Other Physical Units of Microform, by Type of Institution: Aggregate United States, 1968, 1969, and 1971

Type of Institution	Reels of Microfilm			Physical Units of Microform		
	Fall 1968	Fall 1969	Fall 1971	Fall 1968	Fall 1969	Fall 1971
All Institutions	2,213	2,582	3,623	18,968	23,977	37,574
Universities	16,010	18,205	26,649	194,052	239,728	362,175
Four-year Institutions with Graduate Students	2,105	2,619	3,893	15,861	22,954	44,837
Four-year Institutions without Graduate Students	1,001	1,125	1,437	2,500	2,547	3,592
Two-year Institutions	521	680	1,064	144	264	1,215

SOURCE: U.S. Office of Education. National Center for Educational Statistics, *Library Statistics for Colleges and Unviersities,* Fall 1971, Analytic Report (Part C), Washington, D.C., 1973, p. 4 (Table B).

not possible, since the two tables use different measures. Table 7 has calculations for the mean and the 90-percentile, and Table 8 for the 25-percentile, the median, and the 75-percentile.

An examination of library handbooks of about 90 widely scattered community colleges shows that the large majority use microforms for several purposes. The most frequent use is made in the periodical area. Most community colleges maintain back files on microform of magazines to which they also subscribe in their printed form. The practices of the various colleges vary with regard to the starting date for the microforms. At the time orders for microforms are initiated, usually not only the latest available volume is ordered; back files are often ordered at the same time. A favorite retrospective time span is ten years, but some

Table 7

Mean and 90-Percentile for Reels of Microfilm and Physical Items
of All Forms of Microform Except Microfilm Held at
End of Year by Public Two-year Institutions:
Aggregate United States, 1967-1968

Enrollment Size	Total Number	Mean	90-Percentile
1	2	3	4
	Reels of Microfilm		
Two-year Institutions	354,373	679	1,927
10,000 or more	64,251	2,142	3,576
5,000 to 9,999	53,631	1,375	2,830
1,000 to 4,999	197,931	798	2,246
599 to 999	29,219	236	799
Less than 500	9,341	115	324
	Physical Units of Microform Other Than Microfilm Reels		
Two-year Institutions	89,567	172	98
10,000 or more	23,459	782	1,750
5,000 to 9,999	37,629	965	2,620
1,000 to 4,999	17,127	69	95
500 to 999	11,298	91	—
Less than 500	54	1	—

SOURCE: U.S. Office of Education, National Center for Educational Statistics, *Library Statistics for Colleges and Universities,* Analytic Report, Fall 1968, Washington, D.C., 1970, p. 59 (Table 8).

THE COMMUNITY COLLEGE LIBRARY

Table 8

Median, 25-Percentile, and 75-Percentile for Reels of Microfilm and Physical Items of All Forms of Microform Except Microfilm Held at End of Year by Public Two-year Institutions: Aggregate United States, 1970-1971

Enrollment Size	Total Number	25-Percentile	Median	75-Percentile
1	2	3	4	5
Reels of Microfilm				
Two-year Institutions	871,500	195	708	1,849
10,000 or more	211,172	1,763	2,801	4,860
5,000 to 9,999	184,744	888	2,123	3,227
1,000 to 4,999	411,048	257	820	1,651
500 to 999	52,242	25	261	530
Fewer than 500	12,292	—	48	360
Physical Items of Microform Other Than Microfilm Reels				
Two-year Institutions	978,295	—	—	274
10,000 or more	249,708	—	130	1,750
5,000 to 9,999	140,274	—	8	581
1,000 to 4,999	566,208	—	—	458
500 to 999	20,136	—	—	20
Fewer than 500	1,969	—	—	—

SOURCE: U.S. Office of Education, National Center for Educational Statistics, *Library Statistics for Colleges and Universities,* Fall 1971, Analytic Report (Part C), Washington, D.C., 1973, p. 41 (Table C-4).

institutions go back fifteen years or more, and some settle for less than ten years. Some apply the same time span to all magazines; some maintain longer runs for more heavily used magazines and shorter runs for items in less demand. Since microfilm files of back issues are generally not discarded (as may happen with certain magazines in their original form), the passage of years will increase the span of coverage.

There are differences among LRCs as to the kinds of magazines ordered in microform, and there are wide variations among community colleges on the question of whether originals should be retained after microforms have been received—or, if originals are retained, for what period they should be kept.

Usually LRCs do not receive microforms for all magazines to which they subscribe. Some libraries will get microforms only for indexed magazines; others will get microforms only for magazines for which they expect a continuing demand, regardless of whether they are or are not indexed. Most community college libraries do retain the originals for certain periods of time: for one year, three years, five years, or as long as a magazine is deemed of reference value. To retain the original issues for a specified period is a good practice, since in most community colleges use of current or relatively recent magazines is heavy, while use of magazines for previous years is light. This is borne out by findings of periodical use in California junior colleges.[8]

In addition to microfilmed periodicals, a number of institutions retain newspapers on microfilm. Most community colleges would not have sufficient shelf space to keep the original newspapers; also the original newspapers become brittle and are apt to deteriorate. There are great variations among institutions as to the time period a newspaper file is to cover. Many LRCs, when they first subscribe to a newspaper, also order a run covering several immediately preceding years. They may also order a number of shorter segments covering historically significant periods such as the Depression years or World War II. However, a few institutions intend to build complete files, adding lacking years as the funds permit. *The New York Times* is the newspaper for which back issues in microfilm are most often maintained.

A number of library resource centers have enriched their general holdings by acquiring whole collections in microform from firms such as Library Resources Inc., an Encyclopedia Britannica company. This firm has introduced the Microbook System, which uses ultra-micro-miniaturization.[9] The reduction ratio depends on the size of the book pages; the usual reduction ratio is 1:55; for larger page sizes the reduction ratio may go up to 1:90. The Microbook System unitizes information: The contents of one title is placed on one fiche or, if necessary on a fiche and a trailer fiche.

Library Resources Inc. has issued the *Library of American Civilization* and the *Library of English Literature*. There are core collections of both, meant primarily for those community colleges that would not need the complete collections or could not afford to purchase them. The core collection of the *Library of American Civilization* contains about 12,000 volumes, all drawn from the larger set of about 20,000, and the core collection of the *Library of English Literature* will consist of about 2,700 volumes, to be based on the complete collection of about 10,000 volumes.

Another firm, NCR, had also announced publication of collections in ultra-microform.[10] NCR would have used the still higher reduction ratio of 1:150, employing its own photo-chromic-micro-image recording procedure. This method makes possible the creation of fiche that may contain up to 3,000 images (pages) and can therefore hold the contents of several volumes—perhaps as many as ten, depending on their length. It is evident that this method does not aim at unitization of information. In the struggle for acceptance by the library profession, Encyclopedia Britannica's microbook method has apparently succeeded.

Of very great importance to the community college field, as well as to other levels of higher or even secondary education, is the Microform Project of the American Association of Junior Colleges, which was initiated in 1969 and concluded in 1973. It was called the AAJC Microform Project and was designed to increase the use of microforms by making microforms dynamic and active information carriers.[11] It was hoped that the project would encourage the use in microform of curricular material in heavy demand.

The project was divided into four phases and originally was to extend over a five-year period; however, the original plan was changed in part, and the study was concluded after four years' duration.[12] Louise Giles was the principal investigator for phase I (1969-1970), and Dale Gaddy was the director of the project for the subsequent phases. During phase I, programs and courses were identified which represented the broad spectrum of courses commonly taught at community colleges throughout the nation. The major product of phase I was a bibliography of over 4,000 entries of required, recommended, and available readings for ten courses, of which seven were high enrollment courses such as English and three were typically lower enrollment courses (for instance, Spanish). Titles included in this bibliography were to be reproduced in microform (with the permission of the copyright holders). They also remained available in their original print form; in this way comparisons could be made between students using the originals and those using microforms.

Student acceptance and learning effectiveness were explored in five pilot studies undertaken during phase II at four Washington, D. C., community colleges. The response was positive and confirmed findings made by earlier investigators at other institutions of learning: Students who use learning resource materials do accept microforms as readily as the traditional hard copy medium; furthermore, there are no significant differences in knowledge acquisition between those studying from the original form and those using microreproductions.

The original plan provided for the verification of the findings of the pilot study through continued research. However, the U. S. Office of Education modified the plan and stipulated that a microform handbook should be developed during phase III, which ended in June 1973, and became the final phase of the project (the project was originally to consist of four phases).

Microforms are used also as carriers of bibliographic data. For instance, a commercial firm has transferred the more recent compilations of the *National Union Catalog* to microfiche, listing each entry under its LC number as well as in a main entry sequence and in a title index. The system is designed to serve as a search tool for catalog and order data. With the aid of a reader-printer the microforms can be reconstituted into hard copy and can serve as catalog cards. This kind of bibliographic tool is ingenious in concept and highly serviceable, but its acquisition or rental can be economically justified only for a rather large learning resource center.

In Chapter 4 we have referred to learning resource center catalogs in microform and in particular to the catalog in use at El Centro College.[13] A master record of all library holdings is maintained on tape by El Centro's computer center. By use of special conversion equipment microforms are prepared directly from the master tape and are then ready for display in the inquiry stations in the college's resource center. The inquiry stations serve the same function as a card or book catalog.

NOTES

1. The author has discussed several aspects of the subject more fully in the article entitled "Microforms, Microform Equipment and Microform Use in the Educational Environment," *Library Trends* 19, no. 4 (April 1971): 447-66.

2. Princeton Microfilm Corporation, Library Service Division, *The Microfilm Technology Primer on Scholarly Journals,* by Franklin D. Crawford (Princeton, N.J.: Princeton Microfilm Corp. of New Jersey, 1969).

3. E. Stevens Rice, *Fiche and Reel* (Ann Arbor, Mich.: University Microfilms [n.d.]).

4. See for instance: R. A. Morgan Company, Inc., "Microform Readers for Libraries," in ALA Library Technology Project, *Library Technology Reports* (Chicago: May 1970).

5. Dale Gaddy, *A Microform Handbook for Community and Junior Colleges* (Silver Spring, Md.: National Microfilm Association, 1974).

6. Allen B. Veaner, *The Evaluation of Micro-publications: A Handbook for Librarians,* LTP Publications, no. 17 (Chicago: American Library Association, 1971).

7. *Ibid.,* p. xi.

8. John Wetzler, "Microfilm: An Answer to Your Periodical Space Problem?" *Junior College Journal* 37, no. 2 (October 1966): 42-44.

9. William R. Hawken, et al., "Microbook Publication: A New Approach for a New Decade" (Chicago: Library Resources Inc., Feb. 13, 1970) (Processed); see also: William R. Hawken, "Systems Instead of Standards," *Library Journal* 98, no. 16 (September 15, 1973): 2515-25.

10. NCR, *PCMI Library Collections: Here Are the Books Behind Bibliographies* (Dayton, Ohio: National Cash Register Co., Educational Products Department, 1970), preface, pp. 1-4.

11. American Association of Junior Colleges, "Microform Project: A Research Project to Determine the Student Acceptability and Learning Effectiveness of Microforms in Community Junior Colleges," Announcement (Washington, D.C.: American Association of Junior Colleges, July 1970).

12. Dale Gaddy, *A Research Project to Determine the Student Acceptability and Learning Effectiveness of Microform Collections in Community Junior Colleges: Phase III,* Final Report, Contract No. OEC-0-9-180260-3703-(095) (Washington, D.C.: U.S. Office of Education, June 1973); and Dale Gaddy, "A Medium for Spies . . . and Community Colleges," *Community and Junior College Journal* 43, no. 9 (June-July 1973): 8-9.

13. Chapter 4 (p. 95). A similar system is used by the Tarrant County Junior College District, Fort Worth, Texas. El Centro and Tarrant differ, among other things, as to the completeness of bibliographic data which are reproduced in microform.

7

USER SERVICES

The center's resources are, of course, used mainly by the students of the college, its faculty, and its staff. Most learning resource centers, as we will show in greater detail in Chapter 8, permit access also to the public at large.

Student needs and faculty needs do not always fully coincide. These different requirements have generally been taken into account in establishing rules to govern the use of the LRC.

This chapter describes a wide range of activities and services designed to facilitate and promote the use of the LRCs' resources. It deals with circulation, general reference and information work, specialized services that are particularly important on the community college level, orientation to resources, and user studies.

It should be noted that some user services are discussed in other chapters. Services to the general public, and services rendered to other persons not connected with an institution, are evaluated in Chapter 8. A number of services have been briefly discussed in Chapter 5 when certain learning materials, facilities, and equipment were described.

The degree to which an LRC can satisfy its users' needs for learning materials and the kind of assistance offered by the LRC staff in resource utilization are among the most important criteria for evaluating its contribution.

SERVICES TO STUDENTS

Circulation of Materials

In community colleges, as in other institutions of higher learning, general circulating books are usually issued for a definite loan period, two weeks being the most common.

Loan policies for nonbook media vary greatly. Some institutions insist that all of these media and the equipment needed for their operation be used on campus. Other institutions permit home use of some media, for instance, records or slides. Sometimes the decisive factor is course-related-ness. Some institutions require use of items assigned by instructors for study on the LRC premises; others have adopted exactly the reverse policy, allowing withdrawal of assigned items for off-campus use.

General Assistance

The LRC staff considers it a major responsibility to acquaint the prospective user with the center's resources in order that he may use them to his advantage. Later in this chapter we shall describe the principal ways used to accomplish this goal: library orientation and library instruction. We shall also evaluate library handbooks and other library publications that are designed to introduce the user to the library.

Influenced by modern learning theory, the student is encouraged to proceed independently in his studies whenever he is able to do so; active learning is more productive than passive listening. The LRC staff member must be particularly sensitive to an individual's requirements. He must know the characteristics of the various media and be able to discern an individual's needs and expectations. In this way he can bring together the learner and the media that is most helpful in a particular learning situation. The LRC staff member who is responsible for service to the public should not stay in a remote office for extended periods; he should be near the prospective users. He should be a "floorwalker," as some librarians have characterized this modus operandi of being always available and noticing and often anticipating the user's needs.

SERVICES TO THE FACULTY

The faculty has more prerogatives and privileges than the students in all institutions that have come to this writer's attention.

Circulation of Materials

Faculty members often are not bound by any loan period; if a faculty loan period is established, it is usually longer than for students. If items are borrowed by interlibrary loan for faculty members, owning institutions are usually prepared to comply with the loan requests. On the other hand, student interlibrary loan requests are filled only if the lending institution agrees to go beyond the requirements of the American Library Association Interlibrary Loan Code. This loan code does not provide for interlibrary loans to undergraduates.

General Assistance

In an ideal situation the LRC staff members work closely with the nonlibrarian faculty members. As bibliographic experts, the LRC staff offer bibliographic assistance to faculty members as they prepare courses. If necessary, the staff will prepare bibliographies for faculty. A number of institutions offer instructors such special services as table of contents service, usually for up to five periodicals. This service provides reproductions of the tables of contents of periodicals in the instructor's area of interest.

The LRC staff member will assist in designing and producing instructional materials. The producton facilities and services made available are varied. A representative listing of facilities and services is given in Chapter 5.

To establish a relaxed and friendly working relationship with classroom instructors and to encourage their active involvement in the LRC, a number of centers have set aside a special room for the exclusive use of faculty members. In this room outstanding recent professional publications are displayed. Sometimes there is a coffee urn. The total atmosphere lends itself to informal discussions between LRC staff and classroom instructors.

MEDIA CONSULTANTS, OR REFERENCE LIBRARIANS AND A-V SPECIALISTS

Depending on the organizational pattern of the LRC, services for book and nonbook media may be combined or different specialists may be assigned book and nonbook media, respectively. In the first instance a staff member deals with the whole range of media—book and nonbook; in the second instance a librarian deals with graphic media and an A-V specialist with nonbook media.

In general, it is most convenient for a library user if he can obtain all the assistance in his learning efforts from one learning resource center staff member. This staff member should have a thorough knowledge of the communication process and a knowledge in breadth of the whole media field. This person, a media consultant, could suggest book and/or nonbook media likely to be most helpful in a particular learning situation. Usually the media consultant who is a generalist would be able to handle the problems posed by the inquirer without needing to involve another staff member who has specialist knowledge in a specific field. Should it be necessary to refer a problem to another staff member for further handling, the media consultant would do so.

Intershelving of Materials

Proponents of the practice of having the same staff member responsible for book and nonbook media are often also in favor—at least in theory—
of intershelving all learning resource materials. The advocates of this
practice affirm that all media in a modern LRC are to be integrated and
given as complete, as fair, and as equal exposure as possible. Intershelving
emphasizes substance and deemphasizes form. In this arrangement all
media dealing with the same subject are displayed side by side, and the
medium that seems particularly suitable for the purpose can be most
conveniently chosen.

Adoption of intershelving was probably preceded by interfiling of the
cards for all communication media. For instance, at the College of DuPage
interfiling of cards had been a preliminary to intershelving.[1] At this
college the staff felt that interfiling of cards was not sufficient to bring
about a completely coordinated use of all media. As the next step towards
more complete integration of the media, the staff experimented with
intershelving of film loops in the sciences. The experiment proved successful beyond expectation; the practice was next extended to the social
sciences, and finally materials in the whole collection were intershelved.
Equipment for the use of the nonbook media was placed near the materials.

Since tapes can be more conveniently intershelved than records, at
DuPage the information on spoken records was transferred (with the
manufacturers' permission) to tapes. Again for convenience and economy
in shelving, slides were placed into carrousel trays, filmstrips into clip
cases, etc. It is recognized that a few materials are too bulky to be placed
on the shelves. In such a case a dummy is made to direct the user to the
item's location.

Preparing nonbook media for intershelving usually requires more time
and effort than putting them into vertical files or specialized storage
cabinets. The system, moreover, can be truly effective only if the equipment for media utilization is near the shelves on which the media are
placed. Intershelving has gained an increasing number of proponents.
There is no doubt that it stresses the substance of a message rather than
the form in which it is conveyed. It gives concrete expression to the
concept that all materials are within the center's domain and that they
should be made available for coordinated use as conveniently as possible.
At the College of DuPage losses of nonbook items have been relatively
small. They ranged from 1 percent to 2 percent, depending on the kind of

media. At the same institution book losses per year amounted to about 3 percent.[2]

From a practical viewpoint it should not be overlooked that more total shelf space is required if nonbook media are intershelved than if each category is assigned its own file or other separate storage area. For example, the librarian of the new Mount Royal College, whose library is responsible for all learning materials, notes that at this college "no attempt has been made to integrate non-print materials into the print sequence, since this poses problems of having sufficient equipment available in close proximity. At the present time it is preferable [at his institution] to differentiate by medium with integrated access via catalogues and subject resource lists."[3]

CAREER GUIDANCE

Career guidance is considered a very important community college service. Usually the LRC performs this function by maintaining files of pertinent resource materials and by assigning one or more of its members to aid individuals in the interpretation of the materials.

Most LRCs collect those college catalogs likely to be in demand by students who intend to enroll at another institution after having completed their course work at the community college. As a rule the collection of college catalogs is comprehensive for the state in which the college is located and perhaps also for the region of which it is part. With regard to the rest of the nation or to foreign countries, the LRC collects catalogs only from institutions in which students or their counselors have indicated an interest.

The catalogs and the other career resource items are usually kept near the reference desk. However, in some institutions the dependence of career counseling on learning resource center materials is stressed by locating a counseling office in the LRC building. At Tarrant County Junior College, South Campus, Fort Worth, Texas, a large room on the second floor of the library, easily accessible to library users, serves as a counseling unit. It is called the "Opportunity Room" and makes available career materials, including college catalogs. The "Opportunity Room" is in charge of a counselor who, while not a member of the library, has the cooperation of library staff members in providing help to students seeking career information. At Mount San Antonio, Walnut, California, a career information and guidance center has been established and assigned quarters in the library building.[4] This center is an interdepartmental project which involves the counseling department as well as the library. The counseling staff makes one of its members available for counseling service throughout the day and also provides clerical help. Students are assisted in the use of materials and in securing contacts with business firms.

Some career programs have been established on a community-wide basis.[5] Lane Community College at Eugene, Oregon, operates a computer-based information data bank. High school and college students are the principal users of this source, which furnishes data on career opportunities and requirements. Also available at Lane are audiocassettes that give detailed information for specific jobs. Staff support is provided by librarians and counselors. At Golden West College,[6] Huntington Beach, California, the guidance department has been assisted by the learning resource center in implementing a plan using the systems approach. Pre-registration planning guides, guidance packets, and a pictorial inventory of occupational training interest are coordinated to supply career information at the time a student or a potential student is ready to use it.

LEARNING LABORATORIES

Learning laboratory is just one of the names used for a type of facility which has been established in increasing numbers in community colleges. Among the many designations for this kind of facility are the following: fundamental learning laboratory, programmed materials center, learning center, comprehensive learning center, individualized instructional center, study skills center, advancement studies program, and developmental learning laboratory.

A college may have one learning laboratory that serves several subject fields, or there may be several learning laboratories, each one serving a specified area. The learning laboratories may be units of the LRC, they may be independent, or they may be attached to the teaching department they serve. In an institution with several learning laboratories, one may be part of the learning resource center and the other (or others) may be independent from the LRC. There is, however, an increasing tendency for the learning laboratory to be a unit of the LRC.

Learning laboratories have these principal characteristics in common: They make available commercially acquired and/or locally produced programmed self-instructional materials as well as other materials that can sustain meaningful learning activities, they help students pursue special educational needs and interests, and they provide for individualized learning opportunities.

The learning laboratory is, or should be, in charge of a director or co-ordinator who provides each student with an appropriate program. To detect an individual's needs, abilities, and inclinations, he must first be given diagnostic tests. His needs will then become apparent and on the basis of the tests' outcome, and occasionally also on the basis of less formal observation, he is aided in the selection of appropriate programs. It is an essential element of the learning laboratory procedure that there is continuing evaluation as the learner progresses from unit to unit. While an instructor may recommend that a student concentrate on a certain subject and use certain learning materials, the student—as the person responsible for his own learning outcome—may accept or reject such recommendations.

No two learning laboratories are exactly alike. The type of program offered will vary with the kind of student body served. In addition to college level instruction programs, some institutions also have programs on a high school or even an elementary school level. In some institutions the learning laboratory includes materials of general interest, such as interior decorating. Subjects which are nearly always included by the learning laboratories are spelling, reading, speech, study skills, and mathematics. After successfully administering these basic programs, a learning laboratory usually increases the offerings. The courses may extend into practically any subject area of college concern: chemistry, biology, physics, psychology, modern languages, etc.

The key person in the learning laboratory is its director or coordinator. The coordinator should have a background in English, reading, and speech, remedial techniques, and counseling, and he should understand the potential of the various kinds of media. He should be able to draw on a corps of subject specialists to serve as advisors.

The learning laboratory has helped the community college become an open-door college—a people's college. The modern community college accepts everyone who has a high school diploma; it also accepts adults who have not graduated from high school. As a rule it accepts any adult who feels he can profit from college attendance. The learning laboratory is the facility geared to the needs of many who might not otherwise be prepared to participate in all phases of conventional college work. The laboratory accepts students where they are and assists them in reaching their self-selected goal of competence.

This educational facility has been discussed in considerable detail by Joseph B. Carter, director of the division of educational resources of the North Carolina Department of Community Colleges.[7]

Reference is made to three descriptions of individual installations: One is in the library administered by the division of general studies (Tarrant County Junior College District, Northeast Campus)[8]; the other two are administered by the learning resource centers of their respective institutions, the College of DuPage[9] and Portland Community College.[10] The Portland installation is called the "Drop-In Center," to emphasize the informality prevailing in this study area.

COGNITIVE STYLE MAPPING

As we have seen, learning laboratories facilitate individualized learning. Most laboratories are open to all students. They are designed to help students eliminate academic deficiencies by offering remedial programs. Although some students visit learning laboratories on their own initiative, they are frequently assigned to work there by their instructors.

The whole learning resources program lends itself to the individualized learning approach. Such a comprehensive approach is followed at Oakland Community College. The Oakland procedure, which will ultimately include the whole student body, has as its objective the personalizing of educational programs by means of cognitive style mapping.[11] Basic to the program is the conviction that an institution should not use students' individual differences to determine who succeeds and who fails in group competition. Rather, an institution must "adapt to differences in cognitive styles as a means of varying teaching techniques to insure the individual's success in his educational program."[12] The designers of the Oakland Community College plan have been influenced by the writings of Benjamin Bloom who maintains that 95 percent of the students, given sufficient time, the proper kind of help, and suitable learning resources, can learn a subject and reach a high level of mastery.

As Bloom notes, students greatly vary as to which learning methods provide the best results. Some learn well by independent methods, others do well in highly structured learning situations, some show best results if they are assisted by a tutor in a one-to-one relationship, some perform best in small groups, and others in conventional class sessions. These findings led Bloom to the conclusion that quality of instruction should be viewed in terms of its effects on the individual learner rather than on a random group. Teaching may have to be modified to meet an individual's specific needs until it fits his most effective learning pattern. The pattern is likely to vary for an individual, depending on the subject he studies and the previous training he has had. An individual may utilize several methods concurrently and alternately. There also is no "thing of learning" (book, record, movie, TV, etc.) intrinsically superior to all other "things of learning," but there are several—"each appropriate to a particular task."[13]

To discover an individual's traits and determine the learning pattern that would best suit his requirements, Oakland Community College has devised the following procedure. Each incoming student is asked to take a battery of tests, some conventional and some unusual—such as being asked to taste cheese and to assemble puzzles. Certain tests measure the ability to comprehend abstractions, others deal with visual and manual coordination, and still others identify personal characteristics of the person tested. On the basis of the test results a cognitive style map is developed for each student. This cognitive style map shows how the individual derives meaning from his environment. The map shows whether the individual reasons like a social scientist or like a mathematician, whether he is a listener or a talker, whether he is a leader or whether he waits passively until he is directed by others. The cognitive style map and information obtained by teachers and counselors are the basis for a student's personalized education program (PEP). Oakland Community College provides a wide range of resources and facilities to meet each individual's learning needs. There are regular class sessions, small group gatherings, rap sessions; youth-tutor-youth, i.e., instruction by a fellow student; studying in a relaxed fashion in carrel arcades; and studying independently in the LRC, which is provided with books as well as with other kinds of learning materials.

LIBRARY ORIENTATION AND LIBRARY INSTRUCTION

Library orientation and library instruction have been a continuing concern of college librarians. Instruction and orientation have been deemed necessary procedures by community colleges, as they have been by senior colleges and universities.[14]

The terms library orientation and library instruction are sometimes
used synonymously to include all efforts to acquaint a student with the
library, its resources, and their utilization. But usually library orientation
is understood as the activity designed to familiarize the library user with
the physical plant—with the location of facilities and resources. Library
instruction involves the conveying of more detailed information on
resources, as well as their proper and efficient utilization. On the community college level we can find examples of various degrees of library
orientation and instruction.

In general, library orientation is viewed as being fully within the
library's sphere of responsibility. The favorite device of orientation is
library tours, usually scheduled by the library office or by the library's
reference, circulation, or public services departments. Tours may be conducted by members of the library staff or by students who have themselves previously been instructed.

Library instruction covering topics such as the card catalog, the
classification system, indexes, general and special bibliographies, and
government documents may be offered in various ways. There may be
separate library-sponsored courses taught by librarians, or library instruction may be offered as a part of existing courses, such as English or
social science. Library instruction in existing classes may be provided
by the regular instructor, or he may request the librarian to assume
responsibility for the presentation of library information. At the freshman level the general sources and simple search strategies are usually
introduced. English classes lend themselves especially well to these introductory presentations. Library instruction is also offered at more
advanced levels; either the regular instructor or the librarian presents
bibliographic resources supporting study and research in these courses.

There are some advantages to a separate library course. The librarian,
as a specialist in the utilization of library materials, is likely to present
them in a systematic and comprehensive fashion. But since in a separate
course library information is usually not related to the solving of practical
problems, the information may often not seem relevant to a student.
The librarian may give more details than the student can absorb or find
meaningful. The course may actually turn into a watered-down reference
course.

If the library information is conveyed within the framework of an
existing course, the library data can be articulated with the subject and

used to explore it more deeply and thoroughly. Combining the library presentation with an existing course has the further advantage of establishing and sustaining cooperation between the classroom teacher and the librarian.

Nonbook media of instruction are utilized in varying degrees by some institutions as learning and teaching devices. In lieu of making an actual walk-through tour to become acquainted with the library and its facilities, the student may watch a slide presentation, a movie, or a video tape. The presentation may be offered anywhere on campus.

Nonbook media are used not only for library orientation but also for library instruction. A few examples may serve as illustrations.

Mt. San Antonio College, Walnut, California, experimented with specially designed videosonic machines.[15] Five videosonic machines were used to give information about the location of departments and facilities and to provide instruction in the use of periodical indexes and the card catalog, with emphasis on subject headings. One videosonic teaching machine was set up in the central lobby and one in each of the four subject areas. The machine in the central lobby was programmed to answer general questions, and those in the subject libraries were programmed to answer matters relating to pertinent periodical indexes and the subject catalogs. The results of a controlled study showed that students who used the machines made more efficient use of the library than those who did not.

At Tarrant County Junior College, Fort Worth, Texas, information dealing with the catalog, periodicals, and indexes is on short tapes which direct the student to problem-solving tasks.[16] A workbook gives instructions and contains questions. The student locates books and answers reference questions. A comparison of the results of a pretest and posttest shows the increments in learning that have been effected in this individualized learning process.

At De Anza College, Cupertino, California, students have available programmed data covering such fields as the use of subject headings, use of the divided catalog, footnotes, and bibliography. For practive, programmed study sheets are provided with each unit.[17]

The programs in use at Mt. San Antonio, Tarrant, and De Anza facilitate independent learning. They are self-paced; further, they are available at the point the individual needs the explanations for making efficient use of the library's resources.

A film prepared by the College of DuPage portrays its innovative approach to the LRC concept. The film, while based on local practices, should have general appeal; it is available for purchase and preview.[18]

Teaching the use of the library should lead from the simple to the complex. As Patricia Knapp suggests, in the process a student should acquire library competence, i.e., a feeling for the library as an organization.[19] He must obtain an understanding for the interrelationships of the various tools, and he must also see that the library is connected with the world outside. In the Monteith experiment the assignments lead from the less complex to the more involved. In the assignments, all of which were course-related, emphasis was placed on process rather than on content, on principle rather than on fact. The whole sequence was unified in terms of leading logically from one step to the next. While this program was applied in a four-year college, Mrs. Knapp felt that it could be adapted to a two-year school, especially since seven of the ten assignments are intended for the first two years of the senior college.

James R. Kennedy, who describes the procedures used at Earlham College, also emphasizes the need for integration of library instruction with general course work, and he describes the various methods used at Earlham to accomplish this goal.[20]

In practically all studies dealing with the use of the library it has been recognized that the attitude of the instructor towards the library is of primary importance, probably of greater importance than any other factor. Depending on the instructor, the same course will produce different degrees of library use. An instructor who considers the library an indispensable tool for learning and research will consistently engender greater student interest in the library than an instructor who is not so oriented. Virginia Clark has urged that librarians use their time and resources to impart a full understanding of the library's potential to the faculty, so that they become its enthusiastic supporters and transmit their library knowledge and enthusiasm to their students.[21]

In institutions that have adopted the library-college concept, each faculty member necessarily views the library as the area in which teaching and learning occurs and sees himself as the user and interpreter of the library's learning resources. The instructor may work alone or draw on the bibliographic expertise of the learning resources specialist in preparing assignments or solving problems.

Library Handbooks

Library handbooks have been prepared by most libraries. In some institutions they represent the only available introduction to the library and its facilities and resources. Usually, however, the handbook is supplemental or complementary to orientation and instruction by librarians and classroom teachers, or to the use of programmed devices.

What information should a handbook contain? In the early 1960s the Committee on Instruction and Use of the ACRL Junior College Libraries Section sought answers to this question. The committee's work resulted in a concise pamphlet that suggested the topics that should be covered by an "ideal" manual, as well as the most serviceable arrangement of the topics and the format. The committee urged anyone planning a handbook to familiarize himself with manuals already in use in various institutions.[22]

An examination of recent handbooks shows a great variety in form, appearance, design, and range and depth of subjects covered. Most handbooks deal with the following: kinds of materials held by the LRC, circulation procedures, catalog and catalog use, classification system used by the college library, special facilities and services, student conduct, and library staff.

Some LRC handbooks give due emphasis to nonbook resources. More often, they stress the graphic resources and give only scant attention to the nonbook resources and equipment needed for their utilization. Occasionally a learning resources division, which includes a library and an instructional media center, issues separate handbooks for each unit. For example, Orange Coast College, Costa Mesa, California, has provided a college library handbook and another handbook for its instructional media center. This introduces the user to the whole range of nonbook media, to many types of equipment, and to services obtainable at the center.

Usually the handbooks list bibliographies and other important reference books; less frequently, a list of periodicals received is also included. In other instances we find sections on "How to Write Term Papers," "Commonly Used Abbreviations," "How to Review a Book," "Parts of a Book," and on other library-related matters.

Many of the handbooks are beautifully designed; some are illustrated. Some are serious and even austere in their approach; others hope to attract the user's attention by a light, even slightly frivolous style and

by amusing illustrations. The majority use the title handbook or library
handbook, but some again have selected more arresting titles. Usually
all information is contained in a single pamphlet—or two, if there is
one each for the traditional library and for the nonbook media unit.
However, some LRCs have used a folder for each of the topics to be
presented. For instance, Mt. Hood Community College, Gresham, Oregon,
has separate folders for books, magazines, and reference. The catchy
titles that identify the folders are, respectively: "Everything You Wanted
to Know About Locating Books But Were Afraid to Ask. . . ."; "Everything You Wanted to Know About Locating a Magazine Article But
Were Afraid to Ask. . . ."; and "Everything You Wanted to Ask About
Finding Things But Were Afraid to Ask. . . ."

Guides for faculty members also vary. Many institutions prepare one
handbook, which is geared to student use, but must also serve the faculty.
Other institutions have prepared special handbooks for the faculty. The
handbooks for the two groups may be identical except that a few sheets
are inserted which give the faculty member information needed by him
only. This is done at Schenectady County Community College where the
extra information deals with book ordering, special services, and film rental.

Other institutions, among them Miami-Dade Junior College, South
Campus, have a faculty handbook which is differently structured and
formatted. The Miami-Dade faculty library handbook gives information
on the organization of the library and in particular the book request
procedure the faculty is to observe: Although there is a central technical
processing department for all campuses, the faculty member submits his
requests to the South Campus acquisition librarian. Faculty members are
apprised of the kind of reference help they may expect, of the interlibrary
loan procedure, and of special services. Close faculty-library cooperation
is emphasized.

William R. Harper College, Palatine, Illinois, provides a student guide
to the learning resource center and, in different format and with quite
different emphasis in subject coverage, a faculty/staff guide to the LRC.
The student guide limits itself to the essential information a student may
seek. The faculty/staff guide provides flow charts and descriptive notes
for each of the service units. Attention is called to a multi-media systems
instruction manual developed for Harper College instructors using these
facilities.

Many LRCs issue various kinds of publications in addition to student
and faculty handbooks, such as manuals which may serve as guides even if

they are not specifically so designated. At Florissant Valley Community College, St. Louis, Missouri, an instructional resources volume fully describes the whole range of facilities and services available and the procedures to be observed by the user. In the section dealing with audio-visual equipment, illustrations accompany the text. The volume also includes lists of the films, filmstrips, and tapes available at or through the college.

Other LRC Publications

These publications include separately issued book order procedures for faculty members; lists of periodicals to which a college subscribes (sometimes separately published even if a list is included in the student library handbook); acquisitions lists (in some institutions complete, in some selective); and bibliographies, like the comprehensive bibliography on careers prepared at Dutchess Community College, Poughkeepsie, New York. Several libraries issue newsletters. In its *Library Newsletter* Nassau Community College, Garden City, New York, invites students, faculty, and staff to review books or other media received by the library. Accepted reviews are published in the *Newsletter*. Kingsborough Community College, Brooklyn, New York, calls the newsletter of its library/ media center, *op. cit.* The principal items that formed the contents of the Summer 1972 newsletter, a typical issue, were an "Acquisition Sampler," an article by a Kingsborough author, a note stating that "Kingsborough Community College Amnesty on Library Fines Sparks Returns," and a description of a library exhibit entitled "Women, The Continuing Revolution Goes Right On."

USER STUDIES

Orientation to the library's facilities and instruction in the use of the resources are efforts designed to bring about effective and intensified use of the library. Beyond this it is important to know which characteristics of the students, instructors, and academic setting have an impact on library use. A number of studies have been undertaken to isolate such factors. Outstanding are the works of Harvie Branscomb[23] and Patricia B. Knapp.[24] These studies, however, were projected against a senior college or a university background. Richard Hostrop saw the need for a baseline study in depth relating to a community college. The setting for Hostrop's investigation, which is entitled *Teaching and the*

Community College Library, is the College of the Desert, Palm Desert, California.[25] When applying the findings of Hostrop's study to community colleges in general, it must be kept in mind that the study is based on the examination of just one institution, a limitation also affecting Patricia B. Knapp's work, which analyzed the library of only one college, Knox College, Galesburg, Illinois. At the time the Hostrop study was undertaken (1965-1966) the College of the Desert had been in operation for four years. Its student body was rather small—about 1,000 in all, of whom nearly 600 were part-time. Most of the students lived in the junior college district.

It was the purpose of the study to discover a relationship between use made of library materials and such factors as academic success, sex, and amount of course work completed. The study did not attempt to trace the differences between two-year colleges and senior institutions with regard to library use; however, such comparisons have been made in several instances.

Hostrop found that students who did well academically in high school and in college were heavier library users than those whose achievements were low. Academic achievement in high school therefore can be used as a predictor of amounts of library borrowing. At the senior college level Branscomb and Knapp found a less close relationship between academic achievement and library use. In close agreement with the findings for senior institutions, it was found that students who complete the most units use the library more heavily than students who complete a few courses only.

The author also noted a close correlation between pick-up time of library cards and library use. Those who obtained their cards before a stipulated date used the library more heavily than those who neglected to obtain without delay the cards required for withdrawal of library materials.

One might expect to discover a positive correlation between scholastic aptitude and library use. This did not occur on the community college level; Knapp found a slight relationship on the senior college level between scholastic aptitude scores and library borrowing. Socioeconomic conditions, however, have a bearing on library use. Students who came from higher socioeconomic strata made heavier use of the library than did those from the lower socioeconomic groups. Finally, and this agrees with Branscomb's study, females borrowed more books from the open collection than did males.

At the College of the Desert no statistically significant relationships were established between quantities of borrowing and such factors as age of student, marital status, living situation, high school attended, major in college, and number of books in home. Hostrop, like the others who have analyzed library use patterns, underlines that the nature of instruction must be given close attention since its impact is more decisive than any other factors that influence library use. He cites in support the findings relating to library use in two comparable economics courses, one taught at Knox College and the other at the College of the Desert. At Knox the economics course was responsible for more library use than any other course. The instructor at Knox did not assign any textbook, but rather urged his students to obtain information by exploring in the library's total resources. The economics instructor at the College of the Desert was textbook-oriented; the course was responsible for just four library book withdrawals.

A surprising fact is that in many courses a student can attain success, as measured by final grades, without library use. At the College of the Desert faculty members felt that library use is notably or extremely influential on final grades in only about a quarter of the courses taught.

Students who were questioned put the number of courses for which library study is extremely important even lower—at about 10 percent. Hostrop calls the courses that require library use as a condition for academic success library-dependent; more exactly, this is interpreted to mean that 80 percent or more of the enrollees borrowed one or more library items for the course.

Today the LRC is more diversified and can satisfy the particular needs and learning styles of a higher percentage of the student body than could the earlier library. The library-college movement and the stress on independent and individualized instruction contribute to a more intensive use of the LRC. Studies of the learning resource center, comparable to Hostrop's study of a library, will probably be undertaken in the future—these may well show the center to be indispensable, not just to a few, but to the majority of the students who want to reach their educational goals.

NOTES

1. Doris Dunnington, "Integrating Media Services," *RQ* 9, no. 2 (Winter 1969): 116-8.

2. Robert A. Veihman, "Some Thoughts on Intershelving," *Audio-Visual Instruction* 18, no. 3 (April 1973): 87-88.

3. John North, "Towards Decentralization: The Learning Resource Centre at Mount Royal College," *Canadian Library Journal* 30, no. 3 (May-June 1973): 241.

4. Harriett Genung, Dean of Educational Resources Library Center, letter dated October 3, 1973.

5. Max R. Raines, "Survey of Leading LIB/LRC's," *Community and Junior College Journal* 43, no. 9 (June-July 1973): 11.

6. *Ibid.*

7. See for instance: Joseph B. Carter, "Learning Laboratories: A North Carolina Community College Educational Innovation," Presented to the State Board of Education . . . Raleigh, N.C., July 1971 (Processed); and Joseph B. Carter, "The Learning Laboratory or Whatever, A Now Program," A Position Paper (Raleigh, N.C.: Department of Community Colleges, Division of Educational Resources, [n.d.]) (Processed).

8. Virginia Reedy, "Maximized Individualized Learning Laboratory," *Community and Junior College Journal* 43, no. 6 (March 1973): 34.

9. Richard L. Ducote and Beverly R. Bogard, "Developmental Learning Laboratory, College of DuPage, Program and Function Study." (Glen Ellyn, Ill., College of DuPage, January 1970) (Processed).

10. Victoria Spandel, ["Learning Center of Portland Community College"], Portland, Ore. [n.d.], pp. 3-5 (Processed).

11. Joseph E. Hill and Derek N. Nunney, *Personalizing Educational Programs; Utilizing Cognitive Style Mapping* (Bloomfield Hills, Mich.: Oakland Community College Press, 1971); Derek N. Nunney and Joseph E. Hill, *Personalized Educational Programs,* folder (Bloomfield Hills, Mich., Oakland Community College, n.d.); and William Hampton, "Audio-visual Technology: Students Find their Way to Learning With Cognitive Style Mapping," *College and University Business* 52, no. 2 (February 1972): 10, 14, 16.

12. Benjamin Bloom, "Learning for Mastery," *Evaluation Comment* 1, no. 2, May 1968 (Published by the Center for the Study of Evaluation of Instructional Programs, University of California at Los Angeles) (also Reprinted as RELCV, Topical Papers and Reprints, no. 1).

13. James W. Armsey and Norman C. Dahl, *An Inquiry into the Uses of Instructional Technology* (New York: The Ford Foundation, 1973), p. 15; see also: Jerrold E. Kamp, "Which Medium," *Audiovisual Instruction* 16, no. 10 (December 1971); 32-36.

14. See for instance: Verna V. Melum, "A Survey to Aid Your Fall Planning: Library Orientation in the College and University," *Wilson*

Library Bulletin 46, no. 1 (September 1971): 59-66; and Carla L. Stoffle and Gabriella Bonn, "An Inventory of Library Orientation and Instruction Methods," *RQ* 13, no. 2 (Winter 1973): 129-33.

15. Harriett Genung, "Can Machines Teach the Use of the Library?" *College & Research Libraries* 28, no. 1 (January 1967): 25-30.

16. Verna V. Melum, "Library Orientation Programs in Selected Colleges in the U.S.," in Seventh Annual Conference, Junior College Libraries (Rockford, Ill.: Rock Valley College Educational Resource Center, 1972), p. 23 (Processed).

17. *Ibid.*, pp. 23-24.

18. College of DuPage, Glen Ellyn, Ill. "A Place to Learn [Film]," February 1973, produced by Learning Resources Center.

19. Patricia B. Knapp, "Library-Coordinated Instruction at Monteith College," in *The Junior College Library,* ed. B. Lamar Johnson (Los Angeles: University of California, 1966), pp. 31-36.

20. James R. Kennedy, Jr., "Integrated Library Instruction," *Library Journal* 95, no. 8 (April 15, 1970): 1450-3.

21. Virginia Clark, "Teaching Students To Use the Library: Whose Responsibility?" *College & Research Libraries* 21, no. 5 (September 1960): 369-72, 402.

22. Association of College and Research Libraries, Junior College Libraries Section, Committee on Instruction and Use, "Standards for the Ideal Junior College Library Handbook" (Chicago: The Committee, 1963), 7 p. (Processed); also as Alice G. Griffith, "Library Handbook Standards," *Wilson Library Bulletin* 39, no. 6 (February 1965): 475-7.

23. Harvie Branscomb, Teaching With Books (Chicago: Association of American Colleges, 1940).

24. Patricia B. Knapp, *College Teaching and the College Library* (Chicago: American Library Association, 1959).

25. Richard W. Hostrop, *Teaching and the Community College Library* (Hamden, Conn.: Shoe String Press, 1968).

8

COOPERATION AND EXTENSION OF SERVICE

Cooperation among academic libraries has been practiced for decades. Practically all libraries have participated in interlibrary loan activities. Others have also jointly prepared union catalogs and union lists. Still others have agreed on cooperative development of resources, sharing of resources, and centralized processing. In a few instances libraries have agreed to establish cooperative storage facilities. Up to recent years the cooperative activities, outside of interlibrary loan and reciprocal borrowing privileges, have affected only a relatively small percentage of libraries.

During the last decade or so cooperative efforts have greatly intensified and a larger number of community colleges have become involved in them. Cooperative activities have been financially furthered by government agencies, state and federal, especially by grants from the U.S. Office of Education. These efforts have also been aided by private organizations. The major impetus, however, has come from the members of the library profession themselves. Librarians—including those of better-endowed institutions and likely to give more than they receive—have generally taken a positive attitude toward cooperation. They are convinced that their institutions are interdependent and that they must extend mutual support to complement each other.

Cooperation has many facets. We will first deal with interlibrary loan. Then we will discuss library consortia, i.e., formal agreements between the cooperating libraries, which are designed to attain a variety of goals and objectives. We will then focus our attention to two surveys dealing with services to the public at large—one undertaken in 1968, the other in 1973. Then we will consider the U.S. Office of Education's *Library Statistics of Colleges and Universities* (Fall 1971), which now includes data on cooperative and extension services. Next we will deal with new roles some public libraries have assumed in serving a specific college

community. The discussion will be concluded by an evaluation of joint
library service.

INTERLIBRARY LOAN

This is one of the oldest, most widely accepted forms of cooperation.
Unless otherwise stated, the rules of the American Library Association
Interlibrary Loan Code apply. The ALA Code specifies certain important
limitations. It excludes from transactions certain recent materials that
an institution may be expected to own, and—especially important for
two-year institutions—it excludes undergraduates as borrowers. In practice, however, this latter limitation has been removed in quite a number
of instances. For example, some state university libraries make their
resources freely available to students enrolled in junior colleges within
their state. This is the case in Kentucky. Community college students
may use the university's main library by means of interlibrary loan.[1]
Often interlibrary loan limitations have been removed by agreement.
Then, of course, community colleges themselves usually honor requests
from other two-year institutions without reference to the restrictions
of the ALA Code.

The practically universal availability of copying devices has had a
significant effect on interlibrary lending. Some institutions now give
the applicant the choice between borrowing an original work or a copy
of the item; other institutions provide copies only.

Statistical details regarding interlibrary transactions are recorded in
Table 10. It is evident that a considerable number of the institutions—
about half as many as those providing originals—supply copies. It is also
noteworthy that most libraries not only borrow materials but are also
prepared to lend them.

ACADEMIC LIBRARY CONSORTIA

Academic library consortia are based on formal agreements between
cooperating libraries. Most of them have come into being in the last
10 to 15 years under the impact of an increasing desire and need to
cooperate.

The subject of consortia has been explored thoroughly in investigations
undertaken by the System Development Corporation on behalf of the

U.S. Office of Education. The *Directory of Academic Library Consortia*[2] and *Guidelines for the Development of Library Consortia*[3] are the two major products of this study. Also very informative is an article by two of the leaders of the consortia research team, meant for a wider audience.[4] Our discussion relating to academic library consortia is largely based on these sources.

To be listed in the *Directory of Academic Library Consortia,* an organization must meet certain criteria, including the following: The participating institutions must be autonomous; more than half of the members must be academic libraries; two or more of the member libraries must be engaged in activities going beyond the traditional American Library Association interlibrary loan regulations. Each consortium must be organized to pursue activities of benefit to the participating institutions.[5] It should be stressed further that participants in consortia "share system and planning resources as well as operating responsibilities and functions."[6]

Consortia vary in objectives, scope, purpose, activities, composition, and clientele served. As for membership, academic library consortia have a choice of including university, four-year, and two-year college libraries, as well as a minority of nonacademic libraries. They may decide on being homogeneous (all members of the same academic level) or heterogeneous (mixed; members from different academic levels).

The directory lists 125 academic consortia. Six of these consortia consist exclusively of two-year institutions. In another 30 cases there is heterogeneous membership, where junior or community colleges have joined forces with representatives of other types of institutions. Patrick identifies twenty-four cooperative activities and notes the extent to which the various consortia either currently engage or plan to engage in them.[7]

Frequent consortia activities are reciprocal borrowing privileges, expanded (in comparison to the ALA Interlibrary Loan Code) interlibrary loan service, making of union catalogs and lists, and photocopying. All of these are relatively low-cost, high-benefit, low-compromise activities as compared to such cooperative activities as catalog card production. In this instance a large initial financial outlay is required before benefits can be realized, especially if production is computerized. Moreover, agreement may have to be reached on the standardization of certain procedures. There may also be considerable financial implications in agreements relating to specialization in acquisition and mutual notification of intended purchases of expensive materials.[8]

Usually consortia have a number of objectives, but a few specified that they had only one objective, for instance, the development of archives of materials relating to Black Americans. An institution can be a member of several consortia; this may be especially desirable if the several consortia that an institution plans to join have complementary objectives. A two-year institution would find it useful to join a consortium with mixed membership—an effective way of opening to the community college the resources of larger institutions. This does not preclude a community college from holding simultaneous membership in a consortium that pursues goals solely of concern to community colleges. In fact, such dual membership may be very desirable.

The diversity among the consortia can probably be best shown by introducing several typical examples. The Cooperative Library Agreement (part of Kansas City Regional Council for Higher Education [KCRCHE]), mixed as to membership and including several community colleges, sets as its current objectives: "joint purchasing of materials; assigned subject specialization in acquisitions, catalog card production, photocopying services; central resource and storage center; reciprocal borrowing privileges; expanded interlibrary loan service; publication program; special communications service; and personnel training or upgrading." In its plan for the future this consortium projects these activities: "production and/ or maintenance of union catalogs, lists and directories."[9]

The Southwest Academic Library Consortium, again an organization of mixed membership with several community colleges in the group, lists the following as current activities: "reciprocal borrowing privileges, expanded interlibrary loan service; special communications services." The consortium names these projected activities: "joint purchasing of materials; assigned subject specialization in acquisitions and other acquisitions activities."[10]

From among the several consortia consisting exclusively of community college libraries we will bring the following examples:

The Film Library Inter-College Cooperative of Pennsylvania lists in the directory a wide range of current activities—practically all operations a consortium can engage in.[11] However, the president of the cooperative stated in a letter that the organization is strictly a 16mm film library cooperative which has neither extended nor plans to extend its activities to other areas.[12]

The consortium having the most member colleges is the California Community Colleges Library Cooperative.[13] Among its purposes and objectives the consortium notes strengthening local self-sufficiency and extension of the principle of sharing. The current activities include photocopying services, microfiche production, and reciprocal borrowing privileges. According to a note in *Library Journal*, the tentative plans of the consortium include cooperative purchasing, cooperative film libraries, reference centers, and cooperative book cataloging and processing.[14] It is also stated that work is underway on the compilation of union lists of both periodical and audiovisual materials. The statewide California Community College Cooperative consists of twelve regional educational resource centers. The statewide board of directors intends to work with other library systems in the state in carrying out California's total library service plans.

The statewide cooperative was established in 1971; the directory includes, in addition, the San Gabriel Community Colleges Library Cooperative which was founded earlier, in 1969, to serve the region of the San Gabriel Valley and the counties of Orange and San Bernardino.[15] According to information received from Shirley E. Bosen, this was the only region in the California Community College Library Cooperative in which the libraries work under a formal joint powers agreement entered into by all of the boards of the participating college districts.[16] Among the specially noteworthy activities of the San Gabriel Community Colleges Library Cooperative is the sharing of 16mm film and the publication of a union list of serials. The cooperative has assumed, with the Metropolitan Public Library Cooperative, the task of devising and managing a demonstration project in the area of periodical selection and retention, and interlibrary loan.

EXTENSION OF SERVICE TO OUTSIDERS

A community college library may extend its services to students not enrolled in the college without the prerequisite that they be affiliated with any other institution of higher learning with which the lending institution has a reciprocal agreement. A community college may even extend

its services to the general public, with or without restriction. Arguments
may be brought for and against opening the doors to the general public.
The principal argument in favor of library use by the general public is the
fact that the community college is an instittution of the community and
as such should be accessible to any member of the community ("members
of the community" is often, but not invariably, defined as any person
within the college district). On the other hand the collection is formed
to meet the needs of the faculty and student body, and its availability to
the college community should not be encroached upon by extending use
of resources and services to outsiders.

A SURVEY BY E. J. JOSEY AND ASSOCIATES

A survey undertaken in 1968 indicates that service to the community
at large is favored by a vast majority of the two-year institutions.[17] The
survey was conducted under the auspices of the Association of College
and Research Libraries, Committee on Community Use of Academic
Libraries. The findings were presented in symposium format; the chairman
of the committee, E. J. Josey, worked with six other librarians in tabu-
lating and analyzing the questionnaire returns.[18] The sample included
public and private institutions, and in most respects there were no appreciable differences between the practices of the publicly supported
and the privately maintained institutions. Over 90 percent of the libraries
permitted outsiders—persons other than students, faculty and staff, and
their immediate families—use of the library resources. Nearly 85 percent
allowed also unrestricted use of the study space. Only 70 percent of the
institutions allowed noncollege members to withdraw books and other
library materials for outside use. But the 30 percent of the libraries that
stated they did not serve the general public were prepared to allow circulation to some segments of the population. According to the survey
findings, teachers, clergy, other professional people, and alumni have
access to nearly all community college libraries. Regarding the question
whether any limits are set for outsiders who are permitted to withdraw
material, the response was "no" from about 20 percent of the libraries.
Other libraries made restrictions of various kinds, such as number of
books that could be withdrawn at any one time. The restriction most
often applied concerned reserve books, which could not be withdrawn
for home use by outsiders.

Most community college libraries did not find use by outsiders a burden. In general, few such persons had been taking advantage of the privilege of using the library's resources and/or services. However, a small number of libraries—about 20 percent of the total group—reported appreciable outside use. The survey showed that many of the colleges not only allow withdrawal of books but are also prepared to provide information and reference service. The feeling that the community college is to serve the public at large, at least the public of the college district, is pervasive and has been gaining ground steadily.

ENCOURAGEMENT OF USE

Some community college libraries not only allow use of their materials by outsiders but also actively encourage the adult public of the district to avail themselves of the community college library's services. Typical of this trend are statements like the following, which have appeared in library magazines: An Illinois report on the Joliet Junior College's new open-door policy notes that adults in the Joliet Junior College district will be issued library cards by the college, giving them access to the learning center materials and that efforts would be made to bring in best-sellers and other books that would have appeal to area residents.[19] Similarly, the learning center of the Northeastern Connecticut Community College in Winsted honors the library cards issued by all town libraries in the northeastern part of Connecticut. Any materials available to the students are available to public library card holders. The community college has also made its library's telephone reference service available to area residents.[20]

The need of the public to have access to the college library is influenced by the location of a community college. If the college is in a city where excellent public library service is available and where many other institutions of higher learning maintain extensive collections, the general public need not rely on a community college library. The picture is very different in a community that has only nominal public library service and no academic libraries except that of the community college. Here, outsiders may have to turn to a community college library as the only source for library materials and library information service.

A SURVEY OF THE EXPANDING
ROLE IN COMMUNITY INVOLVEMENT

The American Association of Community and Junior Colleges and the

Junior College Section of the Association of College and Research Libraries have recognized that the learning resource centers are likely to play a major part in the expanding role of community colleges in community services, nontraditional studies, and external degrees. For this reason these organizations sponsored a survey to assess the nature and extent of such developments. Since a normative study was not feasible, a study was made of about fifty LRCs deemed outstanding by practitioners throughout the junior college field.

In an analysis of the survey Max R. Raines shows that community involvement has many facets and already is far reaching.[21] Some LRCs have contributed to cross-cultural understanding through exhibits and displays of cultural artifacts. For instance, at Wharton County Junior College, Wharton, Texas, the fine arts division of the college and the learning center have cooperated in promoting various kinds of cross-cultural programs. Foreign students have been encouraged to exhibit materials which illustrate phases of the cultures of their countries. The general public has not only been invited to visit the exhibits but also to contribute to them.

The community needs have also been considered in practical matters. Several LRCs have reported that they maintain career informaton systems that operate on a community-wide basis. Lane Community College at Eugene, Oregon, as already mentioned in Chapter 7, has a computer-based occupational data bank that provides high school and college students with current information on career opportunities and requirements. A librarian and a counselor staff this program, which has the cooperation and support of schools, employment agencies, social agencies, and other community organizations.

Some LRCs have developed programs designed to collect, codify, and package information dealing with political, legal, and administrative problems affecting the community. The legislative reference service of the Bellevue Community College at Bellevue, Washington, is a case in point. The service, which is managed by the reference librarian, is available to faculty and students and also to any member of the community. The latest legislative news is also available through CHESTER, the dial-access retrieval system.

The survey notes several other areas for which programs and materials have been developed. For example, learning resources packages for persons enrolled in nontraditional studies, homemakers, and the handicapped. Finally, a few LRCs have created interagency information exchanges to alert community organizations to work being done by other community organizations.

One of the most comprehensive programs designed to reach the general public has been originated by the Coast Community College District, which includes Orange Coast College at Costa Mesa and Golden West College at Huntington Beach, California.[22] The district operates KOC-TV in coopera- tion with others. The station provides college-level programs, programs for the elementary and secondary levels, and general community and municipal service programs. Integral to the whole design is call-back counseling.

It is noteworthy that the five cities of the district have made a joint powers agreement to develop a cable television network. Moreover, the three entities of higher education in Orange and San Diego counties have joined forces to implement the nontraditional approach to learning by creating Project Outreach, a television project. The agencies supporting the project are the University of California at San Diego, California State University at San Diego, and the Coast Community College District. The educational structure formed by these institutions has some of the features of an open university and has been called a "communiversity" by some writers and practitioners. In its initial stages it utilizes cables, cassettes, correspondence, computers, classrooms, and comprehension centers.

The LRCs are important elements in this multifaceted approach to reaching the public of the Coast Community College District. The centers are open to all people of the district. The centers offer specialized facili- ties; for example, the Golden West College LRC has forty computer terminals providing CAI packages.[23]

U.S. OFFICE OF EDUCATION
LIBRARY STATISTICS

The extension of user privileges beyond an institution's own students, faculty, and staff, and cooperation between libraries have been recognized by the United States Office of Education as "developmental areas that are expanding greatly."[24] On account of this trend and the strong interest of the profession in these matters, the Office of Education has begun col- lecting, recording, and analyzing statistics in these broad areas: libraries participating in interlibrary cooperation programs; libraries providing extended user privileges, and libraries participating in Title III LSCA programs. The federal library statistics give data for individual institutions[25] and in the form of aggregate United States summaries.[26] In our subsequent discussions we will utilize only the aggregate figures.

Some of the activities and programs which have been recorded in the United States Office of Education *Statistics, Fall 1971,* are the concern of a number of the academic library consortia discussed earlier in this chapter. The federal statistics will include pertinent activities and programs if they are in operation, regardless of whether they are performed within or outside of the framework of formally established consortium agreements.

Table 9 dealing with extended user privileges includes several categories. The community-at-large category receives service from the largest number of colleges. The other higher education institutions follow. If we subdivide, by size, the community colleges extending service to the community at large, we find that a higher percentage of the smaller community colleges provide this service. The pattern is reversed with regard to user privileges granted by community colleges to other higher education institutions. In this situation a higher percentage of the larger community colleges extend their services. This may occur because the larger community colleges have more of the materials needed by other higher education institutions. With regard to services extended to the community at large, more of the smaller community colleges are in areas without sufficient or any public library service, and they must, in some respects, perform the functions of a public library.

The statistics were also designed to determine whether certain population groups, which have been singled out by some authorities as requiring special consideration, actually receive it in practice. These groups—the educationally and culturally disadvantaged, the handicapped, and the retired—are being given special attention by only very few institutions. Both the Josey survey and the U.S. Office of Education statistics are concerned with extension of services beyond the college's own members. However, a comparison of the Josey survey with U.S. Office of Education statistics would not be productive since the definitions of the concepts are not identical nor are the categories singled out for special consideration the same.

Table 10 covers three aspects of interlibrary cooperation: interlibrary loan, computer sharing, and cooperative acquisition. While a majority of the libraries participate in interlibrary loan transactions, only a few reported that they shared computers or that they were involved in cooperative

Table 9

Number and Percent of Libraries of Public Two-year Institutions Providing Extended User Privileges, by Type of User: Aggregate United States, Fall 1971

			Extended User Privileges Provided													
Enrollment Size	No. of Institutions	Total Responses	Other Higher Education Institutions No.	Pct.	Education Agencies (excl. Higher Education) No.	Pct.	Educationally or Culturally Disadvantaged No.	Pct.	Handicapped No.	Pct.	Retired No.	Pct.	Community at Large No.	Pct.	Other No.	Pct.
1	2	3	4	5	6	7	8	9	10	11	12	13	14	15	16	17
Two-year Institutions	660	1,151	319	27.7	286	24.8	47	4.1	13	1.1	7	0.6	474	41.2	5	0.4
10,000 or more	55	108	38	35.2	25	23.1	10	9.3	3	2.8	1	0.9	30	27.8	1	0.9
5,000 to 9,999	80	137	45	32.8	38	27.7	5	3.6	2	1.5	—	—	46	33.6	1	0.7
1,000 to 4,999	357	612	174	28.4	147	24.0	16	2.6	4	0.7	4	0.7	266	43.5	1	0.2
500 to 999	123	218	45	20.6	57	26.1	12	5.5	4	1.8	2	0.9	97	44.5	1	0.5
Fewer than 500	45	76	17	22.4	19	25.0	12	5.3	—	—	—	—	35	46.1	1	1.3

SOURCE: U.S. Office of Education, National Center for Educational Statistics, *Library Statistics for Colleges and Universities*, Fall 1971, Analytic Report (Part C), Washington, D.C., 1973, p. 59 (Table C-22).

Table 10

Number and Percent of Libraries of Public Two-year Institutions Participating in Interlibrary Cooperative Programs, by Type of Program: Aggregate United States, Fall 1971

Enrollment Size	Number of Institutions	Total Responses	Interlibrary Loans				Interlibrary Cooperation					
			Provide Materials		Provide Copies		Receive Materials		Share Computer Facilities with Other Libraries		Participate in Cooperative Acquisition Program	
			Number	Percent	Number	Percent	Number	Percent	Number	Percent	Number	Percent
1	2	3	4	5	6	7	8	9	10	11	12	13
Two-year Institutions	660	1,507	534	35.4	277	18.4	602	39.9	24	1.6	70	4.6
10,000 or more	55	144	50	34.7	31	21.5	53	36.8	2	1.4	8	5.6
5,000 to 9,999	80	204	75	36.8	45	22.1	75	36.8	4	2.0	5	7.5
1,000 to 4,999	357	843	297	35.2	156	18.5	330	39.1	16	1.9	44	5.2
500 to 999	123	244	88	36.1	36	14.8	110	45.1	1	0.4	9	3.7
Fewer than 500	45	72	24	33.3	9	12.5	34	47.2	1	1.4	4	5.6

SOURCE: U.S. Office of Education, National Center for Educational Statistics, *Library Statistics for Colleges and Universities*, Fall 1971, Analytic Report (Part C), Washington, D.C., 1973, p. 57 (Table C-20).

acquisition programs. Twenty-four responses (representing 1.6 percent of
the total number of responses) indicated a sharing of computer facilities,
and seventy responses (representing 4.6 percent of the total) noted that
libraries were engaged in cooperative acquisition.

Participation in Title III LSCA Programs is the subject of U.S. Office
of Education Table C-21.[27] The programs concern the following bibliographic services: communications networks, reference services, technical
processing services, and miscellaneous projects. Compared with libraries
serving the more advanced levels of higher education, a smaller percentage
of the community college libraries take part in these programs: Reference
services heads the list with twenty-five instances, followed by programs
dealing with communications networks (twenty-four instances), bibliographic
services (seventeen instances), and technical processing services (three
instances).

THE PUBLIC LIBRARY'S ROLE
IN SERVING THE COMMUNITY
COLLEGE STUDENT

By definition, a public library is accessible to all community residents.
There are numerous instances in which a public library has made a particular effort to gear its work and resources to a community college's
specific requirements. A public library often subscribes to periodicals that
community college students may need and orders books recommended for
class assignments. Some public libraries will even put books on reserve
for these students.

An example of this involvement between public library and community
college is the cooperative project, "Study Unlimited," between the Learning
Resources, Laboratory of the City Colleges of Chicago and the Chicago Public
Library.[28] This project is designed to make multi-media study materials
available to members of the public who are preparing for various tests, such
as the GED, CLEP, and college exemption tests and also for those who wish
to earn credit in TV-recorded telecourses.

The City Colleges of Chicago Learning Resources Laboratory will place
in designated branches of the Chicago Public Library the full resources of
its videotape library, which includes some twenty recorded telecourses each
containing thirty programs. The print materials which accompany the
courses will also be sent to the designated branches. The City Colleges of

Chicago will further provide counseling services at all locations. The Chicago Public Library will make available the facilities and resources required, both book and nonbook materials and the necessary equipment. The public library will also provide a coordinator of the program and additional staff to supervise facilities at each designated location. Enrollment in the program is open to:

1. Regular students at one of the campuses of the City Colleges of Chicago,
2. Students preparing themselves for GED or CLEP tests, and
3. Individuals who wish to pursue study for self-enrichment.

"Study Unlimited" was extraordinarily successful even during the pilot stage of the program.[29] After six months operation there were over 230 students enrolled for college credit in the videocassette curriculum. The program had been expected to draw only about thirty students during its initial stage. "Study Unlimited" offered eight courses from various disciplines. The director of the program, Leslie Sandy, observed that some courses did not "adapt easily to the cassette format" and that therefore additional facilities for such courses have been planned—for instance, science labs for science courses.

OPERATION OF A COLLEGE LIBRARY
BY A PUBLIC LIBRARY

The Memphis Public Library and Information Center (MPLIC) and the Shelby State Community College (SSCC) have made an agreement that became effective in the fiscal year 1972-1973.[30] It stipulates that the MPLIC will be the operating agency of the library serving SSCC. Under this agreement MPLIC exercises overall supervision; orders, catalogs, and delivers books; appoints and terminates employment of SSCC library staff; and sets policies for operation of the SSCC library, with the advice and consent of the SSCC Library Committee.

Shelby State Community College provides space; consults with the head librarian; admits him to faculty meetings and gives him appropriate rank and privileges; provides funds in proportion to services rendered to SSCC students; and encourages use of the SSCC library by the public at large. To this end SSCC will post signs outside of the building informing the public that the college library is part of the MPLIC system. This agreement renders the college library a unit of the public library system. The students of the college have the resources of the public library available and can withdraw materials from the public library simply by presenting their SSCC library card. Both institutions contribute funds for the purchase of books and other materials, each in proportion to the extent the SSCC library is used by the college population and the noncollege public.

It will be interesting to see whether this cooperative enterprise will succeed. Some questions will arise that can probably be answered only after a few years of operation: Will the SSCC library build a collection to primarily satisfy the needs of the college community, or will the acquisition program concentrate on materials of general interest? Will the head librarian be able to manage the SSCC library as he and the college administration find proper, or will he receive conflicting orders from the MPLIC? Most problems, of course, can be worked out if both parties can agree on their mutual needs and continue to see the enterprise as mutually advantageous.

JOINT LIBRARIES

There are relatively few joint libraries in the higher education field. The U.S. Office of Education statistics lists thirteen instances in which one library serves two or more institutions, or one instituion and part of another.[31] This tabulation includes only one joint library with a community college as a participant: the Charles S. Mott Joint Library at Flint, Michigan, which serves the Genesee Community College and Flint College of the University of Michigan. The two institutions have separate materials budgets, with each college selecting materials that then become part of the combined collection. The director of libraries is considered a staff member of both institutions, but he is a direct employee of the community college.

Other community colleges share their facilities with units of universities without forming a joint library. The Grand Rapids Junior College Library also serves the Grand Rapids extension centers of the University of Michigan, Michigan State University, and Western Michigan University;[32] Laredo Junior College shares facilities with the Texas A.&J. University branch at Laredo, Texas.[33]

The Auraria Higher Education Center in Denver is in the process of establishing a joint library complex for three institutions: the Metro

State College (a four-year college), the University of Colorado at Denver
(a four-year college with some advanced programs), and the Community
College of Denver-Auraria Campus. At present each institution is still
served by its own library, but the first step toward combining the facilities has been taken by transforming the Metropolitan technical services
department into the Auraria technical services department. This department orders and catalogs the books for all three institutions with each
college doing its own materials selection.[34]

Joint libraries have also been formed to serve the public and the college community. The one joint library serves both functions. This is
different from the case in which a public library—either from its inception
or subsequently—particularly welcomes the clientele of a college which
itself has a library, or from the situation where a college library welcomes
the public at large, which is simultaneously served by a public library.
In contrast, a joint library is a single entity designed to serve both clienteles. Such a joint college-public library has been established at Brownsville,
Texas. This library, labeled a "college-community library," serves Texas
Southmost College and the community at large. The librarian notes that
the joint service has been beneficial to both groups and has meant monetary
savings for the city and the college.[35]

One type of joint library combination frequently established in the
earlier years of junior college development included a junior college and
a high school. This form has now become rather rare, since practically all
junior colleges have moved from the high school-connected range into the
area of higher education.

Joint libraries are doubtlessly more difficult to administer than libraries serving only one institution. The head of the joint library must be
a person with considerable administrative skill. He must not only be fair
and serve all parties on equal terms, but he must also be able to allay any
anxiety that one group might be favored over the other.

The great advantage of the joint library is that its resources can serve
several clienteles. The closer the interests of the user groups are, the easier
it will be to create a joint venture. Joint operation eliminates duplication
of materials, and the combined amount of funds available for the acquisition of books and other materials will allow the building of a more comprehensive, diversified collection than could have been attained by either
of the participants alone. Technical services will be more economical, and
the public service units can have a larger staff, with varying backgrounds,
to counsel and otherwise assist the library user.

It is advisable to indicate by an ownership symbol which institution has provided the funds for the purchase of an item. In case the joint operation were to be terminated, each institution could identify its property without having to go through the original acquisition records. Division of holdings in accordance with ownership may not, however, represent the best solution. When the joint library operation of Chicago State University and Kennedy-King College was to be discontinued, the library staffs of both institutions recommended to their respective administrations that Chicago State University be given the opportunity to purchase the Kennedy-King-owned items of the combined collection. This recommendation was accepted, and with the funds obtained Kennedy-King was able to buy books that were especially timely and useful in a modern community college collection.

NOTES

1. *American Junior Colleges,* 8th ed., ed. Edmund J. Gleazer, Jr. (Washington, D.C.: American Council on Education, 1971), p. 219.

2. Diane D. Delanoy and Carlos A. Cuadra, *Directory of Academic Library Consortia* (Santa Monica, Calif.: System Development Corporation, 1972).

3. Ruth J. Patrick, *Guidelines for the Development of Academic Library Consortia* (Santa Monica, Calif.: System Development Corporation, 1972).

4. Carlos A. Cuadra and Ruth J. Patrick, "Survey of Academic Library Consortia in the U.S.," *College & Research Libraries* 33, no. 4 (July 1972): 271-83.

5. Delanoy and Cuadra, *op. cit.,* pp. 3-4.

6. Patrick, *op. cit.,* pp. 1, 3; and Cuadra, *op. cit.,* p. 271.

7. Patrick, *op. cit.,* p. 71; see also: Delanoy and Cuadra, *op. cit.,* pp. 199-201, for chart noting activities for each consortium.

8. Patrick, *op. cit.,* pp. 158-9.

9. Delanoy and Cuadra, *op. cit.,* pp. 53-54.

10. *Ibid.,* pp. 176-7.

11. *Ibid.,* pp. 64-65.

12. John Bradley, letter dated November 8, 1972.

13. Delanoy and Cuadra, *op. cit.,* pp. 30-32.

14. "Community College Libraries Form Network in California," *Library Journal* 97, no. 12 (June 15, 1972): 2140-1.

15. Delanoy and Cuadra, *op. cit.,* p. 161.

16. Shirley E. Bosen, Head Librarian, Fullerton Junior College, letter dated November 8, 1972.

17. E. J. Josey, et al., "Community Use of Junior College Libraries - A Symposium," *College & Research Libraries* 31, no. 3 (May 1970): 185-98.

18. George C. Elser, Edward C. Heintz, Barbara LaMont, Richard C. Quick, John E. Scott, and John B. Smith.

19. "North Point (Md.) Library Stores College Collection; Joliet Junior College (Ill.) Opens Library to the Public," *Library Journal* 97, no. 7 (April 1, 1972): 1231.

20. "Conn. Community College Opens Doors to P. L. Patrons," *Library Journal* 98, no. 7 (April 1, 1973): 1075.

21. Max R. Raines, "A Survey of Leading LIB/LRC's," *Junior and Community College Journal* 43, no. 9 (June-July 1973): 10-12.

22. Norman E. Watson and Bernard J. Luskin, "Cables, Cassettes, and Computers at Coast," *Community and Junior College Journal* 43, no. 3 (December 1972): 12-13.

23. Bernard J. Luskin, Vice Chancellor, Educational Planning and Development, letter dated May 29, 1973.

24. U.S. Office of Education, National Center for Educational Statistics, *Library Statistics for Colleges and Universities. Institutional Data, Part A. Fall 1971,* General Education Survey, College and University Libraries, 1971. Explanations . . . Part V. (Washington, D.C.: U.S. Office of Education, 1972), p. 243.

25. U.S. Office of Education, National Center for Educational Statistics, *Library Statistics of Colleges and Universities. Institutional Data. Part B. Fall 1971,* Tables 3 and 4 (Washington, D.C.: U.S. Office of Education, 1972), pp. 97-184.

26. U.S. Office of Education, National Center for Educational Statistics, *Library Statistics of Colleges and Universities. Fall 1971. Analytic Report (Part C),* Tables C-20 to C-22 (Washington, D.C.: U.S. Office of Education, 1973), pp. 57-59.

27. *Ibid.,* p. 58.

28. City Colleges of Chicago and Chicago Public Library, "Study Unlimited, for Student Independent Study. A Cooperative Project Between the Learning Resources Laboratory of the City Colleges of Chicago and the Chicago Public Library," May 8, 1973 (Processed).

29. "Study Unlimited," *American Libraries* 5, no. 2 (February 1974): 66-67.

30. Memphis Public Library and Information Center and Shelby State Community College, "Agreement (between Memphis Public Library and Information Center and Shelby State Community College)," 1972

(Processed); and Larry E. Bone, Assistant Director of Libraries for Public Services, Memphis Public Library and Information Center, letter dated May 2, 1973.

31. U.S. Office of Education, National Center for Educational Statistics, *Library Statistics of Colleges and Universities. Fall 1971. Analytic Report (Part C)* (Washington, D.C.: U.S. Office of Education, 1973), pp. 22-23, 24-25.

32. *American Junior Colleges,* 8th ed., p. 262.

33. *Ibid.,* pp. 504-5.

34. Anthony J. Dedrick, Lead Librarian, Community College of Denver, letter dated June 1, 1973; and Rebecca J. Jackson, Supervisor, Auraria Technical Services, letter dated July 9, 1973.

35. Texas Southmost College, Brownsville, Texas, *The Hunger to Read* (folder describing the Texas Southmost College Library); and Anthony J. Valdez, Librarian, letter dated April 27, 1971.

9

STANDARDS AND GUIDELINES

Librarians and college administrators, governing boards of colleges, accrediting agencies, and other organizations concerned with the status and condition of libraries need sets of criteria, policy statements, goals, measures, yardsticks, and other aids and devices to facilitate the evaluation of libraries or learning resources programs.

In the junior and community college field, serious efforts to establish standards go back at least to the 1920s. We shall describe these early efforts briefly and make some observations on standards in general. Principal attention will be given to the most recent nationally applicable statement, "Guidelines for Two-Year College Learning Resources Programs."[1] We shall also refer to others but give particular attention to the documents that have been issued for learning resource centers in California, Illinois, and Washington.

The scope and purpose of such aids in evaluation extend over a wide range. Felix Hirsch, the former chairman of the ACRL Committee on Standards (1957-1963), describes this variety in scope and purpose and refers particularly to the distinction between guidelines and standards.[2]

To clarify the distinction between the two terms, Hirsch refers to dictionary definitions that note a guideline is broad and general, whereas a standard is much more specific and binding. *The American Heritage Dictionary of the English Language* (1969) explains that a guideline is "the statement of policy by a person or group having authority over activity." In the same dictionary, a standard is defined as "an acknowledged measure of comparison for quantitative and qualitative value; criteria, norm . . . a degree or level of requirement, excellence or attainment." These definitions are intended to apply to any field of endeavor.

Through the years, the ALA Standards Committee and other ALA agencies concerned with the application of standards were hampered by

the lack of precise policy statements and procedural rules that would
insure consistency. In 1966 the ALA Standards Committee was charged
with the development of a "Standards Manual," a task which was completed
in 1973.[3] (The manual was endorsed by the ALA executive board and
transmitted to the ALA council at the 1973 annual conference. The council
referred the manual back to the committee, expressing the view that each
division could handle its own standards. The committee was to report
back at the 1974 midwinter conference.) The proposed "ALA Standards
Manual" (1973) identifies terms frequently encountered in standards.
Three terms were considered of particular importance: goals, standards,
and guidelines. The paragraph entitled "Terms Defined" emphasizes that
the definitions are meant to apply only to "ALA standards and guidelines
and not to the goals, standards and guidelines developed by other associations and institutions." However, standards published by other organizations may be adopted by the ALA. It is further noted that the provisions
of the standards manual are not retroactive. In accordance with general
usage, the ALA considers guidelines as statements that do not have the
force of ALA standards nor the commitment of ALA goals.[4] An ALA
standard is intended as a criterion by which current judgments of value,
quality, fitness, and correctness are confirmed.

ALA guidelines are not required to incorporate the following four
elements, all of which must be included in ALA standards: (1) statement
of principles, (2) detail as to necessary elements, (3) reference to accepted
definitions, and (4) where applicable, formulas and rules of specifications
that can be applied with a high degree of certainty.

ALA guidelines, however, do present a suggested level of performance
or adequacy approved by a unit of ALA giving a desired direction of
development and containing practical methods of procedure and self-
evaluation by which judgments can be confirmed and evidence evaluated.[5]

An examination of documents dealing with standards for libraries will
reveal that terminology has not been uniformly applied in the past.
"Standard" has been the favorite term, used for a wide range of measures
and aids in the evaluation of the condition of a library. If examined in
the light of the proposed "ALA Standards Manual" (1973), some of these
statements would not merit the designation of standards; however, in line
with earlier usage, we shall use the term standards for the whole range
of measures designed to assist in the evaluation of libraries.

FROM EARLY EFFORTS
TO THE 1960 STANDARDS

Early efforts towards establishing standards for junior college libraries are well described by Walter C. Eells in his comprehensive survey of the junior college.[6] Eells deplores the fact that the American Council on Educaton set a minimum collection of 8,000 volumes for a four-year college and established no specific requirement for junior college library holdings. Nevertheless, as Eells notes, many accrediting agencies have been impressed that 8,000 volumes are stipulated for a four-year college and felt that comparable provisions should be made for junior colleges. Eells refers to the American Association of Junior Colleges as one of several agencies that had considerably raised the requirements within a seven-year span. A comparison of the 1922 standards with those adopted in 1929 shows the 1922 requirement was for "at least 2,000 volumes selected with special reference to college work," while the 1929 requirement was for "a working library adequately cataloged, modern, and well distributed of not fewer than 3,500 volumes. . . ."[7]

The concern of the junior college librarians themselves regarding the creation of standards is highly significant. The Junior College Round Table of the ALA assembled in 1930 at Los Angeles at the annual conference and resolved that certain minima should be met in establishing standards for junior colleges. They recommended that the minima for book budget, book stock, and staff should depend largely on the size of the enrollment.[8]

The collection should range (as quickly as possible after the library is established) between 10,000 and 20,000 volumes. As to personnel, it was stipulated that there should be two librarians if the enrollment is less than 500. The staff would be increased to head librarian and three professional assistants if the enrollment was from 500 to 1,000 and would have to be still larger with further increases in enrollment size. These standards were recommended but never formally adopted. It took thirty years before the ALA officially adopted standards for junior college libraries.[9] The 1960 Standards are not essentially more stringent than the 1930 recommendations. The 1960 Standards, like the 1930 recommendations, specify two professional librarians as the minimum number. In 1960 the line between professional and nonprofessional was drawn more sharply.

The 1930 recommendations had established a minimum book budget expressed by a specific figure. As noted by Felix Hirsch, the 1960 Standards did not follow the 1930 recommendations in this area.[10] This deliberate change was made because the purchasing power of money had been changing over the years. Therefore, a percentage figure of the total book budget was adopted. The minimum size of 20,000 volumes was chosen since leaders of the profession agreed that this was the minimum required to have a representative collection. The 1960 Standards stress breadth and quality in book selection. They present desirable administrative relationships; they also furnish data concerning size and characteristics of library buildings. The 1960 Standards recognize that the junior college is a dynamic institution which has to remain attuned to changes in society. It is therefore anticipated that with the passage of time the Standards would have to be revised and modified to meet new needs.

The 1960 Standards had a very far reaching influence and a deep impact on junior college library development. They constitute a professional landmark, as James O. Wallace has so fittingly stated.[11]

THE 1972 GUIDELINES

As the 1960 Standards anticipated, many junior colleges changed in scope and size. Many new institutions were established. Experimentation and innovation were favored by many. These and other influences were responsible for the creation of a new national document. Its present title reads "Guidelines for Two-Year College Learning Resources Programs." This represents a deliberate change from the title of the first draft, which read "Guidelines for Two-Year College Library Learning Resource Centers."[12] The title alteration expresses a change in philosophy and scope. Originally the guidelines were meant largely for activities connected with the learning resource center, a geographically delineated unit within the college. This geographic limitation was abandoned, and the guidelines now deal with the institution's learning resources program in whatever geographic location of the school it functions.

In all drafts the document uses the term learning resources. This indicates a program that concerns itself with all learning and teaching media regardless of form. The document accepts and supports a trend that has led libraries beyond their traditional function of repositories for books and has carried audio-visual centers beyond their traditional function as agencies for showing of films. This trend has favored "a confluence of accelerated development in both areas which is inextricably interwoven."[13]

The Guidelines stress that they are not meant to establish minimum quantitative standards but rather to offer "criteria for information, self-study and planning." Even though they are not standards, they reflect recommended practices. While the Guidelines see a role for variant practices, such variations must be supported by convincing evidence and documentation. The Guidelines recognize that each institution is best served by an organizational pattern suitable for its own goals and objectives, and the Guidelines therefore stress that they are not intended to create one configuration into which all institutions must fit. The Guidelines recognize and expect diversity in organizational patterns.

It is maintained in the document that the learning resources program probably expresses the educational philosophy of an institution better than do any of the other elements which contribute to the quality of instruction. (Some other important elements are faculty, students, finances, methods of teaching.)[14]

The Guidelines consider the learning resources program an indispensable element in the educational provisions of a two-year college. The program is an integral part of instruction. The programs of individual institutions can no longer exist in isolation but must cooperate in the development of networks covering larger geographical units, such as states and regions.[15]

The Guidelines define the role of the chief administrator of the learning resources program and his professional and nonprofessional associates. Responsibility for all learning resources is assigned to a central unit; materials should be placed where learning occurs.[16]

The need for budget planning is discussed and here, too, it is stressed that campus-wide needs are considered rather than needs of individual units in an unrelated form.[17]

The role, academic preparation, and status of the chief administrator and of the other staff members are prescribed. On account of the variety of functions it is advised that each staff member have the specific preparation suitable to his job requirements. No longer is a degree in library science considered to be the exclusive form of preparation. For certain tasks preparation in a related area may be more pertinent and more meaningful. Supportive staff is given due recognition and members of this staff category, too, are expected to have training appropriate for their respective assignments.[18]

Under the heading of instructional systems components appear these categories: staff, facilities, instructional equipment, materials and services.[19] The desirable characteristics of each of these elements are noted in detail.

The chief administrator is assigned a leading role in the planning of the facilities. The requirement that facilities must be geared to instructional goals is strongly emphasized, as is the requirement that a building must be flexible so that it can remain functional in case future changes in educational philosophy occur.

In the area of instructional equipment, selection, evaluation, and inventory control are noted.

A detailed and yet succinct account of materials is given regarding their selection, kinds of materials that may be useful, sources of materials, and treatment of gifts. The obvious requirement that materials must be organized for use is noted, and so is the interdependence of user needs, scope, and character of the collection.

It is made clear under services that a user should be able to obtain the materials he needs and work in an atmosphere conducive to study.

It has been emphasized that the Guidelines are qualitative and not quantitative. Quite possibly, future editions or revisions of the Guidelines will introduce quantitative measures. At any rate the document is meant to be reevaluated periodically. Like the 1960 Standards for junior college libraries, the 1972 Guidelines[20] for two-year college learning resources programs notes that the two-year institutions are in a state of flux, their role is ever changing and expanding, and it is quite likely that future editions of the Guidelines may need to be revised upward.

The Guidelines have broad support. They have been adopted by three professional organizations: the American Library Association (Association of College and Research Libraries), the American Association of Community and Junior Colleges, and the American Association of Educational Communications and Technology. James O. Wallace, who has had a leading part in developing library and learning resources standards and guidelines, describes the events that culminated in the participation of the three professional organizations in creating and supporting the document.[21]

This is the first time that three organizations have subscribed to an identical learning resources program. In the elementary and secondary school area, however, a precedent was set by the fact that two organizations joined in creating and supporting the same document.[22] The organizations were the American Association of School Librarians and the Department of Audio Visual Instructon (DAVI) now known as the Association of Educational Communications and Technology. The document "Standards for School Media Programs," intended to serve the elementary and secondary school, pioneered also in adopting the broad concept of learning and teaching materials.[23] The school document does not deal exclusively with books and audio-visual items, but with all media in an integrated fashion.

A closer comparison between the 1972 Guidelines and the "Standards for School Media Programs" discloses additional similarities. For instance, the title in both documents refers to programs rather than to geographically limited libraries or LRCs. The "Standards for School Media Programs" reflect a coordination of the standards for school library and audio-visual programs, and they urge a unified media program. However, there is one major difference: The Guidelines are qualitative only, while the "Standards for School Media Programs" are both quantitative and qualitative.

The proposed ALA Standards Manual (1973) notes that its definitions apply only to ALA standards, ALA guidelines, and ALA goals. The manual does not apply to standards, goals, and guidelines produced by other organizations and associations. The manual recognizes realistically that other agencies may be concerned with standardization and should be free to establish their own criteria and definitions. Not only national and state agencies in related fields have issued and will issue standards; library associations on the state level have also issued standards and will continue to do so. Felix Hirsch questions the wisdom of formulating state standards since, as he notes, "they often interfere with the proper application of national standards."[24] Hirsch's objection seems to have considerable merit, especially if the national document should contain quantitative data. However, as noted before, the "Guidelines for Two-year College Learning Resources Programs" are strictly qualitative. Some library educators may feel the need for quantitative measures, and it will therefore be necessary for them either to reach back to the 1960 Standards for junior college libraries—a document that has been replaced in toto by the Guidelines—or to utilize patterns recommended by state standards.

STATE STANDARDS AND GUIDELINES

Early versions of the national Guidelines take into account that for self-evaluation or planning purposes quantitative measures may be needed.

It is suggested in these early versions of the Guidelines that the California Standards, "the most comprehensive of the currently available,"[25] could be consulted to advantage. To facilitate their use, the California Standards were reproduced as an appendix in the "Guidelines for Two-year College Library Learning Resource Centers." The final version of the Guidelines no longer includes the advice that a state library association document should be consulted for quantitative measures. Even if such advice is no longer given in the national Guidelines, some evaluators may feel the need for having quantitative measures.

It seems appropriate at this point to sketch the features of several state documents that contain, quantitative data and have been issued within recent years. The documents are for California, Illinois, and Washington (State). In each instance the documents have been prepared by the state library association.

These standards and guidelines are meant to serve the institutions within their respective states. However, since library evaluators in other states may also need quantitative measures, they should be able to utilize the state standards that come closest to their own expectations.

The state standards will be described in the following sequence: the California Standards,[26] the oldest, will be first, followed in turn by the Illinois Guidelines[27] and the most recent, the Washington (State) Standards.[28]

The California Standards were designed to apply to institutions with enrollments of 1,500 or over. Smaller institutions might adapt them to their particular requirements. The California Standards give four service areas for which staffing is computed separately: technical services, public services, audio-visual services, and administrative services.

In the technical services area the staff ratio is one professional to two nonprofessional. The formula goes into specifics. It requires, e.g., one technical service position per 1,000 volumes cataloged by the Dewey scheme, or one position per 1,500 volumes cataloged by the Library of Congress scheme. If outside facilities are used, one position is expected to handle 1,500 volumes cataloged by Dewey or 2,500 by the Library of Congress classification.

In the public services area one staff member is recommended for every 30 full-time equivalent faculty members. The staff ratio is 0.4 professional to 0.6 nonprofessional positions.

In the audio-visual field one staff position is recommended for each

50 to 80 faculty members. The staff ratio is 0.2 professional to 0.8 non-professional.

The formula for determining the size of the book collection has been influenced by the Clapp and Jordan article dealing with criteria of building book collections.[29]

As to periodicals a basic collection of 300 titles is stipulated, to be increased by 1.3 titles for each certificated staff member (FTE) and four titles for each subject field.

A listing of audio-visual equipment within the library and for campus-wide needs is included. Formulas for space modification and a listing of factors that serve budget determination are also given.

The Guidelines for Illinois Junior and Community College Learning Resource Centers were adopted in 1972. The compilers and editors of the Illinois Guidelines were able to utilize the national Guidelines for two-year college learning resources programs. It is clearly noted in the Illinois Guidelines that the Illinois Library Association supports and adopts the national Guidelines.

The Illinois Guidelines are meant to extend the national Guidelines quantitatively and to supplement them. The quantitative section of the Illinois Guidelines is patterned very closely after the California Standards. However, the staff formula for the technical services area has been simplified. No distinction has been introduced between personnel needs for cataloging by the Dewey or by the Library of Congress scheme, and no special notice has been taken of the possible reduction in staff when outside processing service is used. The latest version of the Illinois Guidelines prescribes a minimum basic book stock of 30,000 volumes; this is higher than the basic collection prescribed either in California or in Washington. Illinois has in common with California and Washington a minimum basic number of periodical subscriptions of 300 titles.

The Washington State community college librarians and media specialists felt the need for quantitative standards when they were asked to present a survey of their libraries to a Joint Committee on Education.[30] The authors of the Washington (State) Standards consulted numerous sources, among them standards previously developed in other states. Also examined were the national and state standards for school media programs. Considerable weight was given as well to practices of community colleges that were considered effective in meeting the instructional needs of the students.

The national Guidelines were endorsed and many of the qualitative statements of the Guidelines were underscored and presented with force and clarity in the Washington document. It is stressed that the standards are to be viewed as minimal and that the institutions are expected to surpass them in one or another respect. Since each institution's goal is different from that of other institutions, the areas of superior performance differ from institution to institution.

The requirements set up by Washington are higher in nearly every category than those stipulated by the California and Illinois documents. The Washington minimum standards have taken into account very recent developments in the media field and have made recommendations, for instance, regarding light control, kinds of projectors, and television systems.

The Washington (State) formulas, while comprehensive, are more flexible than those of California and Illinois. In the case of staffing, Washington establishes a minimum of three professional staff members for any library learning resource center. Additional staff is required at the ratio of one professional for each 500 FTE beyond the first 500 FTEs. It is stipulated—as it was in California and Illinois—that the ratio of professional to supportive staff be 1 to 2. Washington gives the total staff needs and leaves it to the judgment of the individual institution to assign staff members where they can be of greatest service.

NOTES

1. American Library Association (Association of College and Research Libraries) et al., "Guidelines for Two-Year College Learning Resources Programs," *College & Research Libraries News* no. 11 (December 1972): 305-15 (hereafter cited as 1972 Guidelines).

2. Felix E. Hirsch, "Introduction: Why Do We Need Standards?" *Library Trends* 21, no. 2 (October 1972): 159-63.

3. American Library Association, Committee on Standards, "ALA Standards Manual" (Chicago, 1973) (Processed); see also: *American Libraries* 4, no. 8 (September 1973): 504.

4. *Ibid.*, p. 9.

5. *Ibid.*, p. 10.

6. Walter C. Eells, *The Junior College* (Boston: Houghton-Mifflin, 1931), pp. 440-7, 780-1.

7. *Ibid.*, pp. 447-8.

8. *Ibid.*, pp. 461-2; also in: Ermine Stone, *The Junior College Library*

(Chicago: American Library Association, 1932), pp. 85-87; See also Fritz Veit, "Personnel for Junior College Libraries," *Library Trends* 14, no. 2 (October 1965): 145-7.

9. Association of College and Research Libraries, Committee on Standards, "Standards for Junior College Libraries," *College & Research Libraries* 21, no. 3 (May 1960): 200-6 (hereafter cited as 1960 Standards).

10. Hirsch, *op. cit.*, p. 161.

11. James O. Wallace, "Two-Year College Library Standards," *Library Trends* 21, no. 2 (October 1972): 223.

12. American Association of Junior Colleges and Association of College and Research Libraries, "AAJC-ACRL Guidelines for Two-Year College Library Learning Resource Centers," *College & Research Libraries News* no. 9 (October 1971): 265-78.

13. 1972 Guidelines, pp. 305-6.

14. *Ibid.*, p. 306.

15. *Ibid.*, p. 308.

16. *Ibid.*, pp. 309-10.

17. *Ibid.*, pp. 310-11.

18. *Ibid.*, p. 311.

19. *Ibid.*, pp. 312-15.

20. *Ibid.*, p. 306.

21. Wallace, *op. cit.*, pp. 228-9.

22. American Association of School Librarians and Department of Audio-Visual Instruction, *Standards for School Media Programs* (Chicago and Washington, D.C.: American Library Association and National Education Association, 1969).

23. Frances Henne, "Standards for School Media Programs," *Library Trends* 21, no. 2 (October 1972): 233-47.

24. Hirsch, *op. cit.*, p. 161.

25. American Association of Junior Colleges and Association of College and Research Libraries, "AAJC-ACRL Guidelines," (1971), p. 266.

26. California Library Association, "Standards for Junior College Libraries" (1968) (Processed).

27. Illinois Library Association, College and Research Section, Subcommittee on Junior College Standards, "Guidelines for Illinois Junior and Community Colllege Learning Resource Centers" (Chicago: Illinois Library Association, 1972) (Final Draft).

28. Washington State Association of Community College Librarians and Media Specialists, "Minimum Quantitative Standards for Washington Community Colleges Learning Resources Programs," Washington State Library, *Library News Bulletin* 37, no. 4 (October-December 1970): 263-76.

29. Verner W. Clapp and Robert T. Jordan, "Quantitative Criteria for Adequacy of Academic Library Collections," *College & Research Libraries* 26, no. 5 (September 1965): 371-80.

30. Washington State Association of Community College Librarians and Media Specialists, "A Survey of the Learning Resources Programs in the Community Colleges of Washington State-1970," Washington State Library, *Library News Bulletin* 37, no. 4 (October-December 1970): 235-62.

10

PLANNING THE BUILDING

During the last decade or so hundreds of new community colleges were established.[1] The time between their founding and the beginning of operation was often too short to permit the construction of college campuses. As a result, some colleges had to use already existing facilities as temporary quarters. Sometimes the old quarters were sturdily built, in good condition, and well suited for adaptation to the community college's needs. In some of these instances it was decided to convert buildings originally meant for different uses into permanent college quarters.

Many different kinds of buildings have been transformed into LRCs. Reporting on the situation in Pennsylvania during the late 1960s, Gertrude L. Oetting says, "A mansion, a bank, a laboratory, a swimming pool, a church, a laundromat—each was destined to become a library in the Pennsylvania explosion of community colleges."[2] This list can be greatly extended if facilities are considered on a nationwide basis. A department store, an air control tower, a barn, a high school gym with an indoor running track are other examples of LRC structures originally designed for other purposes.

Whether these buildings are transformed into temporary or permanent learning resource facilities, the architect has to fit his plans into an already-established physical framework. If an old building is to serve temporarily, only absolutely essential structural changes would usually be carried out to keep expenses at a minimum. However, if an old building is to become the permanent home of an LRC, close attention must be paid to all details that might affect its projected function.

A new building is almost always preferable to an old one originally planned for a different use even if substantial alterations are practicable. The cost of conversion may be very high and approximate the cost of a new structure. An architect should be asked for an opinion as to whether

a solid and adaptable old building can be adequately remodeled on sufficiently attractive terms.

THE BUILDING PROGRAM

The first step in building planning should be the development of the
functional program.[3] The librarian should play a major role in developing
the program. In the process of drawing up specifications the librarian
should consult with the staff and with members of the faculty. The librarian
and the staff would also profit from the advice of a library consultant.

When the functional program has been worked out, it should be given to
the architect so that he can use it as the basis for the architectural plan.
The architect's plan should be submitted to the librarian and his staff and
to the library consultant for their reactions. By observing this procedure,
differing points of view can usually be reconciled.

The functional program should indicate the educational philosophy,
the curricula to be covered, the teaching and learning methods, and the
clientele to be served. Are the students likely to pursue mainly college
preparatory work, will a high percentage be in vocational programs, or
will there be a mix of students with various professional goals? The various
categories of students will present differing needs and are likely to require
different kinds of LRC study facilities.

Needs are subject to change, and it should therefore be possible to adapt
the LRC to changing demands. The building should be flexible. This concept of flexibility is in contrast to the fixed-function concept: This concept is realized if each space is so designed that a specific function can
be performed in it with the highest degree of efficiency.[4] For instance,
the stack area is designed to store books most efficiently and economically
without consideration for its usability as a reading area. Likewise, in a
fixed-function building the main design considerations for a reading room
would be its attractive and inviting qualities. However, this room's floor
would usually not be constructed to support ranges of book-filled stacks.
The drawback of fixed-function buildings is that use patterns, once established, can be changed only with great difficulty if at all. Modular
planning was introduced to remedy this situation. Modular construction
is characterized by equally spaced columns, creating modules of the same
size. The total floor area is solid enough to support stacks. Walls are not
load-bearing and can be removed if necessary.

Building planners need to have a clear picture of the functions to be assumed by the LRC. Is it to be the center for all learning resources or only for books? In recent years this question has almost always been resolved in favor of the comprehensive LRC. The center's structure, therefore, must allow for the utilization of many media. To use Ralph Ellsworth's words: "[It] should be a multi-media house."[5] Since improvements and refinements occur and new media are constantly being developed, the quarters must be flexible. They must allow the introduction of new media. This requirement of flexibility is stressed by practicing librarians and writers in the field. A function that is housed in a building today may become obsolete a few years hence, just as stacks are no longer needed for newspapers since backfiles are in microform and kept in cabinets. To assure full flexibility, we need to adopt the concept of open planning implemented by the use of rearrangeable and reallocatable subsystems, especially lighting, ceilings, and mechanical services.[6] There must be channels for all anticipated conduits, even if not all are to be installed before completion of the building. It can be many times more expensive to install channels after the structure is completed.

A very few instructional technologists have suggested that libraries may in the foreseeable future substitute other media for many or even most of the present holdings in book form. In such a case LRC structures as built today would become outmoded. However, the vast majority of experts in the instructional technology field do not see this as a realistic projection. Books are expected to remain the most important "things of learning" for many decades.[7] It would be extremely costly to convert already existing library collections into machine-readable form and commit them to a computer memory from which the information could be retrieved when needed. It is considered likely that some specialized texts will appear as original publications in computerized form, but these will not include the kinds of books used on the community college level. This means that for the foreseeable future LRC structures will have to be built in basically the same way as today, with floors strong enough to support book-filled stacks. However, with the passage of years, there will be a gradual increase of learning materials in computerized form, and it is necessary that the architect take this into account when devising the mechanical and electrical facilities for a building.[8] Probably there will be increased utilization of microforms before there will occur extensive computerization of learning materials (see Chapter 6).

While use of computers for information retrieval will remain exceptional in the community college field, an increasing number of LRCs will
want to have them available for such housekeeping tasks as ordering,
cataloging, and circulation. In general, computer use for these tasks is not
sufficiently extensive to warrant the assignment of a computer exclusively
to the LRC. It would usually not be necessary to provide a computer room
in the LRC, unless the college's sole computer should be placed in the
LRC building. The inclination to do so would be strong if the learning
resources division should be placed in charge of computer-assisted-instruc-
tion (CAI) and the other instructional and instruction-related computer
activities.

The aim of flexibility does not lessen the need for full and complete
planning. It is necessary to know approximately how many students will
be enrolled by the time the building is completed and at specified subsequent periods, perhaps three, five, ten, fifteen, or twenty years after the
building was first occupied. Projections should be made of the number
and kinds of books, periodicals, and nonbook materials to be acquired by
the time the building is opened and at the same subsequent periods for
which enrollment predictions have been made. Projections of the size
of the faculty and staff for the same periods should also be made. In
quite a number of instances a campus may be built in phases. Therefore,
the possibility of horizontal or vertical expansion of the buildings must
be assured.

While most recent college campuses consist of several buildings, with
the LRC occupying all or the major part of one, there are a number of
examples of colleges occupying only one very large structure that includes
all college facilities. This kind of building is found mainly, though not exclusively, in large metropolitan areas where space is expensive and difficult to obtain. In Chicago, for instance, both Kennedy-King and Malcolm
X, two recently built colleges of the City Colleges system, are each contained in one large building. In such structures, as Richard A. Jones states,
the learning resource center "might form the junction between wings of
different functions or become part of a continuous spectrum located by
their use."[9]

Very few library or LRC buildings have a circular design. The main
disadvantage of circular-shaped buildings is the difficulty in expanding
them. However, esthetic considerations and expected favorable student
response to the unusual have sometimes been the controlling factors,
and a decision has been made in favor of building a "library in the round."

According to reports by its library director, the circular building of Chabot College has met the expectations that "1) It should be the focal point for student interest, and 2) it should fulfill completely its function as the resource materials center for the college."[10] The building is highly flexible; functions and/or types of materials have been separated mainly by arrangements of shelving and furniture. Conduits and outlets have been placed in such a way that future requirements can be met. Furniture and some equipment have been designed both to be functional and to fit into the building pattern. The wood stacks on the second floor, for instance, are not in the usual straight form but are serpentine in order to break the wheel-spoke effect that would otherwise result.

Regardless of the kind of building—remodeled or new, separate or continuous, rectangular or circular—immediately upon entering the lobby the user's attention should be directed toward the "keys" of the learning resource center: the catalog, the bibliographies, and the reference tools.[11] In more and more instances the catalog of an LRC is a multi-media catalog containing cards for all the media in the center. However, as reported in Chapter 4, this pattern has not yet been generally accepted. If book and nonbook media are integrated, the keys area would usually house the bibliographic and reference tools for all media. Reference librarians and/or media consultants should be stationed near the tools since they have the most frequent occasion to consult them.

Since reference librarians and media consultants must frequently refer to periodicals and periodical indexes, these materials should be near the reference department. In most LRCs backfiles of periodicals are in microform. To allow concurrent use of recent and earlier periodical files, microforms and microform reading and printing equipment should be kept adjacent to the periodicals that are still in original form.

Some LRCs are federal and/or state government document depositories. The use of these documents frequently requires the assistance of reference staff. These materials, too, should therefore preferably be kept within easy reach of the reference desk. If LRCs have map collections, the map cabinets should be placed in or near the reference department because in a community college maps serve largely reference purposes.

The circulation services, like the reference services, are part of the units which form the "introduction to the building."[12] In most community colleges general books and reserve books are circulated from a single location. However, if the community college is very large, the reserve collection extensive, and the circulation of both general and re-

serve materials heavy, a separate distribution location and staff may be
justified for reserve books.

When the audio-visual activities are performed by a separate department, audio-visual materials are circulated from a separate distribution
unit. However, audio-visual software is increasingly issued at the general
materials circulation unit. In many instances projectors, record players,
monitors, and other hardware continue to be issued from an audio-visual
equipment distribution point.

As contrasted with the fixed-function building that separates book
stack areas from reading areas, today's modular library allows use of any
area of the library for either or both purposes. Neither of these functions
need be concentrated in a specific area. While stack concentrations are
still found in many recently built large university libraries, in most community college LRCs stacks are diffused and reading areas are interspersed
with stack areas.

Ellsworth stresses how important it is to intersperse tables and other
seating in such a way that readers are not forced to walk through a reading
area to reach the books.[13] The person studying in a reading area should
not be disturbed by individuals consulting materials on the shelves or in
cabinets. The conditions for undisturbed study are best obtained if seating
is provided around the edges of the stacks rather than at ranges of tables
and carrels alternating with ranges of shelves.

As noted repeatedly, LRCs vary as to their policy regarding nonbook
media. In some institutions nonbook software and hardware are kept
separate from books, periodicals, and other graphic media. They are kept
in a separate room or rooms and utilized apart from books. The trend
to bring these materials together has gained momentum. Integration can
be achieved by intershelving books and nonbook software or by placing
cabinets or cases for nonbook media near the book shelves. To make
integration of the media most useful, the equipment needed for their
utilization should also be nearby. However, practices vary. In some institutions in which book and nonbook media are placed together, or even
intershelved, equipment is nevertheless concentrated in a separate room
or rooms. (This may be dictated by lack of outlets at preferred locations.)

The preferences of users as to type of seating vary. Most users select
individual seating at carrels, if given a choice, but an appreciable minority
feels more comfortable with table seating and studying in the company of
others. Various kinds of seating are therefore indicated: about 30 percent

at tables, about 65 percent at carrels, and the rest as lounge seating. (Other writers may suggest different proportions of the several types of seating.) Since some students use carrels only for reading, dry carrels—carrels without outlets and without equipment—are satisfactory for them. It is not necessary to equip all carrels with such items as tape players, slide viewers, television terminals, or connections for lines to computers. Some carrels may be dry, some may have just one item of equipment, and others may be equipped with several different kinds. In institutions with a remote access information retrieval system a certain number of carrels are equipped with the devices that establish the connection with the source of program distribution.

Most LRCs have varying numbers of conference rooms or group study rooms. The total number available varies anywhere from one to ten or even more. The number provided depends on many factors such as size of the library, student enrollment, group study opportunities outside of the learning resource center, etc. Students use these rooms heavily when they are provided. If at all possible, there should be a minimum of three or four such rooms even in a small institution. One of the rooms should accommodate from eight to twelve persons, and the rest from four to six. While students invariably appreciate the availability of these rooms, some librarians find it bothersome that at times the rooms have to be closely supervised. This need for supervision can be minimized if the rooms are enclosed by glass panels. If this should not seem practical, glass panels could be installed in the upper half of the doors leading to the conference rooms.

If the LRC is a multi-story structure, conference rooms should be provided on at least two floors. There should also be at least one soundproof typing room (preferably two or three, depending on size of enrollment), each seating from six to twelve persons. If there are several such rooms, they need not be identical in size.

In university and senior college libraries faculty studies are provided for use by one or two persons and assigned to faculty members who prefer to work near the resources of their respective fields of interest. Faculty studies are not usually found in community college LRCs. However, there is frequently one faculty reading or study room for the exclusive use of faculty members.

In many LRCs there are various other user facilities in addition to those mentioned. Frequently the LRC includes a study skills center. This service has been described in some detail in Chapter 7. The study skills centers are designed for students who need special assistance and learning materials tailored to their special—usually remedial—needs. In some institutions it is felt that students with problems should work in general user areas, rather than being set apart by the provision of special rooms. However, when study skills centers have been provided, they have been well received and heavily used by the students they were designed to serve. LRCs may be equipped with facilities such as group listening rooms, language laboratories, electronic student response classrooms, and business rooms with typewriters, adding machines, calculating and transcribing machines. Such facilities are sometimes provided by the college in other buildings outside of the LRC's sphere of authority.

In surveying learning resource center buildings D. Joleen Bock found great differences in the type of resources included by the various centers.[14] She noted that although some of the centers were located in buildings not originally designed for the broad learning resources concept, they were among the most effective in carrying out a total resources plan.

Most LRCs offer production facilities. Usually there are areas for graphic production, for photographic production, for audio production, and—less frequently—for TV production.

LRC production facilities vary in size and comprehensiveness. Some can meet only simple needs, others approach commercial establishments in their production capacity. The television area usually consists of at least three rooms: a TV studio, a control room, and a production room; the larger installations have two or three additional rooms. For photographic production there is a darkroom; there is also an area set aside for graphic production. Many of the larger LRCs have more than one room for each of these production activities. Some LRCs also have a reprographic center, often with equipment that allows handling of all but the most intricate printing jobs. Secretarial pools are sometimes available for various kinds of office work needed by the faculty.

LRCs may set aside areas for faculty members who desire to produce media themselves. Sometimes production facilities are available to students; a special room may be reserved for them in or near the produciton area, or they may be invited to discuss production problems with production staff members and to work alongside them. If the college has a remote access information retrieval system, the originating and distributing facilities also are generally located in the LRC.

With increasing frequency staff rooms are provided. This is a desirable trend; it is very important to have an area in which the staff can spend their rest periods and their lunch hours.

The preceding description of building elements and their placement includes the units most frequently found in community colleges. However, some areas of concern, less universal, but very important to many institutions, have not been covered in this chapter. For instance, a number of LRCs administer the college archives. The collection of archival materials may be small and may fit into one or two cabinets. On the other hand, the archival collection may be large enough to require a separate archives room. The same may hold true for rare books and other rare documents or for art collections, as well as for other specialized materials.

There are many solutions to the problem of arranging the elements of the learning resource center. We have indicated earlier in this chapter that the keys to the LRC should be placed near the lobby, and that the public services—reference and circulation—should also be immediately visible and accessible to persons entering the library. Since the staffs of the technical services department—those who perform acquisitions and cataloging functions—must refer to the public catalog and to the reference tools for bibliographic checking, their department should be located near the catalog if at all possible. However, to the extent that catalogs are issued in book form, or even on computer display screens, technical processes staff will no longer need to rely on the public catalog. The processing staff's reliance on the public catalog is also lessened when the LRC receives materials already cataloged and otherwise processed, ready for shelving. Under these conditions processing departments need not rely on the keys and can be moved to a location at some distance from the catalog and the reference tools, if space is a problem. The various production areas are usually grouped together. When a building consists of several floors, production facilities are very often located on the ground floor. Archives and other rooms with special materials need not occupy prime space.

FLOOR PLANS

To illustrate the preceding descriptions of arrangement of the elements of LRC structures, floor plans of several LRCs will be presented in this chapter. Common to the several LRCs is broad responsibility for book and nonbook media. The plans are from the following institutions:[15] Rock Valley College, Rockford, Illinois (Plan 1); Dutchess Community College, Poughkeepsie, New York (Plan 2); Fullerton Junior College,

Fullerton, California (Plan 3); Portland Community College, Portland, Oregon (Plan 4); and Mount Royal College, Calgary, Alberta, Canada (Plan 5). Since the patterns of Portland and Mount Royal are unusual, introductory comments relating to these two plans will be made.

Portland Community College.[16] The new campus for this college was planned to provide easy access to all areas. All classrooms and laboratories are so constructed that ongoing activities are visible from the outside. The campus is "an educational shopping center where the student can shop and plan for his education program." In addition to the main instructional materials center, there are also satellite learning resource centers in the several instructional buildings. Here a student may find the resource materials for the subjects taught in the specific building. These satellite centers are connected to the central resource center by a retrieval system.

The instructional materials center forms part of the Mall Complex, the crossroads of the campus. The Complex includes the following four buildings: a. Cafeteria, Food Services; b. Bookstore, Administration; c. Registrar, Business, Counseling; d. Instructional Materials Center. These buildings are connected by a covered, heated mall; the mall area provides space for display exhibits and student activities.

A separate communications building includes areas for the radio and television facilities of the college. The building also houses the facilities for the production of all types of teaching and learning materials. Also located in the building are the offices and materials for the various communications subject fields.

Mount Royal College. The library of Mount Royal College, a community college located at Calgary, Alberta, Canada[17] is of unique design; therefore it is included here even though it lies outside of the boundaries of the United States—the area to which this study is otherwise limited.

At Mount Royal College building planning was preceded by a thorough examination of educational goals and objectives. Since as a community college it accepts as a student anyone who has reached the age of 18, the mix of students yields a very diversified group. Like some other educational planners those at Mount Royal were influenced by the writings of Benjamin Bloom,[18] who points out that differences among the students' achievements are a product more of the educational system than of the student's personal characteristics. Bloom maintains that most students can attain the same educational goals, though at different rates of speed. To minimize the effects of the differences in speed, the college has de-

cided to offer a wide range of learning media in order that a student
can utilize the media most suitable to his learning style. The college has
adopted a learning plan which it calls the Lecture-Discussion-Independent
study model. The majority of the students spend approximately 50 percent
of their time in independent study; about 30 percent of their time is
occupied in attendance at regular lectures which convey general concepts
related to a particular discipline. Small discussion groups, accounting for
the remaining 20 percent of the time, give the student the opportunity
to discuss material presented in the lectures. At the time he begins his
studies, the student receives a course outline giving overall objectives
for two semesters of work, objectives for the individual units which make
up the courses to be covered, and information on available learning resources. Members of the department of educational development services,
which consists of counselors and learning specialists, offer assistance to
the student and evaluate his work.

The planners decided to integrate, to the extent feasible, all teaching
and learning resources into a central area called the learning library.
It was devised to include the total physical and human resources of the
college.

To accommodate the various teaching procedures of the instructors
and the differing learning styles of the students, the facilities were designed to be as flexible as possible. The learning library's adaptability
to changing needs was considered of paramount importance.

The campus was designed for an ultimate enrollment of about 5,000
students. According to a report of the college president, Mount Royal
expected a student population of about 3,500 in 1973.

The learning library occupies the first floor of the three-story college
building. It is L-shaped and located around two sides of the core of the
college building, occupying an area of about 170,000 square feet. This
area holds all the learning resources of the college, most of the teaching
and learning space, and most of the faculty offices. The second and third
floors of the college building are directly reachable from within the
learning library. On these floors are the specialized facilities for laboratories and business machines.

The most unusual feature of the learning library is the provision of
decentralized service points called resource islands. Each island is set
apart for one discipline or a group of related disciplines. Each is intended
to offer one-stop service by providing the materials for all the courses
in a discipline, in whatever form required: books, reprints, pamphlets,

individual sheets, learning packages of self-study materials, audio cassettes and other kinds of nonbook media.

Each island has a basic stock of hardware such as cassette audio recorders, slide and filmstrip projectors, record players, headphones, portable TV equipment, monitors, etc.

The building is supported by columns which form modules of equal size. Each of the columns encloses portions of the conduit network: electrical power, telephones, audio and video distribution facilities, and computer terminals. The control consoles built into the columns have switches, jacks, and plug-ins to establish connections with the desired distribution source. The connections at the columns service both the immediate area and neighboring points, such as offices and study and teaching areas.

About 200 faculty offices are distributed throughout the Learning Library, faculty members being stationed near the resource island of their respective disciplines.

It should be noted that not all learning library transactions occur at the resource islands. The main library, at the north end of the learning library, houses the major book collections and media collections, central circulation, and central reference. The main library performs the normal library functions, and serves also as a warehouse from which the resource islands obtain materials as needed and to which they return materials not in current use. Adjacent to the main library are technical services, A-V services, and the typing and printing units. The college's learning resources division has assumed responsibility for reproduction of nonprint resources through a separate department under a director of instructional development.

The librarian, John North, notes that one of the major problems in the learning library's layout is security, since the plan permits maximum access from all college areas. The planners considered it desirable that students be able to move around without restriction and for this reason there are about 60 exits. Although the external fire exits are provided with buzzer alarms, Mr. North believes that the system can be circumvented. However, between the start of library operations and the time Mr. North wrote the article, no especially large losses had occurred. Another drawback of this plan, as of any decentralized model, is the need for duplication of basic materials simultaneously in demand at several resource islands and at the main library.

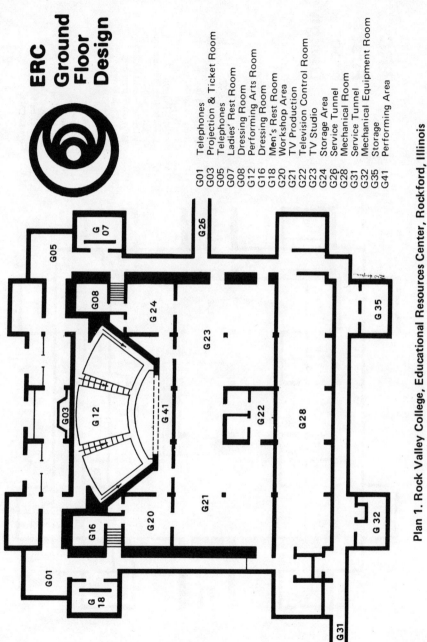

ERC Ground Floor Design

G01 Telephones
G03 Projection & Ticket Room
G05 Telephones
G07 Ladies' Rest Room
G08 Dressing Room
G12 Performing Arts Room
G16 Dressing Room
G18 Men's Rest Room
G20 Workshop Area
G21 TV Production
G22 Television Control Room
G23 TV Studio
G24 Storage Area
G26 Service Tunnel
G28 Mechanical Room
G31 Service Tunnel
G32 Mechanical Equipment Room
G35 Storage
G41 Performing Area

Plan 1. Rock Valley College, Educational Resources Center, Rockford, Illinois

Reproduced by permission of Rock Valley College.

ERC
First
Floor
Design

101 Men's Rest Room
103 Microfilm
104 TV Coordinator
105 Director, ERC
107 Public Services Librarian
108 Public Services Librarian
109 Conference Room
110 Ladies' Rest Room
112 Dark Room
114 Student Typing
116 AV Materials Preparation
117 AV Librarian
119 Listening Facility
120 Technical Processing
121 Catalog Librarian
123 Individual Study Lab
129 Staff Lounge
132 Periodicals
133 Indexes
134 Secretary
135 Card Catalog
136 Circulation Desk
138 Reference Materials
142 Newspapers

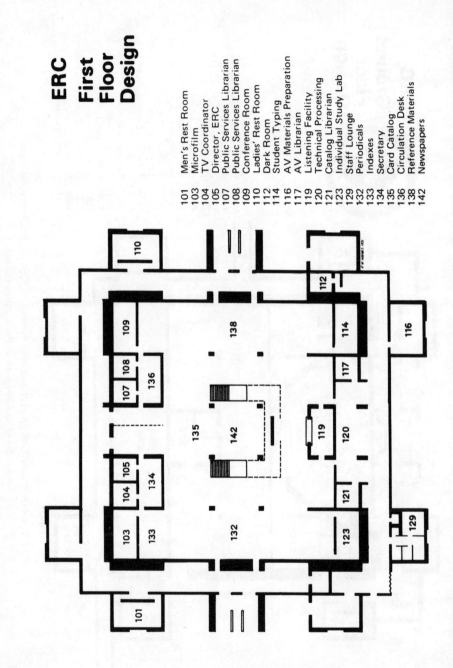

ERC
Second
Floor
Design

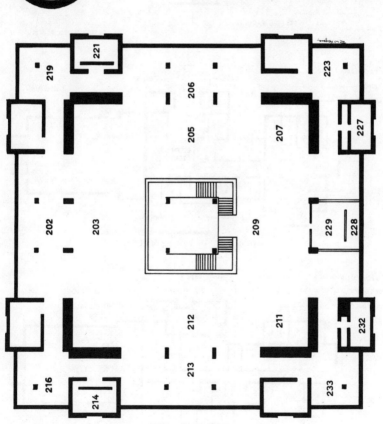

202 Open Stacks (H-N)
203 Carrel Area
205 Carrel Area
206 Open Stacks (P-Z)
207 Reserve Reading
209 Information Desk
211 Reserve Reading
212 Carrel Area
213 Open Stacks (A-G)
214 Men's Rest Room
216 Browsing
219 Browsing
221 Ladies' Rest Room
223 Browsing
227 Conference Room
228 Work Room
229 Reserve Materials
232 Conference Room
233 Browsing

DUTCHESS COMMUNITY COLLEGE

POUGHKEEPSIE. NEW YORK

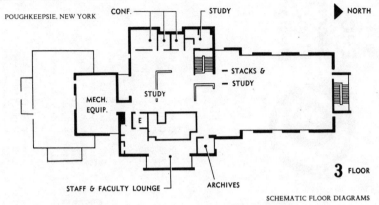

NORTH

CONF.

STUDY

MECH. EQUIP.

STUDY

E

STACKS & STUDY

3 FLOOR

STAFF & FACULTY LOUNGE

ARCHIVES

SCHEMATIC FLOOR DIAGRAMS

OF

LIBRARY

MICROFILM

TYPING

PERIODICALS

COATS

COATS

OFF.

OFF.

LOAN DESK

STACKS & STUDY

REFERENCE

E.

OFF.

TECH. PROC.

SEC'TY.

DIRECTOR

2 FLOOR

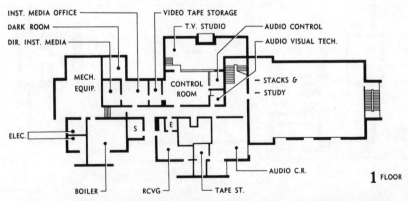

INST. MEDIA OFFICE

DARK ROOM

DIR. INST. MEDIA

VIDEO TAPE STORAGE

T.V. STUDIO

AUDIO CONTROL

AUDIO VISUAL TECH.

MECH. EQUIP.

CONTROL ROOM

STACKS & STUDY

ELEC.

S

E

BOILER

RCVG

TAPE ST.

AUDIO C.R.

1 FLOOR

Plan 2. Dutchess Community College, Library, Poughkeepsie, New York
Reproduced by permission of Dutchess Community College.

FIRST FLOOR

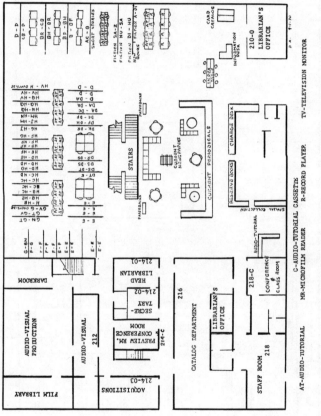

Plan 3. Fullerton Junior College, William T. Boyce Library, Fullerton, California
Reproduced by permission of Fullerton Junior College.

AT—AUDIO-TUTORIAL   C—AUDIO-TUTORIAL CASSETTE   TV—TELEVISION MONITOR
MR—MICROFILM READER   R—RECORD PLAYER.

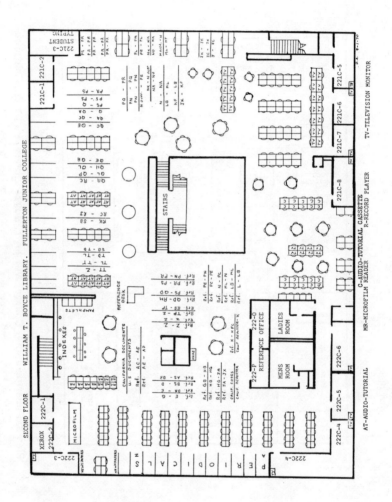

SECOND FLOOR   WILLIAM T. BOYCE LIBRARY, FULLERTON JUNIOR COLLEGE

AT-AUDIO-TUTORIAL   C-AUDIO-TUTORIAL CASSETTE   TV-TELEVISION MONITOR
MR-MICROFILM READER   R-RECORD PLAYER

MALL COMPLEX

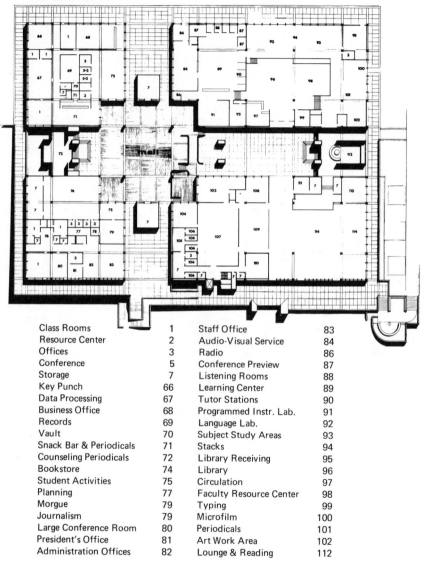

Class Rooms	1	Staff Office	83
Resource Center	2	Audio-Visual Service	84
Offices	3	Radio	86
Conference	5	Conference Preview	87
Storage	7	Listening Rooms	88
Key Punch	66	Learning Center	89
Data Processing	67	Tutor Stations	90
Business Office	68	Programmed Instr. Lab.	91
Records	69	Language Lab.	92
Vault	70	Subject Study Areas	93
Snack Bar & Periodicals	71	Stacks	94
Counseling Periodicals	72	Library Receiving	95
Bookstore	74	Library	96
Student Activities	75	Circulation	97
Planning	77	Faculty Resource Center	98
Morgue	79	Typing	99
Journalism	79	Microfilm	100
Large Conference Room	80	Periodicals	101
President's Office	81	Art Work Area	102
Administration Offices	82	Lounge & Reading	112

Plan 4. Portland Community College, Portland, Oregon, Mall Complex

Reproduced by permission of Portland Community College.

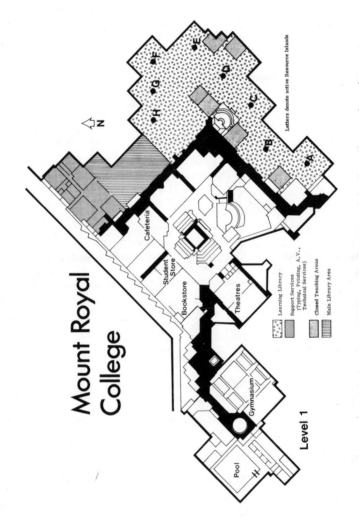

Mount Royal College

N

Level 1

Cafeteria

Student Store

Bookstore

Theatres

Gymnasium

Pool

Letters denote active Resource Islands

Learning Library

Support Services
(Typing, Printing, A.V.,
Technical Services)

Closed Teaching Areas

Main Library Area

Plan 5. Mount Royal College, Learning Library, Calgary, Alberta, Canada
Reproduced by permission of Mount Royal College and John North, College Librarian.

SOURCES

Aspects of planning that are particularly pertinent to the community college level have been emphasized in this chapter. Many other elements, however, need to be considered in LRC building planning, as, for instance, exit control, ceiling height, thickness of floors, quality of lighting, width and height of stacks, possible provision of auditoria, lecture rooms, and classrooms, and location of the LRC building in relation to other structures on the campus.

Some of these subjects are treated in Ellsworth's *Planning the College and University Building*.[19] Ellsworth gives special attention to the planning process. Keyes D. Metcalf's *Planning Academic and Research Libraries* should prove particularly helpful if detailed information is required.[20] In another book, entitled *Library Lighting*, Metcalf urges planners to give greater weight to quality than to intensity.[21] *Educational Facilities with New Media*, edited by Alan C. Green, while concerned with the whole educational plant, gives considerable space to the impact of the newer media on the learning resource center.[22] Educational Facilities Laboratories, a nonprofit corporation, has issued a number of publications that stress the role newer media might play in learning resources building planning.[23]

Also pertinent are the building surveys that have appeared annually in the *Library Journal*,[24] articles by architects[25] and practicing librarians with planning experience,[26] and descriptions of individual structures. Library handbooks and pamphlets issued in honor of an LRC building dedication frequently contain both floor plans and photographs of the building's interior and exterior.

NOTES

1. *American Junior Colleges*, 8th ed., ed. Edmund J. Gleazer, Jr. (Washington, D.C.: American Council on Education, c. 1971), p. 5.

2. Gertrude L. Oetting, "A Mansion, a Bank, and a Laundromat!" *PLA Bulletin* 26, no. 4 (July 1971): 197-203.

3. Harry F. Anderson, "The Architect Views the Building and the Planning Process," in *Junior College Libraries: Development, Need, and Perspectives*, ed. Everett L. Moore (Chicago: American Library Association, 1969), pp. 95-99; and Ralph E. Ellsworth, *Planning the College and University Library Building: A Book for Campus Planners and Architects*, 2nd ed. (Boulder, Col.: Pruett Press, c. 1968), pp. 31-39.

4. Ellsworth, *op. cit.,* pp. 5-10.

5. Ellsworth, *op. cit.,* pp. 14, 16-17.

6. James Hughes and Bob Reed, "The Community College: Review and Preview," *Architectural Record* 147, no. 6 (June 1970): 153; and Alan C. Green, "Places for Higher Learning: Some Ideas and Some Cautions," *Community and Junior College Journal* 34, no. 7 (April 1973): 7-9.

7. James W. Armsay and Norman C. Dahl, *An Inquiry into the Uses of Instructional Technology* (New York: The Ford Foundation, c. 1973), p. 71; see also: Mildred F. Schmertz, "Communications Technology and Its Implications for Library Design," *Architectural Record* 153, no. 4 (April 1973): 134-6.

8. Schmertz, *op. cit.,* p. 136.

9. Richard A. Jones, "Building Planning—Design for Unique and Innovative Centers," *Illinois Libraries* 51, no. 6 (June 1969): 466.

10. Warren B. Hicks, "Center of the Campus: Chabot College Library," *Junior College Journal* 37, no. 3 (November 1966): 39; and Warren B. Hicks, "Chabot Rounds out Resources," *Library Journal* 91, no. 21 (December 1, 1966): 5897-901.

11. Ellsworth, *op. cit.,* pp. 44-46.

12. Ellsworth, *op. cit.,* p. 40.

13. Ellsworth, *op. cit.,* p. 87.

14. D. Joleen Bock, "Two-Year Academic Library Buildings," *Library Journal* 96, no. 21 (December 1, 1971): 3986-9; also, letters dated June 20, 1972, and August 8, 1972. See also: Joleen Bock, "Two-Year College Learning Resources Center Buildings," *Library Journal* 97, no. 21 (December 1, 1972): 3871-3.

15. The author wishes to express his appreciation to the chief administrative officers of learning resource centers (or libraries) for supplying the plans and for granting permission to reproduce them here. The plans are drawn from the following sources: Rock Valley College, Rockford, Illinois. *Educational Resources Center. Planning and Design.* Pamphlet [n.d.]; Dutchess Community College, Poughkeepsie, N.Y. *Dedication of the Library and Falcon Hall.* October 21, 1967; Fullerton Junior College, Fullerton, California. William T. Boyce Library. 1 sheet [2p.] [n.d.]; Portland Community College, Portland, Oregon. *An Educational Shopping Center: The New Campus.* [n.d.]; John North, "Towards Decentralization: The Learning Resource Centre of Mount Royal College," *Canadian Library Journal* 30, no. 3 (May-June 1973): 237.

16. Portland Community College, Portland, Oregon, *An Educational Shopping Center: The New Campus, Portland Community College.*

Portland, Ore. [n.d.] [p. 1] (Amo De Bernardis, President); and "Portland Community College," *Architectural Record* 147, no. 7 (June 1970): 144-7.

17. John North, "Towards Decentralization: The Learning Resource Centre of Mount Royal College," *Canadian Library Journal* 30, no. 3 (May-June 1973): 236-42; Ray Howell, "Mount Royal: Where Islands Move the Media," *Canadian University & College* 8, no. 2 (March-April 1973): 33-4; see also: Mount Royal College, Calgary, Alberta, *The President's Report* (Calgary, Alberta, March 1973) (folder), [p. 1] (Albert B. Pentz, President); W. R. Bate and J. North, "Islands of Media Provide Instruction on Demand," *College & University Business* 55, no. 1 (July 1973): 37; J. A. Barrett, "Design Looks Like a Shopping Plaza and Works Like a Library," *College & University Business* 55, no. 1 (July 1973): 34-5; and Stanton Leggett, "Learning Progress is as Multileveled as the Building," *College & University Business* 55, no. 1 (July 1973): 36.

18. For a brief discussion of Bloom's theories, see Chapter 10, p. 186.

19. Ellsworth, *op. cit.*

20. Keyes D. Metcalf, *Planning Academic and Research Libraries* (New York: McGraw-Hill, 1965).

21. Keyes D. Metcalf, *Library Lighting* (Washington, D.C.: Association of Research Libraries, c. 1970).

22. Alan C. Green, ed., *Educational Facilities with New Media* (Washington, D.C.: National Education Association, Department of Audio-Visual Instruction, c. 1966).

23. See for instance: Alvin Toffler, "Libraries," in *Bricks and Mortarboards: A Report on College Planning and Building* (New York: Educational Facilities Laboratories, 1964), pp. 69-98; and Educational Facilities Laboratories, *The Impact of Technology on the Library Building* (New York: Educational Facilities Laboratories, 1967).

24. Bock, *op. cit., Library Journal* 96, no. 21 (December 1, 1971): 3986-9 and *Library Journal* 97, no. 21 (December 1, 1972): 3871-3.

25. See for instance: Anderson, *op. cit.;* and Jones, *op. cit.,* p. 463-7.

26. See for instance: Louise Giles, "Planning Community College Resource Centers," *American Libraries* 2 (January 1971): 51-54.

11

MOVEMENTS AND DEVELOPMENTS WITH STRONG IMPACT

We have emphasized in other contexts that the learning resource center does not exist in a vacuum but is shaped by the goals and objectives of the institution of which it is a part and also by outside forces and developments affecting education and librarianship.

The present chapter singles out three developments for special consideration. They are: the library-college, open education, and newer media. Comprehension of their essential features is necessary to understanding the direction in which the LRC is moving. Other significant forces that have already exerted or are likely to exert a strong influence upon the community college LRC are unionization of staff, democracy in education, and accountability. These, as well as other influential developments, are generally understood, and therefore not discussed here.

THE LIBRARY COLLEGE

The operations of an increasing number of community colleges have been influenced by the library-college movement.[1] This receptivity to new ideas has been especially evident among the more recently established colleges since they were not bound by tradition and were ready to experiment. The library-college movement had its beginning in the 1930s. It influenced practices in a few colleges even before its concepts were clearly formulated by Louis Shores. His writings, which now cover a span of over forty years, give evidence of the extraordinary role he has played as an innovator, as a catalyst, and as an advocate.

Only gradually did the movement pick up momentum. It began to gain strength in the 1960s when a number of colleges systematically translated library-college concepts into reality. Interest in the movement spread and led to pilot projects and conferences, of which the one held at Jamestown College in 1965 was the most noteworthy. An organization known as Library-College Associates was founded in 1966. In 1968 the Library-College Newsletter was enlarged and became the more substantial *Library-College Journal,* since renamed *Learning Today.* This journal, which bears the sub-title "An Educational Magazine of Library-College Thought," can be profitably consulted both for its articles and for its regular departments. The notes in the department of "Innovations," for instance, are compiled by Louis Shores and Janiece Fusaro. This department, especially, publishes many contributions of interest to the community college LRC staff.

A perusal of the literature shows that there is no unanimity among the advocates of the library-college as to its definition, nor is there unanimity with regard to the order in importance of the essential characteristics of the library-college. Most writers would agree that an institution should meet, at least in part, certain qualifications in order to be considered a library-college. It would accept the concept of the generic book. The term was coined by Louis Shores. (The generic book comprises the conventional printed book as well as all other means of communication—print media other than books, and nonprint media. All media are tied together to form a unified and interdependent media structure.) In the library-college the librarian functions as a teacher and the teacher becomes a librarian. The line of demarcation separating the two becomes blurred and is ultimately nonexistent. Teacher and librarian are equals, possessing diverse skills and combining their efforts in furthering the learning process. In the library-college the more advanced student assists in teaching the less advanced; the student himself is not only learner but also teacher. The entire curriculum consists of library-based study. Obligatory class attendance is abolished. Individualized study takes its place. The learner has the whole range of learning media at his disposal and is able to select the medium most likely to enable him to reach his learning goal.

The library-college movement is designed to affect all levels of higher education. The movement has found considerable acceptance, especially among community colleges. Few community colleges have adopted all the characteristics required to transform an institution into a library-college. However, many institutions have adopted some characteristics of a library-college and operate in certain respects in a library-college fashion. Usually a college does not specifically declare that it has assumed the character, in full or in part, of a library-college after it has adopted some of its features. But occasionally a college goes specifically on record by selecting library-college designations for certain of its activities or for staff members. For instance, in 1970 Pasadena City College created the position of library-college overseer.[2] This staff member was charged with the instructional activities of arranging, filming, and video-taping materials relating to learning; orienting teachers to the library as a bibliographic system; relating media to educational equipment; holding seminars on the meaning of the generic book; and being involved in a host of curricular and co-curricular matters.

OPEN EDUCATION

Traditionally learning leading to a degree or other form of academic recognition has involved class attendance in a campus setting. In recent years it has been felt more and more strongly that education should be available to the many who are not in a position to or prefer not to do their college work in the conventional way. Examples are persons who must work at the time classes are usually scheduled, young mothers, members of minority groups, senior citizens, physically handicapped.

In recent years many flexible programs have been developed.[3] They are known by various names, such as university without walls, open universities, external degree programs, new degree programs, noncampus colleges, nontraditional study programs. All of these programs have in common a stress on achievement and competence rather than a specific period of college attendance, and they also assume that these students are motivated by their own desire to learn. "Education should be a positive act of individual volition rather than a passive acquiescence in an institution's routines and requirements."[4] Usually recognition is given for life experience acquired outside of the academic environment. In some programs a written agreement is drawn up between the student and college representatives, participating instructors, and resource persons. This agreement, often called a personal contract, specifies the goals selected by the student, the learning materials recommended for use, and the various learning modes to be followed.

We have noted that although the various open-education programs have certain common features they take many different forms. Some programs, such as the New York (State) Education Department's external degree program, grant degrees on the basis of examinations taken and passed regardless of whether the student has taken classes in preparation for the degree.

On the other hand Empire State College of the State University of New York (SUNY) stresses on-campus study and a close student-teacher relationship. Empire State has a core faculty at headquarters and resident tutors at twenty regional centers. These tutors make themselves available to students for the development of individualized programs of study and for general help and advice. A student may meet with an instructor or he may be in contact with him by correspondence. An enrollee of Empire State College may use the resources of any of the institutions—about 20— that make up the SUNY group, as well as other institutions and facilities.

Empire State College mainly serves persons living in New York State, just as similar agencies created in recent years in other states usually serve individuals residing or working in those states. A different pattern extends beyond the boundaries of one state and includes participating institutions from various parts of the country. One of the best known is the "University Without Walls," supported by a consortium of about twenty institutions of higher learning. The essential features of the university without walls program are well described in its proposal for an experimental degree program in undergraduate education. Since it is typical of many plans we shall reproduce it in part.

This proposal outlines an alternative plan for undergraduate work which can lead to a college degree. It is called a *University Without Walls* because it abandons the tradition of a sharply circumscribed campus and provides education for students wherever they may be—at work, in their homes, through internships, independent study and field experience, within areas of special social problems, at one or more colleges, and in travel and service abroad. It abandons the tradition of a fixed age group (18-22) and recognizes that persons as young as 16 and as old as 60 may benefit from its program. It abandons the traditional classroom as the principal instrument of instruction, as well as the prescribed curriculum, the grades and credit points which, however they are added or averaged, do not yield a satisfactory measure of education. It enlarges the faculty to include knowledgeable people from outside the academic world and makes use of various new techniques for storage, retrieval and communication of knowledge. It places strong emphasis on student self-direction in learning, while still maintaining close teaching-learning relationships between students, teachers and others. It aims to produce not finished graduates but life-long learners. . . .[5]

There are many forms of open education in operation. A recent survey of the Educational Testing Service estimates their number at between 1,000 and 1,400.[6] If the growth these programs have experienced in recent years continues, it may be expected that by 1980 about 30 percent of all higher education will be provided by nontraditional means.

Since all institutions that offer open-education programs are prepared to make flexible individualized arrangements, senior colleges and universities will probably attract some individuals who otherwise would have enrolled at a community college. However, the community college is likely to remain the most common entry point to higher education, especially for students who need guidance and counseling and who wish to study and learn by interacting with others.

As Deborah M. Nordh notes, many community colleges have already incorporated many features stressed by the advocates of open education.[7] Community colleges as a group have been more flexible, more adaptable to an individual's needs, and more innovative than any other type of higher institution. Some community colleges have for years practiced flexible scheduling and course modularization. Some have given credit for work experience and some have exempted students from certain courses on the basis of success in proficiency tests. Most important, the community college is the American open-door college.

The community college LRC is likely to be affected by the movement towards open education. Since a student may acquire at least part of his background in an informal fashion, he will study independently and wish to rely mainly on LRC staff for advice and assistance. The person engaging in independent study will usually also require a wide range of media, especially the newer media. LRCs will also be affected by a probable increase in telecourses. Learning resource staff will work with subject specialists in planning and developing such courses. Telecourses are intended to reach the still nonserved who for one reason or another find it impossible to attend classes on campus. To assure the opportunity for review or other repeated use, audiocassettes or videocassettes of telelectures will be kept in the LRC, where these materials can be consulted whenever the student desires. In certain fields learning resource packages will be prepared, usually to satisfy a demand engendered by recommendations in courses.

NEWER MEDIA

All agencies which we consider learning resource centers (regardless of their designations) deal with books and periodicals as well as with other types of communication media. The media that have been in use for years or even decades are called the older media. Those developed more recently are known as the newer media.

The older media comprise such materials as films, audiorecordings, discs and tapes, filmstrips, slides, and transparencies. The newer media are the devices engendered by developments in electronics: television, tape recorders, and computer applications. Radio, though in use for decades, is included with the newer media since it belongs in the field of electronics. The adoption of the newer media has usually not caused abandoning the older media but has enlarged the total range of media available for utilization.

The impact of the newer media on instruction has been given thorough attention. The contribution of the Commission of Instructional Technology is outstanding. *To Improve Learning,* assembled under the editorship of Sidney G. Tickton, is probably the most comprehensive two-volume report of the last decade dealing with all phases of instructional technology.[8] Two other publications, addressed to a general audience, have drawn heavily on this commission's work for documentation. One of the publications was issued by the Ford Foundation and is entitled *An Inquiry into the Uses of Instructional Technology;*[9] the other, published under the auspices of the Carnegie Commission on Higher Education, is called *The Fourth Revolution: Instructional Technology in Higher Education.*[10]

In terms of impact on the educational scene the Carnegie Commission likens "the fourth revolution"—the developments in electronics (especially those involving radio, television, the tape recorder, and the computer)—to three earlier developments of far-reaching consequences: the first "revolution" which occurred when the education of the young was shifted at least in part, from the home to the school; the second, the adoption of the written word; and the third, the invention of printing.[11]

Instructional Television[12]

Broadcast television, the form best known to the general public, is used both for educational and commercial purposes. Here the message is broadcast over the air and can be received by anyone with an antenna. Another characteristic of broadcast television is that only one signal (one program) can be sent at any one time on each channel.

Closed circuit television is the form of television most widely used for instructional purposes. Usually cables connect those buildings which are to be included in the campus television network. The network may also be extended into neighboring campuses. One of the great advantages is that several programs can be sent simultaneously through the same cable.

Cable television, commonly called community antenna television (CATV), is similar in concept to the campus-wide closed-circuit television, except that it reaches a greater geographical area. This is possible because specially designed antennas pick up signals from remote places, reinforce the signals, and distribute them. While broadcast television can carry only one program per channel, cable television can carry many signals (about twenty); if more sophisticated equipment is perfected, this capacity could easily be doubled.

Television pictures were formerly recorded by film (kinescope). Now the recording and storage of materials designed for repeated use is often on videotape. Videotape has many uses. It can be transmitted by the television station and it can be played through monitors at any chosen location, as for instance, the classroom, the LRC, or the home. Videotape has an advantage over film: It can be reproduced virtually simultaneously with the time of the original presentation.

Videocassettes are bound to become very important devices especially as increased demand permits them to be sold more cheaply. To utilize this media a cassette player is simply attached to a television set; then a cassette is inserted, and the set is activated by pushing a button. The Carnegie Commission report notes that some technologists expect that by 1985 videodiscs will become available. They can be bound into books and in this way print and nonprint materials reinforcing each other's messages can be made available as combined learning media.[13]

Film

Film has been used as a means of instruction for well over half a century. In former times it was frequently necessary when a film was to be shown to move students out of their regular classroom into a properly equipped area. Film use has acquired new momentum with the introduction and refinement of the 8mm format. It is now widely used to present brief segments—single concepts—of a broader topic. These single concept films have been cartridged and can be handled easily at practically any location. Louis Forsdale believes that 8mm film can be technically improved to such an extent that it could replace 16mm film; it could then become the format for packaging the whole range of moving images.[14] Such a change would make film production less expensive and contribute to a still wider film use.

Microfilm, microfiche, and other microforms have been treated separately, in Chapter 6.

Generation of Images

Speaking of 16mm films in particular and image systems in general, Robert Wagner stresses that we live in a time "when images beget other images—one visual form becoming another." A motion picture may become a still picture by the freeze-frame method; a set of still photographs may become an iconographic film or a television image; film can become videotape; 16mm film can become 8mm film, etc. In all of these transformations the quality and often the effect of the picture is being changed. The educator must not only be able to evaluate how the original image was created (by whom, for whom, and with what intent), but he must also be able to "identify the generation of image which reaches the student, the nature of transformation, and what might have been lost—or added—in the translation."[15]

Computers

We shall not attempt to include computer technology in our discussion of computer use in the field of education. For general background information we refer the reader to texts on computer technology, of which there are many available.[16]

In the learning resources field computers are used largely for management and housekeeping functions. Computers serve mostly in such library operations as ordering, cataloging, serials work, and circulation. So far computers have been used only infrequently in the area of information retrieval and to an equally limited extent for instructional purposes.

George A. Comstock, who surveyed use of computers for instruction in California, assigned instructional applications to five categories:[17]

1. Data processing and computer science. The teaching of computer skills where the computer itself is the main subject.

2. Student problem solving and research. The computer is a tool for learning about a subject outside of computer science.

3. Tutorial. In this instance the computer is the device through which instruction is presented. The computer is used instead or partly instead of an instructor.

4. Simulations, demonstrations, and gaming. Portions of the subjects of instruction—social and physical phenomena—are simulated.

5. Teacher's aid in managing instruction. Use for recording of grades, attendance, assignments; also for guidance of instruction. Comstock's survey showed that so far tutorial use was less than any of the other instructional computer applications.

The lack of development in the area of computer use aimed at supplanting, supplementing, or supporting part of the traditional instructional process is also noted by Armsey.[18] As of now, computer utilization is slight in computer assisted instruction (CAI), comprising drill, practice, tutorial, and dialogue. Use is also minimal in computer managed instruction (CMI), where the instructor utilizes the computer chiefly as a device for planning instruction for an individual student. John E. Coulson agrees that in the near future computer assisted instrucion will remain very limited, but he sees great potential for use in instruction if we stop thinking of the computer as just another audio-visual aid and begin to appreciate its capabilities as a general purpose information-processing system.[19]

Audio Listening Centers[20]

These centers usually consist of a number of carrels that contain tape play-back equipment. The carrels may also be equipped with other media such as 8mm films and slides. These centers have been found useful for many areas of learning: language instruction, speech, and education, to mention some of the most significant applications.

Individual Learning Laboratories[21]

Probably the best known is the one developed at Purdue by Samuel N. Postlethwait for the teaching of biology to freshmen. The assumption is that learning must be done by the learner, and therefore the system is so constructed that the learner is always actively involved. Postlethwait's scheme includes a number of procedures. A student has available taped lectures; he is also referred to textbooks as he might be by a teacher in a live classroom situation; at the proper juncture he is directed to engage in experiments or to view a film, a filmstrip, or some other media. To assure the learner frequent occurrences of success, courses are divided into smaller units. Research has shown that a student is likely to master a subject more easily and rapidly if it is broken down into a number of units. They bear various names, such as coursettes, mini-units, minicourses, concepto-packs, etc.

Minicourses may be segments of more than one comprehensive course. For instance a minicourse may be a component of a complete course in biology and chemistry, and its successful completion would be counted in the fulfillment of the requirements for both the chemistry and the biology course.

Postlethwait's procedure has been used also in fields other than biology.

Dial Access Information Retrieval Systems (DAIRS)[22]

The name of this system is derived from the fact that initially the only means of access was by a dial. This dial is operated much in the same way as a telephone dial. But in recent years manufacturers have introduced push buttons, similar to the kind used for touch-tone telephones, as access devices. Some writers therefore prefer the broader term "remote access information systems" as the designation for these retrieval systems.[23] The purpose of the systems is to make information practically immediately available. Retrieval systems consist of magnetic tape record and replay devices. These are linked to telephone switching devices, and the latter are connected with individual reception points. In some instances a computer is employed for switching. Typically, various kinds of materials which are prerecorded on magnetic audio- or videotape are collected in a central storage center. But a system can also be adapted to receive live broadcast television, closed-circuit television, slides, film strips, and moving pictures.

Access to materials may be random or serial. A system provides random access if a student may obtain a program at any time. We label also as random access the situation where a user, though having access to the program, might find that another has already begun using it. The second user, and any others who might come in at intervals during the program, would have to accept it at the point to which the first user has carried it. (The program can, of course, be replayed for the benefit of those who have missed earlier portions.) Practically pure random access is obtainable at the Oak Park-River Forest High School installation where after a wait of only a few seconds a user obtains a copy of the master tape, which he can use without interference. Serial access means that each user has access only after the preceding individual has completed use of the recorded information.

Programmed Instruction

Programmed instruction is based on a procedure originally designed by Sidney L. Pressey.[24] It was intended to be a testing device. In its earlier years it was considered merely an adjunct to learning; its application has since been broadened.

Programmed instruction is a reproducible program that requires the active participation of the student and assures him of an immediate response as to the accuracy of his answer; as originally conceived, it is self-pacing.

Programmed instruction gathered many adherents who felt that this form of learning need not be merely an adjunct to other forms but could stand alone as an instructional method. B. F. Skinner, e.g., maintained that programmed instruction could be fully self-instructional. Skinner's method is characterized by the small increments into which an informational sequence is divided and by the linear approach. Norman A. Crowder, another advocate of programmed instruction, is noted mainly for supporting branching, an approach that provides for several alternative directions for study, depending on the answer given by the student.

More recent definitions have omitted self-pacing as an essential characteristic of programmed instruction, and programmed instruction is no longer limited to individual use but also utilized in class groups.[25]

Programmed instruction is important per se as a popular teaching device, but is equally important for its general effect on the design and development of all teaching materials. The intensive study of programmed instruction yielded findings on the nature of the teaching procedure and especially on methods of fitting teaching and learning into a particular environment. Programmed instruction appears in many formats—mechanical, electromechanical, and in the shape of books. The book format has proved less expensive than any of the other formats, and it has become dominant.

Parameters for Various Instructional Media

Analyzing educational technology, James G. Miller has prepared a summary table entitled "Characteristics and Cost of Various Instructional

Media (1969)."[26] This table summarizes a number of important parameters for the various educational media.[27] Along with the whole range of the newer media we find books, periodicals, and standard audio-visual aids, as well as lectures and small discussion groups.

If we are to discover which media is most effective in a given situation, we must know what is the optimum learning environment. Research has shown that there is no universally applicable superior learning environment. It differs from individual to individual, for an individual from one time to another, and for the same individual from one learning goal to another. Miller feels nevertheless that criteria of usefulness of the individual media can be established. He proposes that media are most useful if an individual can: a) carry them around; b) use them individually rather than have to coordinate his activities with those of others; c) use the aids anywhere, not only in school; d) schedule use of materials at his discretion and in terms of his own needs; e) control rate of flow of information input and output in the learning process, repeating the process if he finds it necessary; f) interact actively with aids (it is recognized that active learning is generally superior to passive learning); g) have output originating with him influence the next input coming to him; and h) receive inputs in multiple sensory modalities (multiple channels reinforce each other; learning aids that come through electronic networks are more useful because they can reach the student wherever he may be).

NOTES

1. Howard Clayton and Robert T. Jordan, "The Library-College," *Encyclopedia of Education*, vol. 5 (1971): 608-13; Janiece F. Fusaro, "Toward Library-College Media Centers: A Proposal for the Nation's Community Colleges," *Junior College Journal* 40, no. 7 (April 1970): 40-44; Louis Shores, *Audio-Visual Librarianship: The Crusade for Media Unity, 1946-69* (Libraries Unlimited, 1973); Louis Shores, et al., eds., *The Library College. Contributions for American Education at the Jamestown College Workshop, 1965*, Drexel Institute of Technology, Drexel Library School Series, no. 16 (Philadelphia: Drexel Press, 1966); and *Learning Today*, vol. 1-(Norman, Okla.: College-Library Associates, 1968-   ).

2. Louis Shores and Janiece F. Fusaro, "Innovations," *Learning Today* 6, no. 4 (Fall 1973): 70-71.

3. Lee J. Betts, "The Evolution of Open Education; or, Close Your

Eyes and Open Your Mouth," *Community and Junior College Journal* 43, no. 6 (March 1973): 15-17, 92.

4. Ernest L. Boyer and George C. Keller, "The Big Move to Non-Campus Colleges," *Saturday Review* 54 (July 17, 1971): 46.

5. Union for Experimenting Colleges and Universities, "Universities Without Walls: A Proposal for an Experimental Degree Program in Undergraduate Education," Summary Statement (Yellow Springs, Ohio: Antioch College, September 28, 1970), pp. 1-2 (Processed).

6. Betts, *op cit.,* p. 16.

7. Deborah M. Nordh, "Emphasis" [Open Education], *Community and Junior College Journal* 43, no. 6 (March 1973): 10.

8. Sidney G. Tickton, ed., *To Improve Learning: An Evaluation of Instructional Technology,* vols. 1 and 2 (New York: R. R. Bowker, 1970, 1971). Unless otherwise stated, subsequent notes referring to this work are to vol. 1.

9. James W. Armsey and Norman C. Dahl, *An Inquiry into the Uses of Instructional Technology* (New York: The Ford Foundation, 1973).

10. Carnegie Commission on Higher-Education, *The Fourth Revolution: Instructional Technology in Higher Education* (New York: McGraw-Hill, 1972).

11. *Ibid.,* p. 9.

12. Carnegie Commission, *op. cit.,* pp. 19-22; Armsey and Dahl, *op. cit.,* pp. 37-49; National Association of Educational Broadcasters, Research and Development Office, "Television-in-Instruction: The State of the Art," in Tickton, *op. cit.,* pp. 299-312; and Frederick Breitenfeld, Jr., "Instructional Television; The State of the Art," in Tickton, *op. cit.,* pp. 137-60.

13. Carnegie Commission, *op. cit.,* p. 22.

14. *Ibid.,* pp. 15-16; Louis Forsdale, "8mm Film in Education. Status and Prospects—1968," in Tickton, *op. cit.,* 231-9; and Armsey and Dahl, *op. cit.,* pp. 49-51.

15. Robert W. Wagner, "The Generation of Images," in Tickton, *op. cit.,* p. 375.

16. For a concise discussion of basic computer technology and education-related computer technology, see Armsey and Dahl, *op. cit.,* pp. 58-67.

17. G. A. Comstock, "The Computer and Higher Education in California," in *The Emerging Technology: Instructional Uses of the Computer in Higher Education,* by Roger E. Levien (New York: McGraw-Hill Book Co., 1972), p. 225. Also quoted in Carnegie Commission, *op. cit.,* pp. 22-23.

18. John E. Coulson, "Computer-Assisted Instruction and Its Potential for Individualizing Instruction," in Tickton, *op. cit.*, pp. 197-209.

19. Armsey and Dahl, *op. cit.*, p. 67.

20. Carnegie Commission, *op. cit.*, p. 17.

21. *Ibid.*, pp. 17-18; and Samuel N. Postlethwait and Robert N. Hurst, "Mini-courses: Focusing on the Individual and His Learning," *Library-College Journal* 4, no. 1 (Winter 1971): 16-24.

22. Richard B. Hull, "Dial Access Information Retrieval Systems," in Tickton, *op. cit.*, pp. 277-82; R. Stafford North, "Dial-Access as an Instructional Medium," in Tickton, *op. cit.*, pp. 313-21; and David M. Crossman, "The Remote Access Audio-Video Information System," *Library Trends* 19, no. 4 (April 1971): 437-46.

23. Crossman, *op. cit.*, p. 438.

24. Armsey and Dahl, *op. cit.*, pp. 55-58; and Susan M. Markle, "Programming and Programmed Instruction," in Tickton, *op. cit.*, pp. 293-7.

25. B. Lamar Johnson, *Islands of Innovation Expanding: Changes in the Community College* (Beverly Hills, Calif.: Glencoe Press, 1969), pp. 74-75.

26. James G. Miller, "Deciding Whether and How to Use Educational Technology in the Light of Cost Effectiveness Evaluation," in Tickton, *op. cit.*, vol. 2, pp. 1007-27, esp. pp. 1012-13.

27. Carnegie Commission, *op. cit.*, pp. 96-102, esp. pp. 98-101 (Table 2).

INDEX

214

instructional, 154, 206
operations, 113-114
videocassettes and videotapes
utilized, 206
Texas Southmost College, 161
Tickton, Sidney G. *To Improve
Learning,* 205
Trinkner, Charles A. *Basic Books
for Junior College Libraries,*
82, 85
Triton College, course offerings, 7
Two-year college
branch of state college (or university), 10
control and support, 9-12
development, 306
faculty, 9
the future, 12-13
independent junior college
district, 11
main functions, 7-8
multi-institution junior college
district, 11, 12
Two-year post-secondary institution. *See* Two-year college

"University Without Walls," 203-
204
Use of library, influence of instructor on, 138, 143
User studies, 141-143

Veaner, Allen B., 119-120
Videocassettes, 206
Videotapes, 206
Voegel, George H., 76-77 n. 25

Wagner, Robert P., 207
Wallace, James O., 168, 170
Waubonsee College, 115
Wesley College, 111-112
Western Michigan University,
specialist's program, 24
Wharton County Junior College,
153
Wheeler, Helen, 49, *A Basic Book
Collection for the Communi-
ty College Library,* 82, 85,
96 n. 12
Williams, Hayden R., 117 n. 24

ABOUT THE AUTHOR

Fritz Veit is Director of Libraries and professor of library science at Chicago State College. He was educated at the universities of Freiburg, Berlin, and Heidelberg, and was awarded his Ph.D. degree from the University of Chicago. He has published numerous articles on librarianship in scholarly journals.